CW00573518

797,885 Books

are available to read at

www.ForgottenBooks.com

———◆———

Forgotten Books' App
Available for mobile, tablet & eReader

ISBN 978-1-333-36857-9
PIBN 10496033

1 MONTH OF
FREE
READING

at

www.ForgottenBooks.com

By purchasing this book you are eligible for one month membership to ForgottenBooks.com, giving you unlimited access to our entire collection of over 700,000 titles via our web site and mobile apps.

To claim your free month visit:

www.forgottenbooks.com/free496033

THE GATEWAY TO THE SAHARA

ADVENTURES AND OBSERVATIONS IN TRIPOLI

The Arbar-Arsāt

Through Tripoli's byways

THE GATEWAY TO THE SAHARA

ADVENTURES AND OBSERVATIONS
IN TRIPOLI

BY

CHARLES WELLINGTON FURLONG, F.R.G.S.

WITH ILLUSTRATIONS BY THE AUTHOR FROM PAINTINGS
IN COLOR, DRAWINGS IN BLACK AND
WHITE, AND PHOTOGRAPHS

NEW AND ENLARGED EDITION

NEW YORK
CHARLES SCRIBNER'S SONS
1914

To
MY WIFE

PREFACE

TRIPOLI, in Barbary, is the only Mohammedan-ruled state in Northern Africa, the last Turkish possession on that continent, and outside its own confines is little known.

Nowhere in Northern Africa can the life of town, oasis, and desert be found more native and typical than in Tripolitania. How long before the primitive customs of this people will give way before the progressive aggression of some Christian power, and the picture of an ancient patriarchal life be tarnished with the cheap veneer of a commercial vanguard, may be answered any morning by the cable news of the daily paper.

The great dynamic forces of modern civilization cause events to march with astounding swiftness. Tripoli, in Barbary, is already in the eye of Europe; to-morrow the Tripoli of to-day may have vanished.

We have recently skirted the edge of Morocco with the French legions, sojourned for a while

in far-famed Biskra, wandered in Southern
Tunisia and felt the charm and subtile influence of the Garden of Allah, and have visited
the Pyramids—by electric car. But that vast
middle region, Tripoli, where the great range
of the Atlas runs to sand and the mighty desert
meets the sea, has been left unentered, unde-
scribed.

June, 1904, found me a second time in North
Africa; previously it was Morocco, the westernmost outpost of the Orient, now it was Tripoli,
the easternmost state of Barbary. A specially
viséd Turkish passport let me into The Gateway to the Sahara—the first American to enter
in two years.

Within these pages by word and picture I
have endeavored to give an insight into this
most native of the Barbary capitals, its odd and
fascinating customs, industries, and incidents;
a view of those strange and interesting people
who inhabit the oases and table-lands of Tripolitania, their primitive methods and patriarchal
life; an account of the hazardous vocation of
the Greek sponge divers off the Tripoli coast;
a story of the circumstances surrounding · the
dramatic episode of the burning of the United

PREFACE

States Frigate *Philadelphia* in 1804, and of my discovery of the wrecked hull below the waters of Tripoli harbor in 1904; a narrative of some personal adventures which occurred during a trip alone with Arabs over some two hundred miles of the Great Sahara; and a description of the daily life and vicissitudes of the camel and the Saharan caravans, of the trails over which they travel, and of the great wastes which surround them.

In recording the impressions of town and desert it has been my endeavor throughout this volume with pen and with brush to paint with full color, to surround fact with its proper atmosphere and to set it against its most telling background. Events are described so far as possible in their order of sequence, but it has seemed preferable to present them in subject completeness rather than in diary form. The history of Tripolitania has been practically eliminated from the body of the book, being condensed within a four-page "Historical Note."

The native words introduced, are for the most part in common use among the few English and other foreigners, and are usually Arabic or local vernacular modifications of it; throughout the most simplified spelling has been adhered to. Translation is in most cases parenthetically given with the first occurrence of a foreign word and also in the glossary, when a word is repeated.

Of that portion of the material which has already been presented in magazine articles, the main part has appeared in *Harper's Magazine*; the remainder in *The World's Work, The Outlook*, and *Appleton's Magazine*.

My sincere acknowledgments are due to my friend Mr. William F. Riley, of Tripoli, Consul for Norway and the Netherlands, who by his ever-helpful advice and untiring efforts rendered me invaluable service; to Mr. Alfred Dickson, then British Vice-Consul, for his timely help and interest; to the rest of that little coterie of kind friends in Tripoli who showed me every courtesy and attention during my sojourn there—Mr. Arthur Saunders, in charge of the cable station, M. Auguste Zolia, Chancellor of the Austro-Hungarian Consulate, and Mr. W. H. Venables; also to Redjed Pasha for numerous privileges and kind assistance; to the Greek naval officers and sailors stationed

PREFACE

at Tripoli for generous aid in work over the wreck of the United States Frigate *Philadelphia*—in particular to Captain Batsis, Dr. Georges Sphines, and Dr. St. Zografidis; to Mr. David Todd, Professor of Astronomy, Amherst College, for letters; to Rabbi Mordecai Kohen, librarian of the synagogue, and to faithful black Sālam who proved his worth in time of need.

C. W. F.

NOTE TO SECOND EDITION

SINCE the first edition of this volume the prediction ventured in its preface and on its last two pages has been fulfilled and Tripoli has entered a new era of its history. To complete the romantic story and more fully depict the Tripolitania of to-day, two chapters with illustrations have been added to this edition and include the relation of Tripolitania to the Mediterranean question, a résumé of the Turko-Italian War and an account of Italy's real-estate venture in North Africa, from the moral, political, military, and economic view-points.

Side by side with the Italian renaissance of Tripolitania—Libia Italiana—will drift the old patriarchal life of Barbary; the camel and his driver will long compete with the iron horse and for many, many years Arab, Berber, Black, and Bedawee will pitch their tents in the oases and on the sun-scorched desert sands.

CONTENTS

[xv]

CONTENTS

—Date palms—Their value—Markets or suks—
Transportation—Horses—Description of the Tues-
day Market—A market crowd—A knife seller—
Character of Arab merchants—An Arab sharper—
Arab barbers—Fruit—Corn sellers—Butcher shops
—A marabout—Coffee houses—A mental mirage—
Two points of view.

CHAPTER FOUR

Black nomads—Sālam—Slave statistics—Hausaland
Hausas—Slavery—Slave rights—Slave traffic—
Tribute-paying system—Freedom—Sālam's capture
—Slave life—Gambling—Cowries—Gambling away
freedom—Bashaws' persecution—Sālam's master
resists Bashaw—Sālam sold—Kano—Trade of Kano
and Sudan—Tuaregs—Products of Kano—Slave caravans—Kola nuts—Sālam's journey—A Tuareg
fight—Kola nuts—Sālam sold several times—His
master Hadji Ahmed—Escapes to Ouragla—Tends
camels—Second escape—Sufferings of the journey
—Reach Ghadāmes—Sent to Tripoli—Arrival in
Tripoli—Obtains freedom—Sala Heba—Hadji Ahmed again—Plan for Sālam's recapture—Scheme
foiled—A Sudanese dance—A brush with Black
fanatics—Sālam's courage.

CHAPTER FIVE

The masked Tuaregs—Tuareg confederation—Tuareg
territory—Character—Methods of brigandage—
Dangers of the trails—Reprisals—Tuareg convoys
—Adventure of two French officers—Tuaregs of
white race—Religion—Character—Massacre of
White Fathers—Flatters expedition—Marriage—
Women—Social system—Tuareg slaves—First Tu-
aregs seen—Tuareg costumes—Weapons—Shadow-
ing—Unsuccessful attempt to photograph them—
Asgar Tuaregs—Bartering—The Tuareg mask—
The Sect of the Senusi—The telek and other Tuareg
weapons—The Asgars again—The picture obtained.

CONTENTS

CHAPTER SIX

The Mediterranean—Bashaws' Castle—Grounding of
U. S. Frigate *Philadelphia*—The surrender—The
burning by Decatur—Local traditions—Jewish rec-
ords found—Hadji-el-Ouachi—An Arab tradition
—The old Arab's story—Old guns—Bushagour's
houses—More specific results—Start to explore harbor—Discovery of a vessel's ribs below water—The
Philadelphia—Diving—Condition of the vessel—
Second expedition with machine boats and sponge
divers—Size, position, and location of wreck determined—Third and last expedition—Sponge divers
again—Parts brought to surface.

CHAPTER SEVEN

Tripoli's three principal industries—Minor industries
and resources—Tripoli Harbor—Commerce of Port
of Tripoli—Casualties of one month—Quicksands
and reefs—Barbary ports—Arab galleys—Exports
—The sponge grounds—Some unpleasant facts—
Treatment of Greek sponge divers—Greek hospital staff—Methods of diving—Divers' paralysis—
Theory concerning it—Cure—A fatal case—Aboard
a sponge boat—Methods of fishing—A sponge fleet—
Depth and time of diving—Diver and shark—Preparing for the season—Outfitting—Contract conditions—Pay—The day's work—Preparing for the descent—The descent—Obtaining sponges—Qualities
—What the diver sees—Manner of ascent—Brutality
practised—Preparation of sponges—Value—Bleaching—Night on a sponge boat—The end of the season.

CHAPTER EIGHT

Esparto grass or halfa—Esparto regions—Esparto
pickers—Description of grass—Wages—Methods of
gathering—Dangers—Consequences—Loading cam-

CONTENTS

CONTENTS

Night marauders—The old caravaneer's story—A caravan attacked—Value of goods lost—Tripoli's caravan trade diminishing.

CHAPTER ELEVEN

Acquaintance with the camel—An epitome of the desert—His history—Kinds of camels—Bargaining —Breeds of camels—Meaning of dromedary—Riding a baggager—Driving a camel—Camels in market —Feeding—The camel market—Breeding places— Camel raisers—Buying a camel—Biters—Means of defence and attack—Character—Camel doctor— Passing in a narrow way—A mehari or riding camel —Comparison with draft camel—Manner of riding —Equipment—Travelling ability of mehara—Dismounting—Closer acquaintance with the camel— Physical characteristics—Hallil and his white nakāt (she camel)—Drinking—Adjustment of loads— Saddles—Camel's adaptation to environment— Desert songs—Camel lore—A black camel—Manner of driving camels—Punishment—Mortality—Dangers of bad ground—Old Bakri and his blind camel —A camel's last days.

CHAPTER TWELVE

Desert travelling—People met with—Consideration of diet—Clothes—Camping outfit—Obtaining food Birds—Bedawi—Boundary marks—Hard travelling—Muraiche suspected—Arrival at Khoms— The burden of the trail—Audience with Governor— Visit Roman ruins—A Roman harbor—Grounds for suspicion—Men mutiny—Start for Kussabat delayed —Good advice—A late start—View of Khoms— Guard unwelcome — Leadership decided — Night schemes—Apprehensions—Small caravan passed— Followed by thieves—Attempt to ambush—Strategy necessary—Use Muraiche as screen—Ali tries to run—Mohammed attempts to strike—Reached Kussabat—Sleep on a fondūk roof—The reason for treachery—Guard leaves—Journey continued—a brief rest—A night's sleep.

CONTENTS

CHAPTER THIRTEEN

CHAPTER FOURTEEN

CHAPTER FIFTEEN

CONTENTS

—Secret sect of the Senousi—Enver Bey—Desert communication—Airships and automobiles—Italian reprisals—Turks wonderful fighters—The Peace of Lausanne—Some treaty terms—Italian sovereignty proclaimed from Castle.

CHAPTER SIXTEEN

ILLUSTRATIONS

[xxiii]

ILLUSTRATIONS

ILLUSTRATIONS

MAPS

HISTORICAL NOTE

A SKETCH OF TRIPOLITANIA FROM PRE-HISTORIC TIMES TO TO-DAY

TWELVE centuries before Christ, Phœnician traders had worked their way along the southern shores of the Mediterranean and up its oleander-fringed rivers, until their galley keels grated on the fertile shores of Lybia [Tunisia]. Here hordes of armed warriors, swarming ashore, planted their standards high above the fragrant broom which covered the golden hillsides, and as centuries rolled by, Outili [Utica] and other cities were reared, among them Carthage.

At the close of the Third Punic War, Carthage lay in ruins and the whole coast territory of Africa, from the Pyramids to the Pillars of Hercules, became subject to the Romans, and the territory we now know as Tripolitania, a province of the Cæsars.

Three cities, Leptis, Sabrata, and Oea, anciently constituted a federal union known as

Tripolis, while the district governed by their Concilium Annum was called Lybia Tripolitania. On the site of Oea modern Tripoli, in Barbary, now stands. Tripolis suffered the varying fortunes of a Roman African colony, the yoke weighing heaviest under Count Romanus in the reign of Valentinium, A. D. 364. Then came the sacking by the Austerians and wild native tribes from the deserts, encouraged by the policy of Genseric, the invading Vandal king.

Before the reign of Constans II, 641–668, we find the name, wealth, and inhabitants of the province gradually centred in Oea, the maritime capital of Tripolis; 647 A. D. saw the beginning of the great Arab invasion, which, gathering force, sent the resistless tidal wave of the *Jehad* [Holy War] sweeping across Barbary. It broke down what was left of Roman rule, merged the wild Berber aborigines into the great sea of Islam, inundated Spain, flooded even to the gates of Poitiers before it was checked, then, slowly receding, finally found its level south of the Straits of Gibraltar and the Middle Sea.

Since that remote past the flags of various

nations of the Cross have for brief periods flung their folds in victory over this Moslem stronghold. When the caravels of Charles V, of Spain, were making conquests in Mexico and Peru, that monarch presented Tripoli and Malta to the Knights of St. John on their expulsion from Rhodes by the Turkish Sultan, Soliman the Magnificent. Later, in the sixteenth century, Soliman drove them from Tripoli and received the submission of the Barbary States.

In 1714 the Arabs of Tripoli gained independence from their Turkish rulers and for over a century were governed by their own bashaws.

In 1801, on account of the unbearable piracy of the Tripolitans, war was declared between Tripoli and the United States. In 1804, but for the blocking by our government of the scheme and land expedition of General William Eaton when Tripoli was within his grasp, the sixteen-starred banner of the United States, too, would undoubtedly for a time have supplanted the Flag of the Prophet. Thus, not only would the imprisoned crew of the *Philadelphia* in Tripoli have been freed, but our shame as a tribute-paying nation to the Barbary states mitigated. Peace was concluded in 1805.

Thirty years later Tripoli again came under Turkish rule, since which time until 1911 the crescent flag of the Ottoman waved there undisturbed and Tripoli continued to steep herself in the spirit of Islam, indifferent and insensible to the changes of the outer world.

At 3 P. M. October 3, 1911, a war-ship's shell proclaimed Italy's campaign against Tripoli, and for over a year Cross and Crescent again clashed on Tripolitania's shores, drenching its sands in blood.

In the late afternoon of October 18, in the Hôtel Beau-Rivage at Ouchy, Turkish and Italian peace plenipotentiaries had been closeted since ten that morning. Without, the broad terrace flooded with warm sunlight was crowded with its fashionable throng at afternoon tea; from the orchestra flowed the soft strains of a waltz. At exactly 5.45 Naby Bey stepped toward Signor Bertilini and said, " Gentlemen, we will sign," and the Treaty of Lausanne became a fact. Italian sovereignty was proclaimed over Tripolitania and Cyrenaica, the Turk stepped from his last foothold in Africa—christened by modern Rome *Libia Italiana*.

THE GATEWAY TO THE SAHARA

CHAPTER ONE

TRIPOLI IN BARBARY

BRITAIN holds Egypt, France has seized Algeria and Tunisia with one hand and is about to grasp Morocco with the other, but Tripolitania has escaped the international grab-bag of Europe and still dwells native and sequestered among the great solitudes which surround her. Tucked away in a pocket of the Mediterranean, five hundred miles from the main highways of sea travel, transformed and magnified under the magic sunlight of Africa, Tripoli,[1] the white-burnoosed city, lies in an oasis on the edge of the desert, dipping her feet in the swash and ripple of the sea.

I first saw her through my cabin port-hole when, gray-silvered, the half light of dawn

---

[1] The name Tripoli is applied to both the Pashalic of Tripoli and the city, and occasionally to Tripolitania, the territory.

slowly filtered through the tardy night mists and mingled with the rose flush of approaching day. Two silver moons dimly floated, one in a gray silver sky, the other in a gray silver sea. A strip of shore streaked between; in gray stencilled silhouette a Moorish castle broke the centre of its sky-line; slender minarets, flat housetops, and heavy battlements flanked in a crescent westward, and the delicate palm fringe of the oasis dimmed away east. The *adán*—call to prayer— drifted away over the sleeping city and harbor. The gilded crescents of the green-topped minarets in glints of orange-gold heliographed the coming of the rising sun: the shadows of night seemed to sink below the ground-line, and the white-walled city lay shimmering through a transparent screen of wriggling heat-waves.

The coast of North Africa from Tunis eastward does not meet the converging water routes short of its eastern extremity at Suez. Along the seaboard of this territory the Mediterranean laps the desert sand and over the unbounded sun-scorched reaches of Tripoli and Barca, to the border-land of Egypt, wild tribes control the vast wastes.

The great territory of Tripolitania embraces

[2]

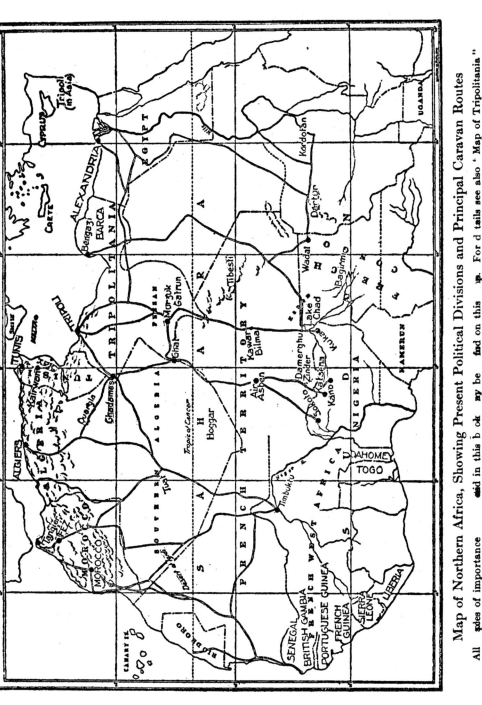

Map of Northern Africa, Showing Present Political Divisions and Principal Caravan Routes

All places of importance used in this book my be found on this map. For details see also ' Map of Tripolitania ' [Chapter Three] and " Map of the Town and Harbor of Tripoli " [Chapter Six]

what is known as the vilayet of Tripoli, the Fezzan to the south, and the province of Barca on the east, governed as an integral part of Turkey. The Pashalic of Tripoli includes that portion of the vilayet extending from Tunisia to the southernmost point of the Gulf of Sidra. Of all Barbary,[1] Tripolitania is most truly African.

It is situated equally distant from the three entrances of the Mediterranean and is the focus of the three great caravan routes from the South. Tripoli's freedom from European occupation may be attributed to three causes: her isolation from the main highways of commerce, the apparent sterility of her desert plateaus as compared with the more fertile Atlas regions of the other Barbary states, and the fact that she is a vilayet of the Turkish Empire.

The anchor chain rattled through the hawsepipe of the S. S. *Adria*. Her nose swung slowly into the wind, a soft south wind laden with all those subtle and mysterious influences of that strange land, tempting one on against its gentle pressure, as though to lure him far back into those desert reaches from whence it came.

---

[1] Barbary (Berbery) included the four states—Morocco, Algeria, Tunisia, and Tripolitania.

A knock at the door of my cabin, and a short, wiry Englishman looked out from beneath a broad panama which shaded his keen, laughing eyes.

He extended his hand. "I'm William Riley; our friend's letters reached me and I've just come aboard; but I say, bustle up, if you want to get through with those Turks at the Custom-House. Perhaps I can help you," and he did as soon as I mentioned certain articles in my outfit.

"It might go badly with either of us if we sit down too hard on this ammunition," he remarked, glancing at the bagging seat of my trousers, as we stepped upon the stone customs' quay from the Arab galley which brought us ashore.

My viséed passport was sent to Redjed Pasha,[1] the Turkish Military Governor. The customs passed, two Arabs with my luggage followed in our wake up the narrow streets of one of the most Oriental coast towns of North Africa— Tripoli, the Gateway to the Sahara.

As we left the Custom-House, Mr. Riley pointed to a well curb on our right. "A few days ago a Greek merchant engaged some men to

[1] Pasha is Turkish, Bashaw Arabic, for chief, Bey or Governor.

clean out that well, which for years has been a receptacle for refuse of all kinds. The first Arab to go down was overcome at the bottom by poisonous gases; a second descended to assist him and was overcome; likewise a third, a fourth, a fifth. More would have followed had not the crowd prevented. All five lost their lives, the last one dying yesterday. The Greek merchant who engaged them was thrown into prison and fined twenty *naps* [napoleons] because, as the Turkish officials charged, the men would not have died had he not asked them to go down."

During my stay within the bastioned walls of Tripoli, my quarters were in a *lokanda* [hostelry] kept by an Italian family. This characteristic Arab house, with its plain-walled exterior and open square inner court designed to capture as little heat and as much light as possible, was on the *Arbar-Arsāt* [Street of the Four Columns]. No one ever brags of the wideness of Arab streets, and despite the fact that the Arbar-Arsāt was a Tripoline boulevard, from necessity rather than from choice I often discreetly retreated to a doorway or side street from an oncoming widely burdened camel.

The Arbar-Arsāt became my friend and chronicler. Through the busy hum and drone of passers-by at morning and evening-tide, through the hot quiet of siesta time and cool stillness of night, there drifted up to my window the story of the life of a picturesque people, replete in the ever-varying romance and bright imagery of the East.

Daily under my window a Black mother ensconced herself in the doorway with her child, where she crooned a mournful appeal to passers-by. Alms are often given these town beggars by their more fortunate brothers, for says the Koran, "it is right so to do." The following, however, may illustrate an interesting but not uncommon exception to the rule·

"In the name of Allah give alms," wailed a beggar to a richly dressed Moor who was walking ahead of me.

"May Allah satisfy all thy wants," replied the wealthy one and passed on. The wealthy one once picked up bones for a living.

The percentage of these beggars and other natives troubled with ophthalmia is very great in Tripoli, as in many Oriental cities, due in part to the fierce sun glare and the fine desert sand blown by the *gibli* [desert wind], but mainly to the flies. So it is not surprising that many of these people become blind through sheer ignorance and lethargy. But then—Allah wills!

Tripoli bestirs herself early. A few steps down the Arbar-Arsāt, my friend Hamet, a seller of fruits and vegetables, and his neighbor, the one-eyed dealer in goods from the Sudan, take down the shutters from two holes in the walls, spread their stock, and, after the manner of all good Mohammedans, proclaim in the name of the Prophet that their wares are excellent. The majority of those who drift along the Arbar-Arsāt are of the four great native races of Tripoli: Berbers, descendants of the original inhabitants; Arabs, progeny of those conquerors who overran the country centuries ago; the native Jew; and lastly, itinerant Blacks who migrate from the South.

The Berbers, like the Arabs, are a white-race people whose countless hordes centuries ago flooded over Northern Africa, coming from no one knows where. That one by Hamet's shop stops to examine some figs. His *baracan*, the prevailing outer garment of Tripolitans,[1] has

---

[1] "Tripolitans" signifies the people of the territory, "Tripoline" a dweller in the town of Tripoli.

[8]

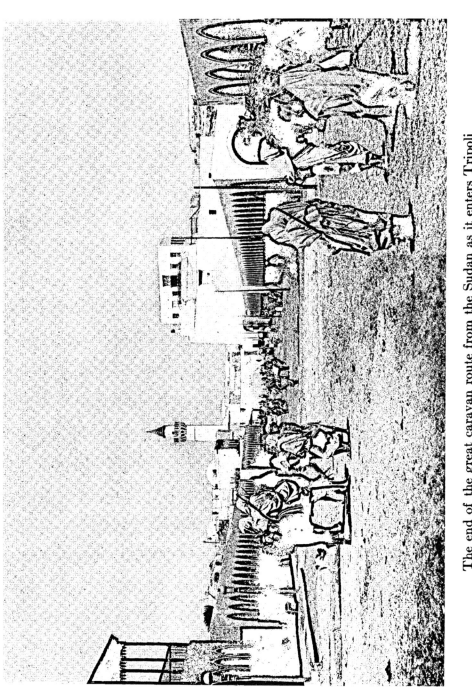

The end of the great caravan route from the Sudan as it enters Tripoli

slipped from his head, which is closely shaved, save for one thick lock of hair just back of the top. Abū Hanifah, the seer, so goes the story, advocated this lock of hair, that in battle the impure hands of the infidel might not defile the decapitated Moslem mouth or beard.

Whatever their station in life, in appearance and bearing the Arabs of to-day are worthy sons of their forbears, who forced kings of Europe to tremble for their thrones and caused her scholars to bow in reverence to a culture and learning at that time unknown to the barbarians of the North.

Look at the swarthy Hamet in full trousers and shirt of white cotton, squatting in the shadow of his shop awning. As he rises to greet a richly dressed Moor, Sāla Heba, the slave dealer, each places his right hand in turn on his heart, lips, and forehead, thus through the *temenah* [greeting], saying, "Thou hast a place in my heart, on my lips, and thou art always in my thoughts." Had these two Arabs exchanged the cotton garments and the gold-threaded turban, scarlet haik, and yellow embroidered slippers, neither would have lost his superb dignity, for either could well have graced the divan of a Bashaw.

The Blacks, mostly nomadic and fewest in numbers, come from the South to escape the crack of the slave whip or migrate in small tribes from the Sudan. At no great distance from Tripoli, under the shàdow of the palm groves of the oasis, a tribe of Hausas have erected their palm-thatched *zerebas*. Within this village they have their chief and laws after the manner of the native life of the interior.

Many of these Blacks are caravan men, but find employment in and about the town. Often along the Arbar-Arsāt I have watched these powerful fellows carry to and from the town wharves and *fondūks* [caravansaries] heavy loads of merchandise suspended on long poles slung across their shoulders. Some of them showed great calf muscles playing under deep-grooved scars like those which slashed their cheeks and temples—brands either of their tribe or of servitude.

Last but not least, however, is the native Jew. In every town of Bàrbary where the Arab tolcrates him there in the *Mellah* [Jewish quarter] he is found. Never seeming to belong there, yet omnipresent from the earliest times, he has managed not only to exist beside his Arab neighbors, but has thriven.

First and most important of the intrusive foreign element are the Turkish military and merchants whose commander-in-chief rules as Pasha of the vilayet of Tripoli. He is in command of the twenty thousand troops who exercise general surveillance over the towns and districts where they are stationed. It is the duty of these scantily clad and poorly paid Ottomans to assist in collecting taxes from the poverty-stricken Arabs, to protect caravans along the coast routes, and enforce Turkish administration in a few leading towns and their vicinities.

Next in numbers are the several hundred Italians and a Maltese colony of fisher-folk who live near the Lazaretto [Quarantine] by the sea. Members of the foreign consulates and a few other Europeans complete the population

In Tripoli the religious classification of Moslem, Jew, and Christian is most emphasized perhaps by their three respective holidays, Friday, Saturday, and Sunday. From the Western point of view this interferes somewhat with trade, but is not felt by those who would regard life as one long siesta. The extent to which even pleasurable effort is disapproved among Mohammedans is shown by the Pasha's reply when

asked to join in the dancing at one of the consulate affairs. "Why should I dance," replied his
Excellency, "when I can have some one to dance
for me?" The same reason was offered by a high
official for his inability to read and write.

As one wanders through the maze of narrow
streets the unexpected constantly delights. Every
turn presents a new picture or creates a fresh
interest and the commonplace is full of artistic
possibilities. One soon overlooks the refuse and
other things objectionable in the compelling
sense of the picturesque. Wandering among
Tripoli's sacred mosques and bazaars, losing one's
self in the romantic maze of a thousand and one
legends, one's mind is satiated with a cloying
surfeit of perfumed romance. It is as difficult to
select from this illusive whole as to tell at what
hour is the supreme moment in which to see her
—when the dew-bejewelled oasis, through which
crawls some slow-moving caravan, lies violet-
colored in the early morning; when in the heat
of the day, sun-scorched, every spot of color
stands out like the particles of a kaleidoscope;
at sunset, when desert and city are bathed in
rose; or in the still night when, blue pervaded,
she rests hushed and ghostlike on the edge

of the silent desert, the golden crescents of her mosques turned to silver and mingling with the stars.

Evidences of the Roman occupation confront one on every hand. Columns of a Pagan Rome support the beautiful domed vaultings of some of the mosques or are set in as corner posts to the houses at every other turn, and the drums thrown lengthwise and chiselled flat are used as steps or door-sills. Beyond the walls of the town fragments of tessellated pavement laid down two thousand years ago are occasionally found. Two Roman tombs decorated with mural paintings were recently discovered about a mile or so from the city. Unfortunately I was too late to see these, as the Turkish authorities at once ordered the places filled in and the spot was soon obliterated by the shifting sand. At one end of the Arbar-Arsāt, in the very heart of Tripoli, stands what once must have been one of the most splendid triumphal arches of antiquity. It is known to the Moors as the Old Arch; to the Europeans, as the Arch of Marcus Aurelius, in whose honor it was erected A. D. 164.

What seems to have been the rear of this triumphal arch now fronts the street, while its

front overlooks a wall, below which some pigs
root and grunt about in the mire. Much to
the interest of a few pedestrians, I climbed the
wall and photographed the sadly obliterated
inscription—an almost inaudible whisper of the
past. Later, inscribed on the faded leaves of
an old album,[1] I ran across a record of this
inscription made over half a century ago. It
read:

IMP . CÆS . AVRELIO . ANTONIN . AVG . P.P.ET .

IMP. . CÆS . L. . AVRELIO . VERO. . AMENIACO . AVG .

SER . — S. ORFITUS . PROCCOS . CVM . VITEDIO .

MARCELLO . LEG . SVO. . DEDICAVIT . C . CALPVRNIVS

CELSVS . CVRATOR . MVNERIS . PVB . MVNEPARIVS .

IIVIR . Q . Q . FLAMEN . PERPTVVS. . ARCV .

MARMORE . SOLIDO . FECIT

The arch appears low and heavy, which is
not surprising, considering that it is half buried
beneath centuries of accumulated rubbish and
wind-blown desert sand. Partly mortared up, it
now serves as a shop for a purveyor of dried
fish, spices, and other wares. Once I entered its
interior to outfit for a caravan journey; many
other times I visited it to admire in the dim light

---

[1] Album in possession of M. A. Zolia, with dates about 1844. It
formerly belonged to Dr. Robert G. Dickson of Tripoli uncle of
Mr. Alfred Dickson, Acting British Consul in 1904.

"In the heart of Tripoli stands . . . the Arch of Marcus Aurelius"

its beautiful sculptured ceiling and the weather-worn decorations of its exterior.

Through these narrow, fascinating streets of Tripoli her thirty thousand inhabitants go to their tasks and pleasures. Between series of arches, which serve the double purpose of re-enforcing the walls and giving shade, awnings are stretched here and there. Under these and in little booths all the industries necessary to the subsistence of the town are carried on.

At every hand one seems to be enclosed by one or two storied houses, whose bare walls with few windows and heavily made doors give little suggestion of the beauties of color and craftsmanship those of the better class may contain. On either side of the streets, particularly in the bazaar quarter, are little hole-in-the-wall shops, as though their owners had burrowed into the walls of the houses, and there, half hidden among their goods, cross-legged they squat, these merchants of the drowsy East, fanning flies and waiting for trade.

Their wares stand out in brilliant display of burnished brass, copper trays, hanging lamps, silver-mounted ebony snuffboxes, and flint-lock guns, handsomely worked saddle-bags and leather money pouches heavily embroidered and of Kano dye. In the quiet shadows of long arcades, men pass noiselessly in slippered feet over carpets and rugs from Kairwan, Misurata, and the farther East. Out in the sunlit streets a few Europeans mix with the native populace. Conspicuous among them are heavily turbaned Moors[1] in fine-textured burnoose and richly broidered vests, in strong contrast with camel men from the desert, muffled in coarse gray baracans. Then there are the blind beggars, water-carriers, and occasionally a *marabout* [holy man], who, like St. John of old, dresses in raiment of camel's hair.

The whole moving mass was like a great confetti-covered stream, here pausing, there swirling and eddying, but ever flowing between banks and islands of brilliantly colored booths with their shimmering Oriental wares. Rising above it all, caravans of camels forged quietly along with soft and dignified tread.

To the casual Occidental observer, undoubtedly the visual impressions are paramount. For the atmospheric color in its semi-tropical brilliancy serves to make more effective and lumi-

---

[1] The term "Moor" is a class more than a race distinction. It signifies a native town dweller and is used throughout Barbary,

nous the variegated detail of local color—of people, houses, mosques, and bazaars. But to one to whom it is a prism through which he views Moorish thought and character in deeper relationship, it has a far-reaching symbolism— the all-pervading influence of Islam.

Spanning the street of the *Suk-el-Turc* [Turks' Market] is a trellis-work covered with grape-vines. Through their green leaves and clusters of purple fruit great splashes of sunlight fall on drowsy Moors. Here most of the official business is transacted, and notaries as well as other public officials have their offices. Near by is the principal mosque, and in the light transparent shadow of its arcade sit the sellers of caps. The bright glare of the sunlight makes it difficult to see into many of the shops, but at the sound of a shuttle one may pause a moment and see an Arab weaving on his loom fabrics of the finest quality and intricate design. Near by in an opening blackened with smoke a barefooted baker moulds coarse dough into flat, rounded loaves.

Down the street the faint intermittent tinkling of a bell is heard   "*Bur-r-ro!*" [Get out!] in warning rasps the high-pitched voice of a camel driver. I dodged quickly into the shop of a silversmith and watched four lumbering camels squdge softly by. To prevent those behind the driver from being stolen, the halter rope of each was tied to the tail of the one ahead, and on the tail of the last camel, as he flipped and flapped it from side to side tinkled a bell.

A wily one of the Faithful, not being rich in this world's goods, turned covetous eyes on a nomadic brother who passed through the town leading a string of six camels. "Allah! Allah ursel el Allah! Could not the brother spare one of his *jamal ℓ*" [camels]. So, dusting the flies from his eyes and hooding himself with his baracan, he stealthily followed. He was aware that near the New Gate the street narrowed and made a double turn. No sooner had the driver and head camel rounded the first corner than the wily one seized the bell attached to the hindmost camel. With a stroke of his knife he severed it from the tail of the animal, and keeping it tinkling, quickly fastened it to the tail of the next, cut loose the last beast, and—"Allah wills" —made off with his prize.

Probably no superstition has a stronger, more universal hold on the Mohammedan than his

" A barefooted baker moulds coarse dough into . . . rounded loaves "

belief that one may cast upon him the influence of the "evil eye." Let a stranger, particularly one not a Moslem, look intently on anything worn or carried on the person of an Arab, and he will straightway, to nullify the spell, wet his fingers and pass them over the object upon which the stranger's gaze is cast. Inquire after the health of his wife, or seek to flatter him, and he raises a protecting hand to his face. Fetishes in the images of hands are seen among the ornaments worn about the persons of the women, symbolized in the decorations of utensils, and occasionally on the exterior of their mosques. Over many an arched portal is the impression of a black hand print to protect its inmates. A number of times a door left accidentally ajar has been slammed to as I passed, on account of the influence which my "evil eye" might have upon the occupants.

Flanking Tripoli on the east is the ancient Castle of the Bashaws. Under its walls and bordering the sea lies the garden of the Turkish Army and Navy Club [known as the Café], which in the cool of the day is the social rendezvous of the foreign element of Tripoli. When the sapphire-blue shadow of the great castle wall had thrown itself across the garden and crept its way over the sandy stretch of the Tuesday Market beyond, and the distant Arab houses sewed a golden thread across the dusk shadows of the coming twilight, together with the little coterie of English residents and other friends, the end of the day was invariably spent about one of its tables. Here, over our Turkish coffee, *mastica*, and *lakoom*, the latest news would be discussed; a recently arrived caravan, the latest edict of the Pasha, anything from the arrival of Turkish exiles to the Thames boat-race or London and Paris quotations on ivory and feathers.

I found out some time after my arrival that I was the first American to visit Tripoli for two years. The sudden alighting in their midst of a stranger had set going at full pressure their speculative machinery, and for a time I was regarded as a spy.

One evening at the Turkish Club we turned our attention from the praying figures of the Moslems in a near-by cemetery to an incoming steamer. Then the conversation drifted, like the lazy wreaths of the cigarette smoke, to the ancient Castle of the Bashaws, which flanks the city on the east. Within its ramparts is a little village, and could its old walls speak, they could tell tales of intrigue, romance, and bloodshed innumerable. I had been through the prisons and barracks for which it is now used, and had talked with some of the prisoners. One was a Turkish exile, a man of education, who for political reasons had sacrificed his freedom for his convictions, and considered himself lucky to have escaped being sent far south to Murzuk with its sense-robbing climate.

"Do you see that spot in the wall, close to the ground and under that corner bastion?" said my friend Riley, pointing to where a small hole had apparently been bricked up. "Well, one afternoon, I was passing here from the *Suk* [market] when a ragged, unkempt fellow appeared in the caravan road there, acting most strangely. He seemed afraid to walk erect, and, though in broad daylight, groped his way about in a most uncanny manner. A crowd collected. Turkish guards soon appeared and conducted him back to the Castle from which he had come. Yes, through that stoned-up hole. You see the poor beggar had been in there for years, down in one of the dungeons below the ground. He had been there so long that no one remembered who he was or for what he had been imprisoned; but somehow he managed to secure a hard instrument and dig his way out. Had he reached the outside at this time of day or at night, he might have escaped. Why didn't he? Coming from the darkness, he found himself blinded by the strong sunlight, and the heavy iron shackles on his feet gave him away. Unless he is dead, perhaps the poor wretch is there now, only a few yards from us— but on the other side of the wall." Riley knocked the ashes from his cigarette and looked thoughtfully at the *Adria* steaming in with the weekly mail.

CHAPTER TWO

TOWN SCENES AND INCIDENTS

FROM the top of my lokanda I could look over the dazzling, whitewashed, color-tinted city, a great sea of flat housetops broken only by several minarets, an occasional palm-tree, the castle battlements, and the flag-staffs of the European Consulates. The mosques, the city walls, and some of the more important buildings are built of huge blocks of stone, but on the whole it is a city of sun-dried bricks, rafters of palm-wood, and whitewash. This material serves its purpose well in a country of heat and little rain, but permitted of a unique catastrophe in February, 1904.

Some miles back of the town in the low desert foot-hills, owing to a cloud-burst, a great body of water was accumulated in a natural reservoir. Suddenly it burst, flooded across the country without warning, and on a bright clear day swept through the oasis and town of Tripoli, gullying its way to the sea. Sweeping around the bases of the houses, the sun-dried bricks at their foundations disintegrated like melting snow, the walls collapsed, and some eighty people perished. For almost a day it cut off traffic along the main caravan road as it led into Tripoli. Great crowds gathered along its banks and on the roofs of the neighboring houses. The next day muffled figures searched amongst the débris in the gully for their lost ones and property.

Often under the blue-green of African nights I would sit in my window, whose broad stone ledge still held the heat of the departed day, and listen in undisturbed reverie to the night sounds of the Arab city, sounds among which the rumble of traffic was conspicuously absent, sounds which took on a personal element—the soft scuff of feet; the prayer calls of Muezzins; far-off cries, voices of an almost forgotten people. From under the palms far out beyond the town, the hoarse bark of a wolf-hound drifts in, as patrolling the mud walls of his master's gardens he warns away marauders. Though early evening, the Arbar-Arsāt is almost deserted. A low, sustained whistle, then down in the dark shadow a dusky figure moves noiselessly by. Soon

The result of the flood

"Muffled figures searched . . . for their lost ones and property"

another whistle from the direction in which he has gone, and I know a second night watchman has passed him along. Thus to a certain extent does Tripoli protect or watch her inhabitants, who for good or ill may have occasion to trace their way at night through her dangerous, tortuous streets.

Drifting over the housetops come wavering pulsations of sound. Then from some distant quarter they take form, and the wild beat of the tom-toms, strangely suggestive of the great elemental nature, heat, and passion of the drowsy and fanatical East, throbs its way nearer and nearer through the maze of dark and deserted streets. Now the long-sustained or rippling resonant notes of the oboes and thrumming gimbrehs are discernible. "Lu-lu-lu-lu!" ring out the shrill voices of women; clash! go the steel cymbals, and a wedding procession turns into the Arbar-Arsāt.

A yelling runner on ahead passes under my window, then in irregular march the procession itself. First, bearers of lanterns of colored glass which throw beautiful prismatic lights on the white-walled houses and illumine the swarthy faces of the musicians who follow them; then more lanterns, diffusing the darkness, glinting in scintillating reflections from the men's eyes, and throwing great slashes of mellow light down upon the heads and shoulders of the muffled forms of the women. In their midst, seated on a donkey, rides the bride, hidden from view under a *palanquin* [canopy]. Again follow lanterns illuminating the dark canopy, etching out the red gold threads of the heavy embroidery from its dark, velvety background.

Just beyond my window the procession halts, wails a song, and moves on. Then the wild rhapsody of a desert people grows fainter; again only the tom-toms sound out in their barbaric prosody and float away over the town and the desert sand. A scavenger dog sneaks by and the city sleeps.

One midnight I watched the moon disk pass behind the minaret of the Djema-el-Daruj [Mosque of the Steps] at the corner and paint the city in silver. On the other side of the Arbar-Arsāt, far down the street, I caught sight now and again of a thief, as, rope in hand to lower himself into the courts, he worked his way along the roof tops. Quick and catlike his wiry figure dropped lightly to a lower level here, or scaled a height there, until he reached the house across the street. Sitting motionless I watched him with interest. Barefooted, he wore only a pair of cotton trousers, while a turban was twisted about his fez. The moonlight played over the muscles of his supple body and glinted a silver crescent from his crooked Arab knife. It was not until directly opposite that he saw me. For a second he stood motionless, then like a flash dropped below the parapet of the house and disappeared.

Many an evening I would saunter down the Arbar-Arsāt; pause long enough at the door of the Djema-el-Daruj to sense the interior of this beautiful shrine, lit only with its suspended cluster of myriad little lamps. These twinkled in the gray darkness like the falling stars of a bursting rocket and shed their delicate glow over the prostrate figures of the devout Moslems beneath them. On straw mattings which covered the marble floor, they turned their faces toward the *kibleh* [sacred niche] and Mecca. I rarely stopped, however, to deliberately peer into this sanctuary, lest I give offence. The next corner brought me to the Street of the Milk Sellers' Market. Knocking at a big green door, I would shortly meet with a cordial reception from my friend Riley.

His house, originally built for and occupied by the favorite wife of Yussef Bashaw, was one of the best examples of the *seraglio* of a high-class Arab. A broad balcony surrounding the court took the place of the living-room, after the manner of the Arabs. Here amidst a bower of tropical plants, carpeted with rare rugs and furnished with all the necessities for a complete home life in the East, most of the family life is spent. Off the balcony were the private living-rooms. After the Arab custom, originally no two were connected and all save one received their light through barred windows opening upon the balcony. Several of these rooms had been converted into one spacious drawing-room and another into a library.

Both Bashaw and Sultana have long since gone. Yussef's bones repose in a mosque of his own name, while under an arched tomb of the Sultanas at Sciara-el-Sciut, the dust which was once the beautiful Lilla lies beneath the wind-blown sands near the sun-scorched desert trail which leads to Misurata. I gazed in fascinating reverie at the worn depressions in the floor tiles and where the edges of the balustrades had become softened and rounded.

One evening, after Sālam, the black Sudanese, had brought us our Turkish coffee, we settled down comfortably on the long wicker seats. The addax horns and native weapons on the walls painted long diverging slashes of black in the lamplight. The lamp shed its rays through the balustrade into the court, and the gnarled old tree which rose from its centre threw fantastic genii shadows on the opposite walls; the soft wind rustled in its canopy of leaves, through which an occasional star scintillated in a bit of blue.

"Riley," said I, "who lives in the big house with the heavy bolted door, near my lokanda?"

"The one with the Roman column for a corner post? Why do you ask?"

"Well, in passing I often look up at the lattice which projects from the window above its portal, and this afternoon when the sun fell full upon it, through its jalousied wood-work I saw indistinctly the face of a girl, then heard a gruff voice, and she disappeared."

"Strange! Those jalousies, you know, screen the only window in the house that looks out on the street. That window is in the *gulphor*—a room strictly private to the master of the house, none of his immediate family ever being allowed to enter without his particular permission. Come!" said Riley; "I will show you," and he led the way to his private study, which had formerly been the gulphor of Arab masters. "Step out here," and I found myself in a little latticed box outside the window. "This hole in the floor allows one to see who may be knocking at the door directly beneath, but it has been known to be used by Moorish maidens as a means of communication with outsiders. By the way, you found no piece of cloth or paper in the street, did you? Odd stories have been associated with that house. It is rumored that a young Circassian girl, mysteriously brought from across the Mediterranean, is confined there in the seraglio of her master."

We talked late, for the night was hot. During the day the silver thread of the mercury had hovered about blood-heat, and now, at midnight, it had dropped only to eighty degrees; but this was nothing unusual in Tripoli. Suddenly the brindled bulldog started from his dozing at his master's feet and with a low growl sprang upon the top of the balustrade which he patrolled, sniffing high in the air.

"A thief on the roof," remarked Riley. "One night, not long before you came, that pup woke me out of a sound sleep. There was the devil of a rumpus in the street outside my door. Backed up against it, doing the best he could with his heavy *krasrullah* [knobbed stick], which all Tripolitans carry at night, was Hadji Ali, a neighbor, putting up a game fight with three big Blacks with knives. Opening the door, I pulled him in; the Blacks started to follow. From behind my revolver I told them that any man who sought my protection against murderers would have it. Ordering them away, I closed the door and made Hadji comfortable for the night."

"What had he done to them?"

"Oh, nothing; they were hired by his enemy, another neighbor. They hid in that archway up the street and sprang out at him as he passed." As I went by the archway on my return that night I hugged the farther wall and carried my revolver in my hand."

It is little wonder that here in the Bled-el-Ateusch—The Country of Thirst—where the

relentless sun enforces rest and the great solitudes seem to brood a sadness over things,
there has been engendered in all the people
a life of contemplation and fatalism little known
and still less understood by thicker-blooded
men whose lives are spent in struggle and ac-
tivity against the adverse elements of northern
climes.

Tripoli is a land of contrasts—rains which
turn the dry *wadis* [river beds] into raging torrents and cause the country to blossom over
night, then month after month without a shower
over the parched land; suffocating days and cool
nights; full harvests one year, famine the next;
without a breath of air, heat-saturated, yellow
sand wastes bank against a sky of violet blue;
then the terrific blast of the *gibli*, the south-east
wind-storm, lifts the fine powdered desert sand in
great whoofs of blinding orange, burying caravans and forcing the dwellers in towns to close
their houses tightly.

Arab character in a marked degree seems to
be the child of its environment and has inherited
many of the characteristics of the great solitudes
among which it has dwelt for thousands of years.
On the one hand the Arab is hospitable and open-

Rows of shops by the Market Gate, where the caravans " outfit "

handed; on the other treacherous, grasping, and cruel; seemingly mild and lazy, yet he is capable of performing extraordinary feats of labor. His religion and literature are full of poetry, but many of their tenets are lacking in his daily life. In his architecture and design the highest artistic instinct is shown, yet the representation of any living thing is forbidden. Stoical and dignified, yet he is capable of being roused by any wandering marabout to an ungovernable state of fanaticism; now you know him, again he is as mysterious and changeable as the shifting sand about him; by nature he is a nomad, a dweller in tents rather than in towns. "Allah has bestowed four peculiar things upon us," say the Arabs: "our turbans shall be to us instead of diadems, our tents instead of walls and houses, our swords as intrenchments, and our poems instead of written laws."

By the creed of Islam all lines are drawn, all distinctions made. Upon the traditions of Mohammed and the interpretations of the Koran the Arab orders his manner of life in polity, ethics, and science, and "Allah hath said it," is the fatalistic standard of his daily life. The teachings of the Koran and centuries of warfare in which women were but part of the victor's loot have in no small degree helped to develop that exclusiveness which is a cardinal principle in the Moslem life, for there is no social intercourse among Mohammedans in the Occidental sense of the word.

The plain-walled house of the Tripolitan Arab, with its heavily bolted .door and jalousied window, is built with due consideration to guarding well the secrets and private life of the occupants, and whether large or small, in town or country, all are of the same plan.

The inner court is the quarters of the mistress of the harem. In many of these are ancient marble columns, while rare old China tiles adorn the walls. Here the mistress entertains companies of women; here they celebrate in their peculiar fashion the birth of a child or wail the burial-song over the body of the dead.

Occasionally a Moorish woman is permitted to visit the mosques at night, accompanied by a servant. Sometimes she calls on a woman friend or with an attendant visits the bazaars. At these times she wears a baracan of fine texture, and a dark blue veil bound around her forehead covers her face. According to the thickness of this veil, her features may be more or less distinguishable. I have noticed that oftentimes the more beautiful a woman, the thinner the veil. Tripolitan women of the middle class have a custom of going about without veils, but draw the baracan over the face instead, leaving a small aperture through which they peek with one eye. Women of the lower class—the countrywomen and Bedawi—frequently go with faces uncovered.

The country Arab converts all his scant earnings into silver ornaments, and these are deposited on the persons of his wives—a veritable burden of riches, for they are constantly worn. I have run across women hauling water under the cattle yoke of the desert walls, literally loaded down with pounds of silver, while the husband sat on the edge of the well-curb and directed the irrigation of his fields.

This silver forms an important function as a barometer of the country's prosperity, to read which one has but to go to the little booths of the silversmiths in the trellis-covered Suk-el-Turc and note whether the country people are sellers or buyers. In 1900, a year of poor crops, $72,500 worth of this old silver, so dear to the womankind of the peasantry, was broken up and exported, chiefly to France.

The Turkish Imperial taxation is under the head of *verghi* [poll and property tax] and the tithe on agricultural produce. During the ten years preceding my sojourn in Tripoli, the total averaged $540,000 annually.

The verghi payable by the vilayet was fixed at a sum equivalent to $408,000. Only in two years was this obtained, ın 1901 and surpassed in 1902. Both were years of bad harvests, showing the tremendous pressure which must have been brought to bear on the peasants by the authorities. During the past thirty years the trade of Tripoli has been stationary, with an average annual value of $3,850,000—exports balancing imports with remarkable regularity.

Though the Tripolitan ıs quick to learn he has little creative genius, and his constitutional apathy is a formidable barrier against departure from his primitive customs and traditions. In the deserts certain tribes live by means of reprisals and by extorting heavy tolls from caravans. In the vicinity of the populated districts there are marauding bands of thieves, and in the towns and *suks* [markets] are scheming ne'er-do-wells. But

from my observation, most of the people hard-earned their bread at honest labor: the artisan in the town, the farmer in the country, the trader and caravan man on the trails.

CHAPTER THREE

WHILE the vilayet of Tripoli is a purely agricultural province, a very small area of these barren, inhospitable wastes is cultivated or cultivable under present conditions, and one need not look far for the primary cause—the yoke of Turkish taxation. "Give me until to-morrow and I will pay my verghi," I once heard an Arab farmer say to a Turkish tax collector.

"Then give me your camel."

"She and her foal were sold at Ramadan [Annual Fast]," was the reply.

"Ha! thou kafir [unbeliever], thy baracan will fetch little enough," and without a murmur the Arab was stripped of the garment.

The district which lies between the crumbling eastern extremity of the Atlas known as the Tripoli Hills and the sea forms almost the entire present productive soil of the vilayet of Tripoli, being two-fifths of its 410,000 square miles. In this narrow strip, Arabs, Berbers, and Bedawi cultivate cereals, vegetables, and fruit trees. Here one is transported into an Old Testament land, to a people who still cling with childish tenacity to the picturesque and crude customs of ages past. There amid a flock of sheep is Joseph; Rebecca is filling an earthen water-jar at a desert well, or perhaps a young Bedaween sower after the first autumnal rains have soaked the ground, goes forth to sow. With a rhythmic swing of the arm he broadcasts seed. An elder member of the family, perhaps the old sheik himself, follows with a crude iron-tipped plough drawn by a camel, cow, or dilapidated ass. About four inches of soil are scratched up, but enough to turn under the seed, and the rest is left to nature. After the grain is garnered it is flailed or tramped out under hoof on some hard-packed spot, and a windy day awaited, when it is thrown in the air, and wheat and chaff are thus separated.

The soil, however, is so fertile, that with abundant rains the harvests are surprising in their yield. The seed sown is occasionally wheat, guinea corn, or millet, but generally barley, the staple food of the Arab.

Through lack of rain the Tripolitan can count

on only four good harvests out of ten. This also affects the wool production, and in bad years the Arab, fearing starvation, sells his flocks and his seed for anything he can get. Through lack of initiative and encouragement added to the burden of heavy taxation, fully one-half of the cultivable soil lies fallow, and the Arab cattle-raiser or peasant sows only sufficient seed for his support through the coming year. Any surplus which may be acquired, however, generally finds its way into the hand of the usurer and the tax gatherer, so that the Arab stands to lose by extended cultivation.

An oasis originally meant a habitation which presupposed the existence of water, but has come to mean any cultivated spot. It is usually developed where springs or surface water are to be found; otherwise wells are sunk and the land irrigated by water drawn from them in huge goat-skin buckets.

Selecting some satisfactory spot, the Arab digs his well, sets out his palms and orange-trees, and shortly under their shadows raises fruits and vegetables. In the cool of the day he hauls water to the well-top in the goat-skin buckets, to be automatically spilled into an adjoining cistern.

This filled, a gateway is opened through which
the sparkling liquid rushes, finally trickling
away down the little ground channels by which
the garden is irrigated. Camel, cow, donkey, or
wife may be the motor power used to bring the
water to the top of the well. This is achieved by
hauling the well rope down the inclined plane of
a pit. There was one well I used to visit in the
oasis of Tripoli that was tended by an old blind
man. Down into the pit he would go with his
cow, turn her about, then up again. When
something went wrong with the tackle he would
lean dangerously out from the slimy well-curb
or crawl along the rope beam over the opening
to adjust the rope—no easy feat even for a man
who could see.

From the desert at the back of the town one
looks across a sea of sand surrounding the heavy
battlements. The coast and part of the city
walls are screened by a narrow five mile oasis of
date-palms a mile wide, which raise their chiselled
shafts high above the houses and mingle their
gracefully feathered tops with the needle spires
of the minarets. It is not its beauty alone, however, which makes the date-palm queen among
trees: its shadow is protection from the heat; its

leaves are used for mats and thatching; its wood for building and fuel; its fibre for ropes and baskets; its juice for drinking, and its fruit for food; even its stones, those which are not exported to Italy to adulterate coffee, are made into a paste fodder for animals. No less than two millions of these regal beauties are grown by the Arabs in the vilayet of Tripoli, and great quantities of the fruit finds its way to the arid plateau lands of the Fezzan, whose inhabitants make it their principal diet.

Outside the town walls, or at established spots within the oasis, suks are held on certain days of the week. To these, over the sandy highways through the palm groves, passes the native traffic—small caravans of donkeys and camels loaded with the products of agriculturists, and shepherds with their flocks of sheep, which patter along in a cloud of sand dust.

I once saw a little donkey on the way to market supporting a corpulent Arab, a bag of corn, and a live sheep. Now and again the little burden bearer showed its fatigue and disgust by lying down in the road. Nothing of that nature, though, could disturb the imperturbable son of Allah, who held in place the corn and the sheep

Road through the Oasis of Tripoli

"Over the sandy highways . . . passes the native traffic"

and stood astride the ass, forcing it to lift him as it regained its feet.

The horse is used only for riding. Some fine breeds are found among certain tribes of the Tuaregs and others in the extreme south, or are owned by the wealthy Arabs of Barbary. Those seen about the towns and oases are ordinary specimens and are abominably treated. The Arab generally uses a cruel bit, goads his horse unmercifully with the sharp corners of his broad, scoop-like stirrups of steel, and has a bad habit of drawing it up sharply out of a full run. He is greatly aided in this feat by the character of the Arab saddle, which is undoubtedly the model from which our Western stock saddle originated. The horse-riding Tuaregs have a stirrup which in size is the other extreme of that used by the Arabs, it being just large enough to admit the big toe. Those Tuaregs who infest the northern deserts and the Asgar and Kelowis Tuaregs who control the Tripoli-Sudan trade routes, use the riding camel.

The Suk-el-Thalat [Tuesday Market] is held just without the walls of Tripoli on a broad stretch of sand bordering the sea, and the Friday Market farther out in the oasis.

One morning before dawn I passed through the Castle Gate to the Suk-el-Thalat. Many others, mostly merchants from the town, were moving in the same direction. There was Hamet's one-eyed neighbor. Like many others, he carried a little portable shack, under which to spread his wares. I climbed to the top of the high wall of a square enclosure. In the early light the gray and white baracans of the people merged into the tone of the sand, and I could sense the great noiseless mass of humanity moving below me only by the dark spots of faces, arms, and legs. Then the sunlight flooded a scene as truly barbaric and pastoral as any in the days of Abraham.

A palette of living, moving color, this red-fezzed, baracaned humanity wormed its way between piles of multicolored products of the oasis—scintillating brass, copper, and silver utensils; ornaments, brilliant cloths, and leather trappings from the antipodes of Tripoli trade—Kano and Manchester. Most of the populace were merchants from the town, others tillers of the soil from the oases and plateau lands, half-naked Blacks from the neighboring suburb of Sciara-el-Sciut, caravan men and camel raisers from the tribes of Zintan, Orfella, and the Weled-Bu-Sef. Darkly clothed Jews were much in evidence, also wild desert men from the far south and nomadic traders from anywhere. Here the high, round fez, modern rifle, patched brown suit, and heavy shoes bespoke the Ottoman soldier, and the occasional glare of a pipe-clayed sun helmet, a European.

In the wall's shadow just below my perch squatted a vender of knives. For culinary use? Not by Mohammed's beard! A knife is a thing to slay with; none but infidels, Jews, and Christians at repast would portion food with such an instrument. Prospective customers crowded about him; some drew the crooked blades from their brass-mounted sheaths and bargained at their leisure. Instinctively they preferred to barter, but this method of trade has been greatly superseded by the use of Turkish currency, although napoleons and sovereigns pass in the coast towns as readily as *paras* and *medjidies*.

The following extract from a letter of a leading British resident of Tripoli will give an insight into the character and business methods of the Tripoli town Arab.

The *good* old Arab is fast *dying* out, only a few remaining of the old school. When I came here seventeen years ago [and not made my fortune yet] I sold hundreds of pounds to the Arabs, entering the goods to their debit in my books, calculating the amount with them, and they always paid up without any bother. When a man was ill he would send word and when well again would come round and bring the money. The new and present generation cannot be trusted. . . . They are learning tricks from the Jews and find they have to do them to be able to compete. It is quite a common thing for Arabs here to fail and offer 20 per cent. to 25 per cent.; before you never heard of an Arab smashing he has learned all the vices of the European . . . and has slipped the good points of the Arab.

The rural Arabs are thoroughly ignorant, superstitious, and suspicious when they come into town, knowing that the Jews, most of the Europeans, and the town Arabs are all on the lookout to take him in. He is hard-working and tills in his garden or field with his family, coming into town on market day to sell his produce and buy his little supplies.

The world over the *paysan* is the natural prey of the sophisticated and unscrupulous urbanite. But the methods by which these leeches extract their ill-gotten pelf is as varied as the conditions under which it must be obtained.

Watch that Arab yonder; the one who has just turned in by the camel market with his flock of sheep. He soon stops and huddles them all in a bunch about him. It is early yet and he refuses the low offers proffered by several passers-by.

"B'is salāmah! On thy peace, uncle pilgrim," and a keen-visaged Moor greets him with the Temenah.

A primitive method of transportation

Carrying h avჳo als o merchandise from the Custom-House

"Gedash! [how much] has been offered thee for thy flock?"

"Four medjidies [$3.52] a sheep."

"What dog of an unbeliever has offered the price of his own skin to one of the Faithful? Thy sheep are fat and of good kind and by Allah are worth double, but hold, givest me one per cent. if I sell for twice that which is offered thee? Well said! Come then to yonder fondūk at the edge of the Suk and we will there place thy flock for safety." The Moor draws from his leathern money bag a few paras and pays for the stabling, the fondūk keeper naturally supposing him to be the owner.

"Now," said the leech, "let us take one sheep and go back to the Suk with it" Then through the crowd they pick their way, the leech carrying the sheep across his shoulder.

"Hold, brother, may Allah lengthen thy age. Stay thou here with this sheep, while I seek a customer."

Tired of waiting, and with growing suspicion the man from the *wadān* [country] at last hurries back to the fondūk, only to find that the leech had long since taken the flock and disappeared.

The wall upon which I had been seated enclosed a rectangular yard of several acres in which bulky loads of the wild *esparto* grass, or *halfa*, as the Arabs call it, were being removed from the camels, eventually to be shipped to England for the manufacture of paper.

Patches of blood stained the sand outside some neighboring shacks. They are but the sign of the Arab barber, who, in addition to his tonsorial accomplishments, like the barbers of old, performs simple surgical operations, and our striped barber-pole is but an ancient symbol representing a twisted bandage.

Passing through the produce quarter, I picked my way through heaps of grain, piles of melons, tomatoes, and other stuffs which made gorgeous spottings of color as they lay in the brilliant sunshine, or under the violet shadows of the shacks which were shifted from time to time as the sun wore around. Under a tattered piece of old burlap two Sudanese roasted fodder corn; men scuffed noiselessly by over the hot sand, pausing here and there to ask, "Gedash?" "How much?" Often they squatted down in front of the goods and sometimes spent an hour or more bargaining.

I soon came to the Arab butcher shops. Suspended from heavy poles the meat hung dressed and ready for sale, and one cannot help being impressed with the very evident fact that practically no portion of the animal is considered unsalable. The nature of the Oriental climate has rendered certain kinds of food detrimental to health, and this with the Arab, as with the Jews, has led to a division of animals into clean and unclean. Those for the diet of the Faithful must be killed in a prescribed way. According to the Turkish law of the country, it must be killed in the early morning, and by reason of the extreme heat must be sold by the night of the same day.

Within an open spot a wild, unkempt fellow holds forth to a circle of sober-visaged hearers. His long hair and fantastic garb at once stamp him as a marabout, or Mohammedan wandering monk. His kind are conspicuous characters among the people upon whom they live as, generally bareheaded, staff in hand, they drift along the desert trails through the oases and towns. Most of these half-demented caricatures of humanity dress in filthy rags and claim lineal descent from Mohammed. Attributed as they are with supernatural powers, it is little wonder that they are venerated by the superstitious

Moslems. At Ramadan they are very much in evidence, and have been indirectly responsible for holy wars and the direct cause of many uprisings and revolutions

The arrival of a large caravan from the Sudan is a great event, and as it reaches Tripoli groups of women shrill their cry of welcome. Many small caravans may be seen in the Suk when market is held.

Frequently toward the end of the market day I would drop into one of the numerous little coffee-houses which border the easterly end of the Suk. Low benches lined its sides, and from a dark corner on one of these, I would watch my Arab neighbors smoke thoughtfully over their slender thimble pipes of *kief* and *hashish*.

Between me and an Arab opposite the hazy smoke wreaths curled and lost themselves on the heat-laden air. As the hashish lulled his feverish brain to sleep in the Fields of the Blessed, perhaps through its fumes he saw miraged the events of a time when his sires unfurled their banners before Poitiers, flaunting them for centuries in the very eyes of Europe from the walls of Toledo and Granada, and Basquan valleys echoed the Mezzin's call.

Market outside Tripoli's walls, Castle and cemetery on the right

Through the smoke mist I saw but a representative of a poor tax-ridden people. I saw the great caravan trade through which they acquire their main exports, ivory, feathers, and Sudan skins, now almost gone, and her principal export, esparto grass, further back in the *jebel* [mountains] and growing more sparsely each successive year. Leaving the coffee-house I crossed the deserted Suk, just as the great red lantern of the sun lowered from sight and painted the spaces between the date-palms with bold slashes of red.

CHAPTER FOUR

SĀLAM, A HAUSA SLAVE

AMONG the many nomads who camp for a
time in the oasis of Tripoli or on the outskirts of the town are occasional tribes of
Blacks, who have wandered across the Great
Desert. These are very clannish, and do not
mix much with the inhabitants of the towns, not
even with those of their own color. Perhaps the
most interesting of these Sudanese are the
Hausas, to which people Sālam [1] belonged.
Sālam, like many others of that splendid race
who inhabit the Negro states of the far Sudan,
had once taken his slim chances of escape across
the desert wastes, arriving at last in Tripoli,
where, as in numerous other North African
towns under Turkish or French control, a slave
may obtain his freedom by becoming a Turkish
or French subject.

During my sojourn in Tripoli, Sālam at times

[1] Sālam has been previously mentioned as the servant of an
English resident in Tripoli.

was placed at my service by his master. The picture of this Hausa, when he first smiled in an appearance at my lokanda, is still vivid in my memory

It was one hot August night an hour after the evening prayer had wavered from the minarets across the housetops of Tripoli. I was sitting alone; my doors opened out on the broad balcony which surrounded the inner court. The night wind rustled softly through the upper branches of an olive-tree; a booma bird croaked hoarsely on its nest; the candle flickered. I must admit I was inwardly startled as I looked up from my writing at a white burnoosed figure, which had suddenly emerged from the darkness and now stood beside me. It was Sālam. I remember how black his hand looked in contrast with the white note from his master which he delivered to me.

His short, well-built figure was wrapped in six yards of baracan. From this bundle beneath the red fez, his face like polished ebony mirrored the candle flame in brilliant high lights, and below a heavy beak-like nose, his white teeth glistened and his deep-cut tribal scars criss-crossed in blacker shadows his cheeks and temples. He received my answer: again the light flickered and Sālam disappeared as quietly as he came.

Far away to the south, six to eleven months as the camel journeys, south where the caravans end their long voyages and the Great Desert meets the forests, is the land of the Hausas, that great organized Black Empire. There, in the town of Merādi Katsena, Sālam was born. His town was like thousands of others which lie scattered over the width and breadth of the Central Sudan, their mud walls and thatched roofs baking under the tropical sun of Hausa-land.

Though short in stature, the Hausas, figuratively speaking, are mentally head and shoulders above any of the numerous Black tribes of Africa. They have a written language resembling Arabic and the traveller through the Sudan who speaks Hausa can be understood almost everywhere.

Despite the fact that the Hausas are a commerce-loving people, slavery from time immemorial has been a national curse. For centuries the noiseless tread of laden slaves has worn deep-rutted paths below the forest level, packing them hard as adamant and weaving an intricate sys-

Sālam, the Hausa
Equipped with a spear and a shield of rhinoceros hide

tem of narrow highways through the jungles of Hausaland. Incomprehensible as it may seem, it is nevertheless a fact that only a few years ago at least one out of every three hundred persons in the world was a Hausa-speaking slave.[1]

Notwithstanding horrible atrocities committed by slave-holders, slaves have always had certain rights of their own. Sometimes their condition is better than before captivity, and it is not unusual for head slaves to be slave-owners themselves and to be placed in positions of high trust. One noted instance is that of Rabbah, an ex-slave of Zubehr Pasha, who by direction of the Māhdi became governor of the great eastern Hausa state of Darfur.

The slave traffic, based as it is on a tribute-paying system, has had a most demoralizing effect, and until the recent extension of the British sphere of influence permanent security of life and property was unknown. Slaves sent out with the *garflas* [caravans] often travel as far north as Tripoli and other towns in Barbary where freedom could be had for the asking, but

[1] Charles H. Robinson, in "Hausaland," says: "It is generally admitted that the Hausa-speaking population number at least fifteen millions, *i. e.*, roughly speaking, one per cent. of the world's population, . . . and at the very least one-third are in a state of slavery."

through fear or ignorance many return south again to their bondage. The sum necessary for a slave to buy his freedom, subject as he would be to arbitrary taxation and recapture, is prohibitive, so only escape remains with its attendant risks.

As Sālam trudged beside me through the oasis of Tripoli, or during quiet hours spent together in my lokanda, he told me of himself and his people. In order to appreciate the circumstances surrounding Sālam's capture, one must understand the conditions in his country. A state of feudal warfare between many neighboring towns is a chronic condition throughout Hausaland. The tribute-paying system rather than a state of war was responsible for slave raiding, for vassal chiefs and towns were obliged to include large numbers of slaves in their annual tribute. The powerful Sultan of Sokoto demanded from the Hausa states three-fourths of his tribute in human beings—and got them—ten thousand coming from the King of Adamawa alone. It was in one of these slave-raiding expeditions that Sālam was first made a slave. At the time he lived at Midaroka, where he had been taken by his brother-in-law, Lasunvadi, after the death of his parents.

SĀLAM, A HAUSA SLAVE

"I was cutting fodder in the open with Lasunvadi's slaves," said Sālam. "We had stopped work to await the approach of a great number of horsemen, thinking they were some of our own people. 'They are warriors of Filahni!' suddenly cried a slave and we fled for the brush. I was among those captured and taken to Filahni. The journey was hard; some of the slaves attempted to escape and were clubbed to death. I was then fourteen years old and valuable, so I became the property of Durbee, the Bashaw's son. Durbee was just to his slaves, and we fared well. He had a great many horses which means wealth and power in my land, for every horse means a mounted warrior.

"My work was about my master's compound, but often I would steal away and sleep in the shade of a papaw tree, or watch the scarlet-breasted jamberdes flit about, and the monkeys chase and swing among the branches. Sometimes Durbee himself would find me and shake me awake. 'For what do I give you yams and *dawa?*' [bread] he would say. I would reply, 'Haste is of the devil and tardiness from the All Merciful.' 'Hubba! thou lazy mud fish,' he would shout, and it would be many days before my back would heal from the welts of his rhinoceros hide."

Working when made to, sleeping when he could, a year passed. In the evening he watched the slaves gamble about the fire, often staking anything of value he might have acquired. As slaves and cowries form the chief currency of the people, these are naturally the principal stakes in games of chance. The little white cowrie shells found on certain parts of the African coast are, so to speak, the small change of the country. Several years ago the value of a single cowrie was about one-eightieth of a cent, *i. e.*, two thousand equalled a quarter of a dollar. The inconvenience of this "fractional currency" is evident, considering that three-quarters of a million, weighing over a ton and a half, were paid by a king to an explorer for a few rolls of silk. Consequently, the check-book of wealthy Hausas, when travelling, is an extra number of slaves, one of which from time to time they cash for cowries.

The shells are also worn about the person as a protection from any evil influence, or the "evil eye." Five selected cowries, for gambling, may be found in the possession of most Hausas. Hardly second to the curse of slavery in Hausaland is that of gambling and the passion for it among these people is unrestrained. It takes its most insidious form in the game of "chaca," played by tossing up the five cowries, the result depending upon the way they fall. At times there is no limit to the stakes, and the escutcheon of Hausaland might well be five white cowrie shells on a field of black.

Sālam once told me that a friend of his master was playing one evening after much *lakby* [a palm wine] had been drunk. "Everybody was excited," said he, "for the 'evil eye' was on him, and time after time his cowries fell the wrong way. Losing first his wives, then his horses, he turned to his opponent and cried, 'Throw again; if I lose I am your slave.' The evil spirit of the hyena appeared in the darkness—and he lost."

In Hausaland, as in the rest of native Africa the Bashaws and powerful natives are generally the judges, and not only the poor Hausa, but the owner of too many horses, slaves, and wives, must be careful how he treads, lest he arouse the apprehension or envy of his Bashaw, who loses no time in presenting "requests" for gifts. These demands are continued until his subject is sufficiently weakened or ruined.

Now Durbee had a cousin who had been unfairly appointed Bashaw by the Sultan of Sokoto. Despite the feeling of injustice which rankled in Durbee's breast, he loyally complied with his cousin's demands for horses, until his favorite black horse, his *akawali*, alone remained. One morning as Sālam sat in the porch of Durbee's house, a giant negro arrived to take the akawali and to summon Durbee before the Bashaw.

"My master," said Sālam, "was not feeling sweet, and seizing his war spear said threateningly, 'Take him if you can! Bur-r-ro! Go, tell my cousin a Bashaw does not go to a Bashaw, and my akawali stays with me. Tell him that before the shadows of the date-palms have darkened the doorway of his house I will meet him to fight.'

"That afternoon Durbee mounted his horse, took his shield and weapons, and went out alone. Some of us followed to the edge of the palm grove, and as the appointed time drew near he rode out in the open. There on the hot sands he awaited his enemy. The hour of the challenge passed, but the coward never came. Durbee kept his akawali, and before the annual fast of Ramadan gathered his retainers about him and supplanted his cousin."

A Hausa Bashaw

"There on the hot sands he awaited his enemy"

SALAM, A HAUSA SLAVE

Shortly after this Durbee made a journey to Sokoto to make his peace with the Sultan and left Sālam with a friend in a neighboring town. This man treacherously sold him for two thousand cowries [$25] in Kano, the great emporium of Central Africa.

Within its fifteen miles of mud walls, twenty to forty feet in height, swarms a mass of black and sun-tanned humanity. In the open markets caravans of Black traders from the Congo come in with their long lines of donkeys weighted down with ivory, gold dust, and kola nuts, halting perhaps beside a garfla all the way from Tripoli with European goods and trinkets, or from the salt chotts of Tunisia and Asben, for salt is scarce in the Sudan.

Here Arab merchants from the Mediterranean and the Red Sea meet those from the Niger and the Gulf of Guinea, and no small number of the two million nomads who pass through every year are Hausa pilgrims bound for Mecca. The *hadji* [1] or pilgrimage by the way of Central Sudan, Tripoli, or Egypt has brought the Hausas in touch with other peoples and has contributed much to Hausaland's civilization.

[1] The term hadj, or hadji, is applied both to the pilgrimage to Mecca and to one who has made the journey.

Among this heterogeneous mass are occasionally seen those fierce white-skinned sons of the desert, the Tuaregs. You can tell them at a glance as, lean and supple, with an easy panther-like tread, they glide through this congested human kaleidoscope. Tall and picturesque, with long spears or flint-locks in their hands, and maybe a broadsword across their backs, apparently seeing nothing, they observe all. Perhaps they are here to trade, but more likely to keep close watch of departing caravans bound northward through their territory, that their sheiks may exact homage and heavy tribute, or failing in this may loot.

It is estimated that Kano clothes over one-half of the great population of the Sudan. In the towns of Central Tunisia, two thousand miles away, I have seen the indigo and scarlet cloths of Kano hanging next to those of Kairwan and Sfax, and piled in the Arab fondūks of Tripoli, hundreds of camel loads of her tanned goat-skins ready for shipment to New York, and I have watched the natives in the markets barter for sandals and desert slippers of Kano dye.

On his way to Kano, Sālam passed many slave caravans. Some of the wretches came in bound with thongs or under heavy yokes. One method was to fasten ten to twenty slaves together, one behind the other, by shoving their heads through holes cut every few feet in a long wooden yoke. Sometimes one of these human strings thus fastened together would make futile attempts to escape, pathetically jogging in step through the bush or forest until soon run down by their merciless pursuers. Now and again, as they staggered by, Sālam saw a slave, too weak and exhausted to walk, hanging limp by his neck, his feet dragging along the ground, his dead weight adding to the insufferable tortures of the others hitched to the same yoke.

At such times, unless near a market, the sick are despatched by their drivers who, not wishing the trouble of unshackling a wretch, resort to the simple expedient of decapitation, thus releasing soul and body at one cruel stroke.

In the fifth month of the dry season, during Sālam's stay in Kano, the caravans bound north being in haste to leave before the rains began, his master gathered his men and goods together, the camels and donkeys were loaded, and they started on their journey across the Desert, the Great Solitary Place. They took plenty of kola

nuts packed between damp leaves in baskets.
These they chewed to give strength to travel far
without food.

"A month's journey," said Sālam, "brought
us to the outlying territory of my people, and one
night we passed a spot where there was once a
village of Tuaregs under two sheiks. On one
of my visits there with Lasunvadi, a dog came
sniffing along and a Tuareg struck him with
a knife, whereupon the dog's owner killed the
Tuareg. The men of both sides came running
from all directions and fought till there were not
enough left to bury the dead. Those who were
not killed left the village, and the place was
called Djibana, the Place of the Cemetery of the
Dog."

At Zinder, Sālam's master was obliged to pay
homage and tribute in order to pass through
the territory controlled by its fierce inhabitants,
the Asbenawa, who were under the Bashaw of
Sālam's native town, Katsena. One glimpse of
Sālam's tribal marks, and they would have freed
him and destroyed the caravan. Knowing this,
his master gagged him and did him up tightly in
the middle of one of the camel loads. Here,
jolted and bumped against other camels, unable

to move and nearly suffocated, he was confined during a day's march, and when taken out more dead than alive, his limp body was thrown over a donkey. For months they marched north over the sand and rocky lands of the Desert. Now and again a garfla man paid his last tribute to the sands and added his bones to the many others bleaching in the sun beside the caravan trails.

At last they reached Ghadāmes, and in the course of a year, having passed through the hands of several other masters, Sālam was sold to an Arab by the name of Hadji Ahmed, who sent him into the desert to raise camels.

It was one night in my lokanda that Sālam told me of his escape.

"From time to time," began Sālam, "my master made journeys to distant towns, even as far as Tripoli, leaving the slaves for months without food save what we could gather ourselves. One morning while the stars were still bright and the dried grass wet with the night dews, I left on a *mehari* [running camel]. By midnight of the second day I arrived outside the walls of Ouragla, among some tents. Near one of these the mehari stopped of his own accord, and dismounting, I hobbled him and lay down under a palm-tree to sleep.

"I was startled the next morning at the sound of a voice I well knew, and peered out from under my baracan. Within six camel lengths of me stood Hadji Ahmed, my master, and his head slave

"'Hubba!' said he to the mehari, 'thou lump of swine's flesh! How came you here?' I knew then that the mehari had led me into a trap.

"'Gibani! the mehari is hobbled. What does this mean?' said my master to the head slave. Seeing I was about to be discovered, I jumped up and ran angrily toward them, exclaiming, 'Who should have brought it here but me, whom you left without food!'

"'Who showed *you* the road?' cried he, laying hold of me.

"'My hunger!' Whereupon they both set upon me and flogged me and the next day I was conducted back home.

"Before my master returned from Ouragla, I planned again to escape with Bāko, another slave; we would avoid the towns and go far north, so one day when we were alone branding camels we selected the fastest *mehara* [running camels] in the herd and started.

"For seven days and nights we travelled without stopping. The hot sun beat down upon our heads; the second day a sand-storm dried up what little water we had in our goat-skins. By turns one of us, tied in his saddle, slept while the other led his camel. Sometimes we would slide down from the humps and allow the mehara to graze as we walked along. We found no water, and the beasts began to show signs of thirst and uttered strange cries, groaning and gurgling as they redrank the water from their stomachs.

"One midnight—I shall ever remember it, Arfi [master]—we skirted the outlying palms of an oasis. Everything was very clear in the moonlight, and *water was there,* but we dared go no nearer the habitations for fear of capture, knowing Ahmed was not far behind us.

"We tightened up the saddle straps, for the mehara had grown thin and the soft parts of their humps had almost disappeared. Bāko's saddle, made for loads, was hard to ride and had produced boils, so he often sat behind it to vary the motion.

"As we were sick and weak, every stride of the

mehara sent pain through us. We knew that we could not much longer cling to our saddles, so we lashed each other on. The last time that Bako fell to one side I was too weak to help him, and he rode with his head hanging lower than his heels. The camel ticks burrowed into our skin, our tongues were cracked and bleeding when the mehara at last staggered into Ghadāmes.

"Some days after the Turkish governor of that place sent us here to Tripoli with a caravan, to be taken before his brother the Bey [Redjed Pasha]. Many in the towns came to the Tuesday Market to see the caravan come in, and among them I saw the fat form of one of my former masters, Sāla Heba—the one who had sold me to Hadji Ahmed. He watched us enter the Castle, where we obtained our release, and as I came out a free man he approached me: 'You are a stranger in the town. I live here now. Come and work for me.' So I did, though I well knew the old pig had heard of my escape.

"One night I was awakened from my sleep by Heba holding a low conversation with some one in the court. The other voice I recognized as that of my last master, Hadji Ahmed, and I listened from the roof as they planned my recapture by inducing me to go south again as a caravan man.

"The next morning Hadji Ahmed called for me and said: 'You have your freedom now. Come as a driver and I will give you three medjidies [$2.64], clothes, and a month's wages of three more in advance, to go back with the garfla.' I agreed, and taking the money, went out with him to buy a new burnoose and other clothes. 'Now,' said he, 'go to the Fondūk-el-Burka where the caravan is being loaded.'

"Taking the bundle, I chuckled to myself as I turned up a side street where lived Sidi Amoora, who kept open house for slaves and often provided them with money. There I left my bundle and hid under the sea wall, not far from the house, Arfi, where was once the consulate of your country. Hadji Ahmed and his men ran all over town in search of me and at last one found me asleep wrapped in my new burnoose.

"'Bu-r-r-o! Get out. The garfla is going. Hurry! Your master is angry.'

"'I have no master, I am a Turk now,' said I. Leaving me, the man returned with Hadji Ahmed, who angrily ordered me off, but I laughed and said:

"'Lah! [No.] I know your schemes.'

"'You refuse to go? *You*, my slave, dare steal my money as a tick would bleed a camel!' he cried threateningly, but I sprang from his grasp as he attempted to seize me.

"'Give me the clothes and the medjidies,' he commanded.

"'Lah! I have use for them. I go to the Bey to pay for a protest against you.'

"At this Ahmed was greatly scared, though more angry, but I was safe enough there by the sea wall, as free as Hadji himself, who well knew the Bey could punish him and confiscate his goods.

"'Never mind,' said he; 'here are three more medjidies.' I took them.

"'Kafir!' said I, 'thou white-faced horse with weak eyes!' And that was the last I ever saw of him, but I often went to visit the fat Heba to inquire after his health and to show him my new burnoose."

"But the medjidies, Sālam?" I laughingly queried. The dark eyes met mine for a moment; the pupils seemed to contract fiercely. Then a black hand disappeared under the folds of his baracan.

Sudanese Blacks announcing a religious dance

"I bought this," said he, and drew from its sheath a beautifully worked dagger, the crooked blade of which flashed silver in the lamplight.

Not long after Sālam had related his narrative to me a most unexpected event occurred. One hot morning, from out the sounds of the Arab town life, came the faint rhythmic cadence of distant-beating tom-toms. As their echoes vibrated up the narrow Street of the Milk Sellers' Market, I went out in time to meet a small company of Blacks. They were parading the town by way of announcing to their race the event of a religious dance, to be held near the palm groves of the oasis outside the town.

Late that afternoon found me in company with Sālam headed in the direction of their rendezvous. Sālam was dressed in his best fez and baracan, with a little bouquet of blossoms tucked behind his ear. In one hand he carried—as was his custom on auspicious occasions—a piece of discarded copper cable which he had picked up as a prize at the cable station. Turning a corner of a building on the outskirts of the town, we came into full view of a barbaric Sudanese dance.

Forming a great ring seventy-five yards in diameter was a wild lot of some two hundred

Blacks,[1] surrounded by twice as many excited
spectators. Its limits were fixed by poles, from
whose tops the green flag of the Prophet occasionally fluttered in the hot breeze. Most of the
participants wore gaudy-colored vests, below
which hung loose skirts weighted here and there
at the edges. Each carried a heavy krasrullah,
and there seemed to be certain understood forms
which they observed in the dance. For nearly
half a minute the tom-toms, re-enforced by the
squawking oboes and clashing cymbals, would
sound out their wild strains in regular cadence.
Meanwhile the dancers would beat time, holding
their clubs vertically, scuffing up the hot sand and
uttering strange grunts. Facing one another in
pairs, they would accentuate the beats by sharply
cracking their clubs together several times.

At sudden flares of music they would turn
violently round and round, sending up great
clouds of orange sand, their weighted skirts
swirling out almost horizontally about their
waists. Then they would bring up short, each
opposite another partner, with a crack of their
clubs; and so the dance went on.

[1] These were nomads and of two tribes, the Ouled Bedi from Bedi
and the Ouled Wadi Baghermi. Baghermi is near Kuka, just west
of Lake Chad. Both places may be found on maps.

My presence and black camera box seemed to arouse their suspicion and animosity. These fanatics had been dancing for hours in the hot sun and were crazed with the intoxicating lakby until they had reached a state of religious frenzy of which I was not aware until too late.

Pushing my way through the circle of onlookers, I took a picture of the barbaric crew dripping with perspiration, Sālam urging me to be quick. An old man and a tall, ugly-looking brute broke from the ring and ran toward me. Click! went my camera a second time when, without warning, from the crowd behind came a volley of stones; some struck me; the rest whizzed by into the centre of the ring, striking one or two of the dancers. Those nearest left the dance, and joined the several hundred black, sweating devils who had surrounded me. Sālam sprang between me and the old chief, asking him to call off his tribesmen. But Sālam was of a tribe unknown to these Sudanese nomads and no attention was paid to him.

"Shall I go for guards, Arfi?" said Sālam.

"Yes," said I, and slipping back from the crowd he disappeared. The whole thing occurred so suddenly that I had not realized the

[73]

significance of the danger until he had gone and I found myself in the vortex of this frenzied human whirlpool.

Only a few individual faces stood out of the crowd, the two who left the ring and a loathsome individual, seemingly a marabout, who spat at me. Those behind jabbed me with the ends of their clubs. Those in front, led by the old man, gesticulated and shouted and shook their clubs above their heads. Meanwhile, bruised from one of the stones, I limped as slowly as my impatience would permit across the open space and managed to work my way alongside the stand of an Arab fruit seller. Here, to disguise my mingled feelings of anger and apprehension, I bought some figs. Discarding the poorer ones, I proceeded to eat the rest in the most approved native fashion, affecting meanwhile a steadiness of hand which quite belied me.

Instead of quieting the crowd, my attitude served to make them more furious. They yelled and threatened in my face, while I clung tightly to my camera box and wondered how much resistance there was in my pith sun helmet. I had no weapon and it was better so, for one would have been useless against these fanatics.

" We came into full view of a barbaric Sudanese dance "

The bi

attitude

peared.

the wor

ing aside

confronts

from me

tribe in

not poet

   If the

tion wo

his grea

his club

short fi

speaking

significat

glowered

second s

with us

   "Salai

pulling b

sprang f

me. At

a scuffle

their rif

corted t

The big negro stepped forward in a menacing attitude toward me as Sālam suddenly reappeared. Unable to find guards, he had passed the word and returned to my assistance. Thrusting aside one or two who blocked his way, he confronted the Black and drew his attention from me by deliberately insulting him and his tribe in language which I afterward learned was not poetical.

If the affair had not been so serious, the situation would have been laughable. Puffed up to his greatest height stood the big Black, wielding. his club above his head. Below him Sālam's short figure was gathered back, every muscle speaking defiance, as he crouched with his insignificant piece of copper cable upraised. Both glowered at one another like wild beasts. A second more and the game would have been up with us both.

"Sālam!" I said sharply, at the same time pulling him back. But his blood was up and he sprang from my grasp. A sickening fear seized me. At that moment a shout went up, there was a scuffle, Turkish guards thrust them aside with their rifle butts, and dispersing the crowd escorted us safely back to town.

There was only one reason which led me to request that no troops be sent to gather in the ringleaders. Sālam's life afterward would not have been worth the hide of his desert slippers.

CHAPTER FIVE

THE MASKED TUAREGS

TO the Arab are generally accredited the control and ownership of the Great Sahara, but in reality there, far away from the coasts, a people as mysterious as the trackless sands—the masked Tuaregs—are the real rulers and buccaneers of the Desert. Their homes are in the very heart of those arid wastes, whose vast solitudes seem shrouded in mystery, and where over it all one feels at times, even in the sunlight, an uncanny brooding.

In the vicinity of Timbuktu dwell the Aweelimmiden tribe, the westernmost of the Tuareg tribal confederation. In the very centre of the Sahara and in the rugged Hoggar Mountains, under the Tropic of Cancer, live perhaps the most bloodthirsty of all—the Hoggars. In the deserts in the vicinity of Ghadāmes and Ghāt, where the border line of Tripoli seems to open its mouth, roam the Asgars, while to the south of Tripoli the

Kelowis infest and control the regions through which pass two caravan routes from Tripoli to the Sudan. Every southbound caravan from Tripoli is forced to pass through Tuareg territory. For this privilege the garfla sheik must in person salute the Tuareg Sultan and pay a toll according to the wealth of his merchandise, in addition to a fixed tariff, which is levied on all caravans. And woe betide the luckless caravan whose independent sheik refuses to pay tribute or which is caught in the meshes of tribal wars!

The Tuaregs are masters of a territory half the area of the United States in extent. It reaches from Barbary to the Niger, from the fever-laden districts of Semmur and Senegal on the Atlantic to the land of the wild Tebus, who occupy and control the deserts east of Lake Chad. Out of the million and a half square miles of Tuareg territory scarcely more than the area of New York City is cultivated land, and even this, in most cases, is saved only by a constant fight against the relentless march of the drifting sand. Fearless and enduring must a people be who can live, travel, and thrive in such a desolation.

Mounted on swift mehara, fleet-footed horses,

or depending only on their own hardihood and endurance—now here, gone to-morrow—these fierce adventurers, mysterious and as shifting as the sands over which they rove, occasionally drift northward for trade, to forage, or in the pursuit of plunder.

At times they are seen in the most important suks of the northern Sahara and of the Sudan, perhaps to convoy caravans, to spy upon them, or with garflas of their own.

These suks are in the great marts where the people from long distances meet to trade; so, too, they are naturally the focal points of the caravan routes.

Tripoli caravans which cross the Sahara often travel from three to four thousand miles, involving enormous outlay, great risks, and sometimes taking two years for the round voyage—all for the sole purpose of exchanging the merchandise of the north for the wares and products of the Sudan.

From Morocco to Tripoli I had heard vague rumors of these strange rovers of the yellow main, of their cunning and their relentless ferocity; but only once had I met any one who had ever actually seen a Tuareg, one of the Godforsaken, as the Arabs call them. Shortly after my arrival in Tripoli I set out to get information about them. But information was scarce, save along one line—the pillaging of caravans.

One night, as was my wont, found me at the home of my friend Riley.

"Only Old Mustafa," he commented as he joined us on the balcony which surrounded the inner court. Old Mustafa was one of the shrewdest Arabs in Tripoli. Fifteen years before he picked up bones for a living; now he was one of the wealthiest merchants in the town. But in the past few years much of his wealth, invested in the caravan trade, had been emptied out on the desert by the Tuaregs, Tebus, and Gatrunys. But a little while before a rider had come with bad news from the south on a mehari from Murzuk. Details were meagre, but the home-ward-bound caravan had been attacked between the Bilma oasis and Kawar, on the Chad trail. This trail is the most direct and westerly of the two main routes, and had been considered fairly safe by reason of the recent British occupancy of Kuka at its southern end. The other, to the south-west, by way of Ghadāmes, Ghāt, and Aīr, of late years had proved a costly risk. The great menace to the caravan trade is the Tuareg. It is he who is generally responsible for the looting of the garflas: perhaps indirectly, as in the case of a recent attack by the Rashada, a wild Tebu tribe from the east of the Ghāt route, which had suffered the loss of some camels through a border invasion of Tuaregs. Failing to regain possession, they took it out of the next Tripoli caravan, at a small oasis called Falesselez, and carried off some eighty loads of ostrich feathers and three hundred and eighty loads of Sudan skins. It was a good haul for one raid, but hardly a circumstance, as compared with the Damerghu affair, about half-way between Kano and Aïr. This caravan was one of the largest which had left Kano, consisting of thirteen thousand camels, not to mention donkeys, goats, and sheep. This time it was being convoyed mainly by Kelowi Tuaregs, and started from the south. When about half-way between Kano and Aïr it was attacked by the Damerghu, who had an old score to settle with the Kelowis. They literally got away with the whole outfit to the amount of nearly a million dollars' worth of animals and goods. Old Mustafa was not caught in this raid, which nearly caused a commercial crisis in

Tripoli and left the bones of twelve of her best caravaneers beside the trail.

Paradoxical as it may seem, the Tuaregs are not only despoilers of the caravan trade, but also make that trade possible through their protection as escorts. For, when tribute is paid for safe-conduct through their territory, these swarthy warriors, mounted high on their lurching mehara, accompany the caravan to the outskirts of the territory, or, as sometimes happens, agree to protect it through adjoining dangerous districts. On these occasions they will fight as for their own with all the ferocity of their leonine natures. During the march, however, should one of these eagle-eyed adventurers spy some object which strikes his fancy belonging to a caravaneer, the latter is informed of that fact, whereupon the object changes owners—even to the stripping from his back of his baracan.

"Where can I find the Tuaregs?" I asked.

"Well," replied M. Zolia, eying me quizzically, "most people are afraid that the Tuaregs will find them. Their nearest town is Ghadāmes, twenty days' camel's journey—if you're lucky. Not within the memory of any of us Europeans here in Tripoli has a Christian ever been permitted by the Turks even to start on that route, but a number have *tried* to enter from southern Tunisia.

"Let me tell you of one daring attempt made by two young French lieutenants. One was of the Spahis, the other of the Engineers, both stationed in southern Tunisia. Knowing that permission to make the journey to Ghadāmes would be refused owing to frontier difficulties, they obtained leave, ostensibly for a trip to Algiers.

"An Arab guide had been secured, and that night three muffled figures mounted on mehara sped along the starlit sands toward Ghadāmes. At one place they stopped to rest near the *kouba* [saint's house] of a marabout; then, leaving it and its solitary occupant, continued on. After a fatiguing journey the white walls and date-palms of their goal appeared on the horizon, clear-cut against the blue sky. As they drew up to the gates of the city, however, they were met by a menacing, jeering mob—for the marabout's eyes were keen and his mehari fresh

"Amidst cries of *Roumi! Yahudi!* and volleys of stones they were forced to retreat for their very lives. Fearing an attack, they took a circuitous route devoid of wells, and after super-human exertions staggered back to their starting-point."

I well knew the futility of obtaining permission from the Pasha to travel in that direction; besides, my contemplated route lay south-east. But, being anxious to get at least one glimpse of a Tuareg, I persisted in my inquiry.

"Well, you might cross their trail in the desert," replied M. Zolia, "and by some chance you might run across them right here in Tripoli, for occasionally they come in with the caravans, or to trade."

"Then I could knock off a sketch."

"A sketch!" ejaculated Riley "Gad, man, don't try any white man's magic with your pencil or camera on those fellows. That black camera box of yours, with a glass eye pointing at them, they would regard as an evil thing. They might think you could cast a spell over them, and one method of breaking it would be to stab the evil one casting it. 'Dead men cast no spells' is their motto. Keep away from them; don't even appear too curious. They are childishly super-stitious; you might unwittingly offend them by some trivial act, and their knives are long."

Strange as it may seem, the Tuareg is of the white race, and, were it not for the fierce exposure to sand-storm and desert sun, these swarthy children of nature would undoubtedly count many of a Saxon fairness among them. In their veins flows the blood of Berber ancestry, and in their language is preserved the purest speech of that tongue. The ancestors of these tribes were likely the most liberty-loving of that independent race, and probably, rather than be subjugated, they retreated into the vast spaces of the Great Desert. Here, at certain centres, they have towns built under the shade of the towering date-palms of the oases; but most of their life, often without food and shelter, is spent on the march; a wild sally here on a caravan, or a fierce onslaught there into an enemy's territory from their borders, then the rapid retreat and the dividing of the loot.

They seem to have drawn their religion from the countries bordering the north and south of their territory, for it embodies certain forms of Mohammedanism of their Arab neighbors, combined with more or less of the fetichism of the Sudanese. Their daily life is a defying of the deathlike wastes, and it is but natural that the lonely vigil of night, the yellow gloom of the sand-storm, and all the mysterious phenomena of those deserts over which they roam, should be associated by these people with the jinn and evil spirits with which their legends and folk-lore abound.

"Never promise more than half of what you can perform," runs a Tuareg proverb, and travellers and French army officers have claimed for the Tuareg steadfastness of character, the defence of a guest, and the keeping of promises. This, however, was not borne out in three instances where small bands of the White Fathers [French missionaries] relied upon the Tuaregs' word for a safe escort, only to be murdered when far on their journey; nor in the case of the Flatters Expedition, which left southern Algeria to study questions of railway communication across the Sahara. This ill-fated company left Ouargla, Algeria, about a hundred strong—French native tirailleurs, Arab guides, and camel drivers enough to attend to the caravan of some three hundred camels all told. Attached to the party were a number of Tuaregs. Week after week they toiled in measured march south, passed Amgid, and entered the very heart of the

Hoggar country. Here they were led into a Tuareg ambush. Those who escaped took up, without adequate transport or provisions, a fearful retreat over their trail, harassed by Tuaregs and dying from starvation, sickness, and exhaustion. Every Frenchman succumbed, and at last four survivors, covering a distance of fifteen hundred kilometers north, crept back to Ouargla.

These incidents give a different side of Tuareg character, and are more in accord with the accounts I picked up in Tripoli. Nevertheless the Tuareg undoubtedly has many admirable qualities.

Although polygamy is permitted by their law, it is said it is never practised; women hold property in their own right even after marriage. Most of their women can read and write, and, often pretty and delicate featured, they spend a part of their time within their tents of goat-skins or camel's hair teaching their children.

The Tuareg social system is on a well-organized basis; in it appear four distinct strata of society: the Nobles who are the pure-blooded Tuaregs; the Iradjenatan, half-blooded descendants of Nobles and their vassals; serfs, hereditary descendants of weaker tribes or of freed slaves, who, often banding together, go out on foraging affairs of their own, passing like mysterious phantoms over the sands. In the small hours of the morning they come down with a rush on some unsuspecting *douar* [village]. Sunrise finds them miles away, red-handed with their loot. Lastly are the Bellates, or Black slaves, who become much attached to their masters, often refusing their freedom when offered, preferring to retain their Tuareg citizenship rather than seek their homes in the Sudan. The Tuaregs resort to the same method of branding their slaves as do the Arabs—slashing out strips of flesh from the calves, cheeks, or temples.

One stifling morning in mid-July a surprise awaited me. Only the noise of a disconsolate camel or the drone of some drowsy insect among the courtyard plants of my lokanda drifted on the heated air. I paused a moment on the threshold, as we are wont to do, perhaps through primeval instinct, then stepped out into the narrow, sun-baked street. Just ahead of me another crossed it, cleaving its way between the white-walled Arab houses. My ear caught the soft scuff of sandalled feet, a white garment flapped out from beyond a corner stone, then two tall

A raiding band of Tuareg serfs

figures swung suddenly around the corner. Tuaregs! There was no doubting it, for their faces were masked behind the dark *litham* [veil mask], through whose open slit two pairs of eyes looked catlike and fixedly at me—then we passed.

Giving them barely time to get beyond my lokanda, I ran for my camera and into the street again, but the Tuaregs had disappeared. They could not have gone far, and being strangers in the town, would not have entered any Arab house. My surmise that they had turned down a street leading to the bazaar quarter of the town proved true and I was soon following in their wake.

Draped gracefully over their lean, supple figures, in a way which a Roman pretor might have envied, was a light *haik* or *kheiki*, from which protruded the white sleeves of a gray Sudanese tunic. White *kortebbas* [trousers] reached to their feet, on which were lashed their *ghatemin*, sandals of tooled leather, secured by crossed rawhide thongs passing between the toes and secured at the ankles.

One carried a long spear, and crosswise over his back a beautifully proportioned two-edged sword hung in a richly worked sheath; the other bore an Arab flint-lock, and up the sleeve I knew each concealed a wicked knife. They shortly turned into the trellis-covered Suk-el-Turc, and at a call from an Arab stopped before the small wall opening of a shop.

Only round golden spots of sunlight percolated through the heavy clustered vines and purple fruit and scintillated on their copper bead necklaces and silver amulet cases; but the narrow, crowded mart was too dark to risk a shot with my camera, for I must insure the success of my first attempt, before their suspicions were aroused. From the covering of the booth of a Jewish silversmith I watched the transaction with interest.

The Arab was bartering for their weapons, and, after Arab custom, transcribed his conversation in imagination on the palm of his hand with his index finger. Unlike the Arab, the Tuaregs seemed to disdain haggling over the price, and after an occasional low guttural grunt, by no means lacking in intonation, brought the trade to a sudden termination. One of them threw back the sleeve of his tunic and slipped the leather bracelet of a long knife scabbard from the wrist of his left arm. Handing scabbard and weapon to the Arab, he gathered up a handful of piasters and moved on with his companion.

I slipped from my retreat, noted the Arab booth, and dodged after them for two hours as their path interlaced through the maze of tortuous streets, but no chance presented itself. Owing to my distinctive European dress and glaring white sun helmet, it behooved me to be doubly cautious both for the success of my undertaking and my safety. But I made the most of the opportunity to study carefully their appearance and manner.

Both were men of tall stature, at least six feet in height, I should say. This was accentuated by their wiry, catlike figures and the style of their litham: a mask in two pieces with broad flaps, one crossing the forehead, the other the lower part of the face, suspended from the bridge of the clean-cut aquiline nose or just below it. They adopt this covering, it is said, to lessen the evaporation in throat and nostrils, and rarely remove it even when eating or in the presence of their families. Over the mask was wrapped, turban-wise, a piece of white material, the crown of the head being left bare. From this aperture, the *tadilmus*, a lock of black hair, projected skyward.

They walked with an easy, even-paced lope,

swinging well from the hips, commencing the forward stride of one leg before the other heel had left the ground. Every motion of their supple, catlike bodies gave a sense of muscles trained to perfection.

A glance showed them to be men inured to the most brutal hardship, in which the pitiless extremes of rain and sand-storm, heat and cold, hunger and thirst, and the fortunes of war were but common episodes in the day's work. The Arabs of Tripoli treated them with the greatest respect; not once were they jostled by the passing many. Yet these nomads, stoical as they were, seemed by their guarded glance, not altogether at ease thus removed from their desert trails, and they viewed many things with simple curiosity.

Such were these desert children who strode on ahead of me. Up one street, down another, past the Mosque of Dragut, the Mediterranean freebooter, then up my own street, the Arbar-Arsāt. Here they were hailed by the one-eyed dealer in goods from the Sudan.

Twice I felt sure they had noticed me. It was now high noon and the siesta time found us the only occupants of the sun-baked street. I was too near them to turn back, and as I neared the

little booth where they had stopped their bartering for an instant they turned their shifty eyes upon
me with a look that informed me that my morning's work with them was at an end.

Late that afternoon I joined Riley and the rest
at the Turkish garden, and as we sat about one
of the tables I recounted the morning's episode.

"Yes," he remarked dryly, "Sālam told me
that when marketing in the Suk-el-Turc this
morning he noticed you following them. I sent
him after you with some good advice, but you had
gone. Why, man, you don't suppose for a
moment that those beggars, who can trail a
camel after a sand-storm has passed over his
tracks and who can scent an enemy almost before
he pokes his nose over the horizon, failed to detect you chasing after them in full sight—eh?
They are Asgars, and what's more, they're
Senusi."

The Senusi were the most powerful and fanatical sect in Islam. Three-quarters of a century
ago this powerful fraternity was founded by a
sheik of that name, having for his end the purify-
ing of Moslemism and the extermination of the
infidel. Tripoli, and Bengazi, down the coast,
were at one time the centres of his field of opera-

tions; but now Wadaı, ın the Central Sudan, is its headquarters. The Senusi, so far as I know, wear nothing by which they may be distinguished as do many of the other Mohammedan sects, and every member is sworn to secrecy.

Its influence is so powerful, yet so intangible, that it is a difficult influence for the invading Christian nations to deal with, as France has found to her cost. To the Senusi has been attributed the cause of some of the most violent uprisings and oppositions against the invasion of the French in the Sahara. Not only the Asgars, but the Kelowi are strong adherents of this sect, particularly those residing in Aïr and Ghāt. It is said that the plot against the Flatters Expedition has been laid at the door of the sect.

"How did you know they were in town?" I continued.

"Why, half of Tripoli knows ıt. Tuaregs enter a suk or town for one of three reasons—to trade, to buy camels, or to spy out information regarding an outgoing caravan. Generally they don't bring enough stuff to load down a month-old camel, and they certainly don't pay Tripoli prices for camels, when they can lift them on the trail. So draw your conclusions, as the caravan men and merchants draw theirs. These Asgars will probably hang around the Suk over market day or perhaps longer, keeping an eye on the number of camels purchased, and loaf around the rope shops and other places of caravan out-fitters, picking up any stray bit of gossip which may drift their way. Of course, they may be honest, but the chances are even. Don't repeat your game of this morning with Senusi Tuaregs," continued my friend, as we parted at the Street of the Milk Sellers' Market.

The following morning, before the sunlight on the neighboring minarets and housetops had changed from rose to gold, found me at the Arab shop in the Suk-el-Turc. There, in a dark corner on a pile of old silks, lay the long Tuareg *teleks* [daggers].

"Gadesh?" I inquired. The Tripoline named his price, and I took the coveted weapons back to my lokanda.

The dagger is the Tuareg's main weapon, and has two unique characteristics. Attached to its scabbard is a broad leather ring through which are passed the left hand and wrist; the knife lies flat against the inner side of the arm, its handle grasped by the hand, for the Tuareg evidently goes on the principle that "a knife in the hand is worth two in the belt."

Strangely paradoxical to all the symbolism which plays so important a part in the religion of the orthodox Mohammedan, is the character of the telek handle, for it is in the form of the cross, the symbol of the hated Nazarenes. A number of theories have been advanced by way of explanation, but the most reasonable and substantiated seems to be that it is a relic of the time when this people were Christians, during the Roman era, before they were driven from their more northern habitations by the Arabs. The cross is also found in Tuareg ornaments, and in the handle shapes of their two-edged war swords.

I would venture an opinion, however, that these weapons have no religious significance whatever to the Tuareg, but were patterned after the cross-hilted, double-edged swords of the invading Crusaders, for not only did the Crusader land on the heights of Carthage and other points along the North African coast, but for a number of years Tripoli itself was occupied by the Knights of St. John, who came in touch there with the nomadic desert tribes. They must have left many a graven crucifix, sword, shield, and rosary on the field of battle, and as part of the loot of the Moslem soldiery when the defenders of the cross were driven from Tripoli by Soliman the Magnificent.

The one-eyed Sudanese dealer had bearded these tiger-cats in their dens in the oasis and had come back to the town with a bow and quiver full of their steel-pointed arrows and two goat-skin pillows. The last were ornamented with black and red dye, and from their surfaces small strips and squares had been cut out, producing an attractive geometric design. These leathers, filled with straw or grass, serve the Tuaregs as cushions when on camel-back, or as pillows in their tents. The arrows were wonderfully balanced, having a delicate shaft of bamboolike wood, and the vicious-looking barbed points were beautifully designed. It is said that the Tuaregs do not poison their arrows, but the one-eyed Sudanese handled them carefully and cautioned me against pricking myself with the barbs.

Later in the morning found me in the Suk, camera in hand. This time I risked the sun and substituted for my pith helmet a straw hat, to draw less attention to myself. For an hour I meandered about, searching through the narrow channel ways of the Suk, banked with produce and handicraft articles of town and country.

I had almost despaired of again setting eyes on the Asgars, when, as I rounded the tent of a dealer in goat-skin water buckets, there were the Tuaregs—three of them—all squatting before the tattered tent of a Black, eating ravenously of roasted fodder corn,

This time I would let *them* cross *my* path, and I waited unobserved under the shadow of the wall of the Halfa Suk.

Having gorged themselves, they crossed the market. I anticipated them first at one point, then at another. Either they turned aside before reaching me, their faces were in the shadow, or some Arab exasperatingly blocked my view. Then they headed for the camel market, so I hurried by a circuitous route and arrived begrimed and perspiring at the farther end of a long line of camels. Examining a camel here and there, they gradually worked their way toward me.

The third Tuareg was evidently a serf, for he wore a white litham. He carried a long, gracefully shaped lance, which I would have liked to buy, but an experience of trying to buy a hauberk from a Riffian in Morocco had taught

" From the near side of a camel, I took the picture "

me better than to attempt, as a Christian, to buy a weapon offhand from men who live by the sword. A few yards more and they would be near enough. The sun flooded full upon them, and their amulets containing their charms dangled and sparkled in the light. Two were intent upon a camel to the right; the other, as he came straight toward me, turned his head for an instant to the left. Stepping quietly from the near side of the camel, I took the picture, and knew that the "white man's magic" had not failed me. Turning my head quickly, I directed my gaze thoughtfully afar off.

"Ugurra!" snarled one of the Tuaregs, and he menacingly flipped from his left arm the fold of his haik, revealing on his wrist, just below his dagger band, a heavy stone of jade or serpentine, an ornament, it is claimed, they use in fighting.

The other two turned instantly, and for a moment all the ferocity of their animal natures seemed to leap through their eyes. Their gaze shifted from mine to the mysterious black box beneath my arm.

"Ugurra!"

Then they turned and glided stealthily along their way out into the desert from whence they came.

CHAPTER SIX

THE DISCOVERY OF THE UNITED STATES FRIGATE "PHILADELPHIA"

FROM time immemorial the Mediterranean has been the arena of naval strife and piracy. Men chained to the galley thwarts, exhausted and broken in spirit, have suffered under the heat and cold, and writhed in anguish under the lash of Pagan, Mohammedan, and Christian. But against the long horizon of its history—from the American view-point—one wave looms very high, on whose crest is a burning frigate, and high above her mast-heads we trace through the saffron smoke clouds a name—DECATUR.

On the eastern end of Tripoli's water front, formerly one long line of fortifications, rises the Bashaw's Castle, its thick walls towering over the harbor some ninety feet above their sea-washed foundations.

By the courtesy of Redjed Pasha I saw something of the interior of this ancient pile, which enclosed within its walls a little village of its own. Passing from large open courts of elaborately colored tiles, through labyrinthine secret ways to the prison, I mounted its high terraced ramparts. Rounding over me, the great dome of unbroken blue stretched away to meet the darker mirror surface of water.

To the north-east, parallel to the shore, extends a dangerous line of rocks, now poking their jagged surfaces through the dark blue of the bay, now disappearing under its waters. It was on these hidden crusted tops, three miles east of the harbor entrance, that the grating keel of the United States frigate *Philadelphia* first warned Captain Bainbridge that they were aground. The guns having been hove overboard, her defenceless condition compelled her surrender that afternoon, October 31, 1803.

Much of my time in Tripoli during the summer of 1904 was spent in efforts to obtain data relating to the capture and destruction of the *Philadelphia* by Lieutenant Decatur in command of the ketch *Intrepid*—not only for its local significance, but also with a view to locating the wreck. I questioned representatives of the European governments in the town, waded through countless files of official documents, dusty consular reports, and private journals, but for many weeks my search proved fruitless. Hearing finally that in the *dibriamim* [local records] of the Jewish synagogue an attaché of the French consulate had once found certain valuable historical data, I determined, if possible, to investigate these archives. Consequently, a meeting with Rabbi Mordecai Kohen, librarian of the synagogue, was arranged by the acting British consul, Mr. Alfred Dickson.

On July 14, in company with Tayar, a young interpreter, I found the rabbi buried in a pile of old books in the library of the synagogue. Touching his hand to his forehead, he welcomed us; then brought from a dark corner a musty old book on magic and science and a glass sphere on which he had pasted paper continents. These proved to be his two greatest treasures, which he exhibited with all the unconcealed glee and pride of a child. Then, drawing from a shelf a small volume and a manuscript, he led the way to the British consulate, where, in company with Mr. Dickson, we seated ourselves about a table in a cool north room, and the rabbi proceeded to decipher the brief facts.

He had donned his best attire, consisting of a pair of yellow slippers, an under layer of loose Oriental trousers, and several vests, covered by a dilapidated European overcoat, which he wore only on occasion. Surmounting all this was his greasy fez, wrapped in a tightly twisted blue turban, which he removed only on occasion and never unwound; turban and fez by force of habit had become a sort of composite capital which adorned his partially bald head. His deepset eyes cast furtive glances from time to time as he read first from the small volume, then from the manuscript.

The book proved to be a modern Turkish publication in Arabic entitled a "History of Tripoli in the West," and briefly mentioned the circumstance of the burning of an American war-ship in the harbor. The manuscript was a local history compiled by himself from the papers and journals of an old rabbi, Abram Halfoom, who had lived in Tripoli most of his life and died in Jerusalem some eighty years ago. It contained information covering the period of our war with Tripoli and revealed a few new details concerning the *Philadelphia*. Transmitted through three interpreters, I failed to get at the real Hebraic point of view of the writer. It briefly stated, however, that Yusef Bashaw was a bad ruler, had equipped a number of corsairs, and that the crews of the captured vessels were sold like sheep. His captains, Zurrig, Dghées, Trez, Romani, and El-Mograbi, set sail from Tripoli and shortly sighted an American vessel. Zurrig left the others and daringly approached the ship, annoying her purposely to decoy her across the shoals. She stranded, but fired on the other vessels until her ammunition gave out, whereupon the Moslems-pillaged her. The American Consul [1] was very much disheartened and tried to conclude arrangements similar to those recently made between the Bashaw and the Swedish Consul; but such an enormous tribute was demanded that no terms could be reached, so by order of the Bashaw the vessel was burned.[2] From time to time the corsairs brought in several American merchantmen. Soon the American squadron arrived, blockaded the harbor for

[1] Rabbi Halfoom evidently mistook Mr. Nissen for the American consul, but we had none at the time. Mr. Nissen was the Danish consul, and voluntarily acted as agent for the American prisoners, and happened to occupy the house formerly used as the United States Consulate.

[2] This, of course, was an erroneous idea. It may have been purposely circulated through the town, particularly among the inhabitants other than Mohammedans.

twenty days, and bombarded the Tripolitans, who returned their fire and did great damage.

Such were the first gleanings of my search for local traditions concerning this event which made such a profound impression in both Europe and America, and which Lord Nelson said was "the most bold and daring act of the age."

More specific results came through a chance acquaintance. During my wanderings through the maze of narrow alleys within the walls of Tripoli I fell in with an old Arab, Hadji-el-Ouachi, from whose combination of lingua Franca and broken English I gathered much information. During one drowsy siesta time, as we sat over the muddy Turkish coffee in the shady spacious court of my lokanda, I questioned him regarding the lost frigate.

El-Ouachi stimulated his recollections with a pinch of snuff.

"There is a tradition among my people," he said, "that many years ago there came to Tripoli a big American *markab harbi* [ship of war], and when I was young, like you, Arfi, one Hadji-Ali, an old man, told me that the Americans came at night and burned her in the harbor and she sank by the Lazaretto near the end of the Mole toward the sea."

"But are there no old men now among you who saw this ship?" I asked, by way of testing the accuracy of his knowledge.

"Lah!" He shook his head. "For that was in the days of my fathers. Then the Arabs were a strong people! But I have a friend, old Hadji-Mohammed Gabroom, whose father often told him about it. If we find him now at his coffee off the Suk-el-Turc, he may tell us. Shall we go?"

Passing out into the hot glare of the early afternoon, a few minutes walk brought us to the Suk, where, just before one enters the Street of the Tailors, and the shops of the workers in silver and brass, we came to a small coffee booth. Here, back in the farthest corner, wrapped in the numerous folds of his brown baracan, squatted Hadji-Mohammed Gabroom, a dried-up, sinewy old man, stroking his scraggly beard and sucking at a long pipe-stem. Looking out from under the heavy overhanging brows, and almost lost in the wrinkles of his tanned, sun-parched face, a pair of black beady eyes glittered like two sand beetles. After several salaams we drank of proffered coffee and El-Ouachi stated our mis-

" We came to a heap of . . . rust-eaten cannon "

sion. The fascinating little eyes glowed like live coals, as with almost a look of hatred they searched me through. For a moment the fire died out of them and the old man seemed to lose the sense of his surroundings as though groping in the long-forgotten past. Then, ın the slow, measured manner of the Arab chronicler, he spoke:

"Many times has my father told me the story thus: 'In the year of the Hegira, 1218, during *awasit* [the second ten days of the month] of the month Rajah, my son, the sails of strange ships are seen to the north where the Khafkan and Khafikin [the eastern and western horizons] meet. The *amtar* [rains] have begun, the nights are cold, and few people walk abroad. In that time, there comes from Bengazi way an American ship, which chases a felucca with one mast gone. The Arab *Rais* [captain] knows many passages through the reefs and invites the big ship to follow where the water is shallow. Allah wills! and the big ship is aground.

"'All the corsairs, feluccas, and many small boats filled with armed Arabs swarm around her, as on the Suk-el-Thalat when the market is held. The Americans fight with their small guns and

[107]

wound six of our people, but the Arabs are too many. Soon they capture the ship and bring many Nazarenes to the castle, and it is a great *tarab* [jubilee] in Tripoli. Yussef Bashaw puts the officers in a dungeon in the middle of the Castle, under the terrace. The sailors are bastinadoed and driven like the black *mamluks* [slaves]; they are empty of wallets, apparent of poverty and destitution, with no means of sustenance save the loaves of black bread given them by their masters. In the cold water for many days these Nazarenes shovel sand from a wreck, by the Suk-el-Thalat, build up the broken places in the Castle, and carry heavy loads.

"'The Arabs bring the big ship from the rocks of Bogaz-el-Kebir [the Big Harbor] and anchor her off the Fort and Lazaretto. While the people loot her, from his small boat, one Bushagour, an Arab sailor, sees a white thing in a big gun, and finds two bags of silver medjidies [probably Spanish dollars]; he puts them back quickly. When the night is black he takes again the money in his boat, buries it in the sand near where lies the Lazaretto, and goes back to the big ship, where he is a guard; three days later he buys unto himself two houses.

"'We bring the guns of the Nazarenes from. the water, and make the ship look like new, and put our corsairs close around her. She lies off the Castle in the harbor many days, with the red crescent flag of our people floating over her. Those who dwell in the gardens outside the city and in the wadan take little boats to look at her. At Ramadan they unfurl the green flag of the Prophet from the mast-head, and her guns tell the faithful that the days of fasting are over and they are to prepare for the feast of Beiram.

"'Yussef Bashaw asks much money from this new nation, but Sheik Hadji Mohammed Bet-el-Mal tells Yussef that these American people will not let him keep the ship long. Yussef Karamauli only laughs and tells the Sheik he talks like a woman. Yussef Bashaw feels very safe because the town is full of armed Arabs and all the forts and corsairs are manned, with guns loaded. I, my son, am stationed at the Bab-el-Bahah [the Gate by the Sea], and sometimes at the Inner Gate by the Castle. I keep my best flints in my gun and leave its lock-cover in my house. We feel so safe that only ten Arabs are left to guard the ship.

"'Many days pass and the days of Ramadan are over. In awasit of the month Dzul ca'da of the Hegira 1219 we fear an attack, for we see strange sails when the sun is high; I am a special guard at the gate of the Castle. One evening, shortly after the sun has gone down in the land of the west, there is seen a ketch standing into the harbor. We think she brings goods from Malta, but on her deck are American men dressed like the Maltese and her hold is full of men. They know the gates of the city are shut, and that the Rais-el-Kebir [Captain of the Port] will not give them *practique* [quarantine clearance] until the morning. Long after the muezzin has called the faithful to prayer, and the city sleeps, out of the stillness of the darkness a great cry comes over the water. They attack and slay certain of our guards in the big ship, the rest flee in fear for themselves. They start fires with gourds and bottles filled with spirit and oil. Suddenly flames like the tongues of evil spirits rise from the American ship. These Americans have wise heads; when they lose their ship, they lose it to everybody.

"'Our town is soon in great confusion. Men cry aloud, our women screech, and the great cannons from the Castle ramparts boom. Many think the Castle is fallen. Everybody runs into the streets with his gun; some rush into the gardens at the back of the town, only to meet many coming in from the country and Bedawi village camps. I climb on a housetop better to see this matter, and with me is old Mohammed-el-Ouayti. Soon many hundreds of people pour in from the Black village at Sciara-el-Sciut and from Tajura and Zanzour. Below us the people are rushing through under the Inner Gate of the Bab-el-Bahah, crowding to the water front to meet the enemy, like a great wadi rushing to the sea.

"'Together we watch the fire of the ship. She begins to burn first in the middle; then much powder explodes. The great smoke cloud spreads its wings like some evil bird over the harbor and soars to the upper regions of the darkness, its red talons always taking something from the face of the earth, which it carries toward the outer sea. The Nazarenes, fearing for themselves, turn back in flight, and we watch their ketch disappear in the darkness through Bogaz Jeraba out to the Middle Sea. Soon the harbor is light as day and redder than the sands of the Sāh-ra [Sahara] when the sun is low in the west. When the breath of Allah blows back now and again, the big tongues change their course and lick out at the Castle, making its walls and ramparts red as blood, like some monster dragon as it spits back its fire guns.

"'For three days the ship burns and the sky at night is like this brass on the handle of my *khanijar* [dagger]. Garflas afar off on the desert see it—yea, even plenty of people see it from beyond the Jebel Tarhuna, Fassato, and the farther Jebel, four days' journey as the camel travels. For many years after this she yields her iron and brass to the Arab and Maltese fisherman; for everything that is an object of search resteth not. Such is the story of the Nazarene ship. Know, then, what I tell thee, my son, and keep it in thy memory. Allah wills! Allah is great!'" [1]

The old hadji tapped the kief out of his pipe, slid off the seat into his slippers, and reefing up his skirts about him, mounted his small donkey and disappeared down the Suk.

---

[1] It has been a much-mooted question whether it would have been possible to take the *Philadelphia* from the harbor. Decatur, however, had no choice. "Proceed to Tripoli in company with the *Siren* under Lieutenant Stewart," read Preble's orders, "enter that harbor in the night, board the *Philadelphia*, burn her, make good your retreat with the *Intrepid*." One thing is certain, the chances were evidently against the success of such an undertaking, as must be evident to any one who has actually been over the ground. I do not believe it would have been possible under the circumstances.

In response to my inquiry in regard to the houses bought by Bushagour, I followed El-Ouachi as he clumped along through the Suk-el-Turc. Reaching its northern end we passed east of the Arch of Marcus Aurelius and ascended the street which follows the base of the remaining fortifications, known as the Battery, between the Castle and the Molehead. We soon came to an iron heap of discarded rust-eaten cannon. On one of these El-Ouachi seated himself. Above him was a simple broad expanse of sunlit wall, broken only by its arched portal and the edges of its crenelated profile vibrating in the intense heat of an African summer afternoon.

"These old guns, Arfi," he said as he shifted his baracan over his left shoulder, "were on this fortress in the days of my fathers, and threw their iron balls at the American frigate as she lay off the Castle. After she burned, some of her guns were mounted on these very walls and used against an American fleet."

He presently led the way a short distance up a narrow street, stopping in front of two plain-walled houses. Years of accumulated rubbish had perceptibly raised the level of their thresholds and the dirt dado of the outer walls, so that to enter one must descend.

"These houses, Arfi," he continued, "this one with the hand print over the door to keep off the 'evil eye,' and the one next, Bushagour bought with the two bags of money. Within their walls each has a large court and good rooms. His children's children live here now, but we cannot enter, for the women are there, and these people like not the Christians. Some years ago there was a great explosion in this fortification where the powder was stored, the walls of the whole town were shaken, part of this fortress was broken in many places, houses fell and people died, but these fell not."

As we reached the Bab-el-Bahah, El-Ouachi pointed his lean, henna-stained finger in the direction of the remains of the Mole.

"*Beyond the Molehead, Arfi, the tradition of my people says, the wreck of the big American corsair lies.*" [1]

Following this clue, early the next morning, July 12, before the usual forenoon breeze could

---

[1] On my return to the United States I investigated the original data relating to the capture and burning of the *Philadelphia*, and further corroborated the Arab tradition from original and official sources; from the reports of Commodore Preble, who issued the orders to destroy the frigate; Lieutenant Decatur and Midshipman

Machine-boat and diver from Greek Navy at work over the *Philadelphia*

blur the glassy surface of the harbor, I was at the sailors' coffee-house near the boat builders' ways, where by arrangement I met Riley, Mr. Venables, an English missionary, and a Maltese fisherman. Equipped with grapples, lines, and a *maria* [a bucket with a glass bottom] we seated ourselves on the dirty thwarts of the clumsy craft, and were pulled to the vicinity where Arab tradition said the wreck of the frigate lay. Using the maria, for a light breeze had ruffled the placid surface of the water, the boat was rowed slowly over the ground, describing large spirals, as from time to time we set new starting-points. As I eagerly gazed through the clear glass into the transparent depths, all the wonders of a sea garden passed beneath me; dark violet spots of ragged rocks lost themselves in patches of light sea-green sand, which threw into stronger relief an occasional shell-fish or schools of delicate little sea-horses. Beautiful forms of sponges, coral, anemone, and sea mosses opened and shut or gracefully waved, disturbed by some under-current or one of the shining iridescent fish,

Morris, who carried them out, and [through the courtesy of Mr. James Barnes] from the journal of William Ray, one of the imprisoned crew of the *Philadelphia*, who was in Tripoli at that time, and who, under orders of his Tripoline captors, assisted in trying to clear the wreck of the *Philadelphia* after she was burned.

which, like some gorgeous spectrum, vibrated in unison with the grasses, or turning upward its scaly side, darted like a shaft of silvery light through the green and opalescent depths below.

In less than an hour my search was rewarded by seeing the broken ends of the great ribs of a vessel protruding through dull-colored eel-grass., I noticed that this grass seemed to follow the line of the ribs, and carefully noted its character, to further aid me in my search. Examining these closely, no doubt was left in my mind but that they belonged to a large vessel, and I ordered the boatman to let fall the rough stone which served as an anchor. The lead gave us two and a half and three fathoms.

Hastily undressing, we dived several times. Riley first succeeded in buoying the spot by going down with the line and slipping it over one of the ribs. While on the bottom I carefully examined the timbers. These were honeycombed in certain parts in a peculiar way. The continual sea swash of a century seemed to have made its inroads at the softest places, and they gave every appearance, in form, of partially burned stumps. The wood seemed almost as hard as iron. Much of it was enclosed in a fossil crust, and only by repeated efforts I succeeded in breaking off a small piece. The many winds from the Desert and the shifting shoals of sand had filled in and around the frigate, and her keel must have lain buried nearly two fathoms deeper than the present sea bottom. The freshening breeze made further investigation impossible; so after taking bearings and leaving the spot buoyed, we returned to the shore, landing amid an awaiting, curious crowd of Turks, Arabs, and Blacks.

Six days later, through the courtesy and interest of the officers of the Greek war-ships *Crête* and *Paralos*, a ship's cutter and machine boat with divers were placed at my disposal. On this second expedition my principal object was to determine more carefully the size, position, and location of the wreck, which are given on the chart reproduced on the next page.

My third and last expedition was on the morning of August 3. The divers managed with pick and axe to break off pieces of her fossilized sides, and from her partly buried timbers brought to the surface an eighteen-pound cannon-ball,[1] together with part of the wood in which it was

[1] This solid shot corresponded in diameter to the bore of some of the discarded guns at the Battery and was found in the port side forward. It is now in the Naval Museum at Annapolis.

embedded. The ball and adjoining wood were completely incrusted with an inch of fossil matter. Several other pieces of wood brought up con-

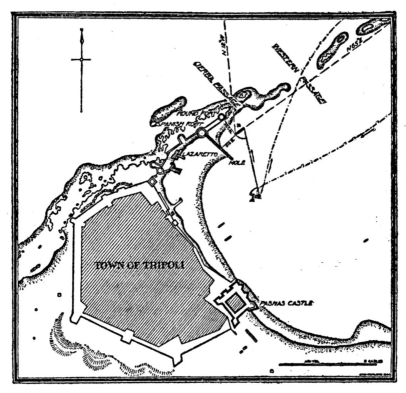

Map of the Town and Harbor of Tripoli

A—Position of the *Philadelphia* when attacked by Decatur. Dot and dash lines indicate the course of the *Intrepid* on entering and leaving the harbor February 16th, 1804. Heavy dotted lines indicate the *Philadelphia's* course as she drifted after being fired.
B—Present position of the *Philadelphia*. Long dash lines indicate her bearings.

tained iron bolts, also copper nails, which probably held down the sheeting below the waterline of her hull. There her skeleton timbers will lie until obliterated by the Desert sand shoals, the quiet work of the shell-fish, and the myriad small creatures of the sea.

CHAPTER SEVEN

THE GREEK SPONGE DIVERS

O F Tripoli's principal industries three stand
out pre-eminently—sponge gathering, esparto picking, and the trans-Saharan caravan
trade through which the principal resources respectively of sea, coast, and Desert, including the
Sudan, are made marketable exports. Besides
these, great quantities of cattle [in good years],
eggs, mats, old silver, woollen cloths, and other
local products are shipped annually, going mainly
to Great Britain, France, Turkey, Italy, Malta,
Tunis, and Egypt. One article only, Sudan
skins, finds its way to the United States, which
supply depends upon the security of the trade
routes. These skins go to New York for the
manufacture of a cheap grade of gloves or shoes.

Tripoli Harbor affords better protection to
vessels than many on the North African coast;
but because of dangerous reefs and shoals it
is a most difficult harbor to enter, particularly

in stormy weather, for the Mediterranean is as varying in her moods as are those peoples who inhabit her shores. Under the gentle zephyrs and clear skies of summer she is as peaceful as Hadji under his awning in yonder Suk; but in winter, when, under the spirit of the north wind, she comes ripping, lashing southward, foaming down in a seething froth on the reef-lined shores of Barbary, she is as wild and fanatical as some mighty horde of Moslems driven by the spirit of the Jehad.

Off some of the Barbary ports vessels frequently lie for weeks awaiting fair weather before they can discharge their cargoes, and the list of casualties for the amount of shipping off the North African coast must be large. In 1904, 543 sailing vessels and 271 steamers entered Tripoli Harbor. Some of the risks which these vessels incur in these waters may be noted from the following, which I quote from two letters received from Tripoli. The author writes:

On Wednesday, December 6 [1905] at 6.25 P. M., we were at the Turkish Club as usual. I saw a rocket go up . . . and said, "There is the S. S. *Syrian Prince* . . . expect me home when you see me" . . . went aboard and stayed there until Sunday, December 10th . . . threw overboard about 620 tons of cargo and got her off at 1.35 A. M., Sunday. I had the salvage steamer *Denmark* here . . . towing at her . . . had five hours' rest the whole time . . . we all worked like devils to get her off before bad weather came on, . . . which did come twelve hours after, and one hour of it would have made a total wreck of her . . . have done nothing else but see into recovering the jettisoned cargo, selling it by auction and writing reports to Lloyds and the Salvage Co., London. Then a beautiful, three-masted steel barkentine of 220 tons has gone on the rocks at Zleiten down the coast, and this means work.

A following letter written shortly after this reads:

Have had no time to write as I had a steam launch smashed up, and on December 22 [1905] a British steamer, the *Collingham*, got on a reef. Have salvage steamer here and am working day and night. . . . I got her off, . . . but she is badly damaged.

Such is the record for one month off the port of Tripoli alone.

The seaboard of Tripolitania can well afford to boast of its share of maritime destruction. The dangerous quicksands of the Major and Minor Syrtes of the ancients are in the bight of her coast-line: sands whose fatal suction, downward-drawing, has claimed many a Roman trireme, many a caravel and stately ship of the line, and many a modern vessel of steel. To the treacherous reefs off Tripoli harbor we owe the loss of the *Philadelphia*, and it was off Tripoli, in a gale, that the United States Dry Dock *Dewey*, on her famous voyage to the Philippines, came near meeting disaster.

In Tunis, Algiers and other ports in the two French North African colonies, good harbors have been constructed and vessels unload at the quays; but in Tripoli and Morocco all cargoes are transferred in lighters or galleylike row-boats, and little protection is offered vessels lying at anchor. Arabs on the whole are good sailors and are not lacking in courage. One Mediterranean captain told me that the best crew he ever had was made up of Moroccans— descendants perhaps of the old rovers of Salli and Rabat.

When in the heavy Arab galleys, I never tired of watching the swarthy Islamites handle the mammoth sweeps. Barefooted, each man would clinch the thwart in front of him with his toes, rise with the loom of the oar to a standing posi-tion, then with a grunt throw himself back with all his supple strength. To "catch a crab" under these conditions was a serious matter. The way in which they handled these enormous sweeps was remarkable, forcing the ponderous galleys through the water at the rate they did. Many of the sweeps must have been over twenty feet in length.

Some idea of the relative importance of Tripo-

li's leading exports ma...r instance, out of a
considers that in 19... about $2,000,000, sponges
total export trade ...,000 or over a fifth, esparto
amounted to $... grass to $630... or over a third, and goods from
the trans-saharan caravan trade to $314,000 or
over one-sixth. The other remaining three-
tenths of her exports were comprised of the
products of the oases and towns on or near
the coast.

The methods of gathering and marketing these
three leading exports are as interesting as they
are unique and hazardous, and the men engaged
in them as picturesque and dirty as they are hard-
working and fearless—the sponge diver on his
restless sea of brine; the esparto picker in his
waving sea of sun-dried grass; the caravaneer on
his shifting, burning sea of sand.

In the eastern half of the Mediterranean, along
the coast from Tunis to the Levant, including the
islands of the Ægean Sea, stretch great regions
of sponge colonies. Those extending for three
hundred and fifty miles along the North African
coast, from the Tunisian frontier to Misurata on
the east, are known as the Tripoli grounds, and
here with the last north winds of the rainy season

come the sponge fleets from the Greek Archipelago. I well remember the night at the Turkish Club that I obtained my first insight into the
life of the Greek scaphander.[1] A party of us, as
usual, sat about one of the tables after tennis and
throwing the discus by the shaded court under
the southern lee of the town wall.

Near by, the dark sapphire-blue walls of the
ancient Castle of the Bashaws stood silhouetted
against a west of yellow amethyst. Its great
shadow had crept across the garden to where we
sat, on over the dry bed of a neighboring wadi,
finally lengthening across the Suk-el-Thalat,
where the distant Arab houses stood out—a level
golden line from the dusk shadows of the purple
twilight.

"Yes, sewn up in a bag!" The speaker was
one of the Greek naval officers. "It was in the
Gulf of Sirte, two years ago," he continued. "A
diver from one of the machine boats had gone
down for sponges, and crawling over the bottom
of the sea came upon a large bag. Perhaps the
thought of sunken treasure caused him to rip
open more hastily its half-rotten threads. . . .

[1] Divers who use the *scaphandra* or machine [air-pump, suit,
helmet, and tube].

Well, there were two of them in it; both were found to have been sponge divers."

"Buried at sea?" I queried.

A peculiar smile played for a moment around the white teeth of the olive-skinned Greek. "Yes, but we could find no record of the burial!"

"And that case of the diver in a sponge boat off Derna?" added an Englishman. "Paralysis didn't creep fast enough, and he was only dead wood aboard, so they buried him alive in the hot sand of the Sahara. Even after he was dead some thieving Arabs stole his clothes."

"Well, there may be cases of foul play," the Greek admitted, "yet they are insignificant compared with that deadly enemy of the scaphander —diver's paralysis. Why, out of the seven hundred scaphanders working on this coast, from sixty to a hundred die every year, and, sooner or later, hardly a man escapes from it in one form or another. Of course these conditions are due, in great part, to the ignorance and brutality of the men engaged in the industry. On the other hand, there have been captains from Ægina, who have been in business for fifteen years and have never lost a diver. With those two vessels in the bay yonder," and he waved his hand toward two white-painted craft, "the hospital-ship *Crête* and the corvette *Paralos* and a sponge diver's hospital on shore, the Greek Government is doing everything possible to remedy the conditions. But, owing to the extensive area of the sponge grounds and other causes, it is almost impossible to keep close watch and detect those who violate the laws."

One bit of interesting information led to another: the common diver, who dives naked with a piece of marble and line, suffers only slight affections of the ears; with the scaphander or helmeted diver, the greatest danger occurs in the rapid ascent, producing sudden relief of pressure, dangerous symptoms appearing only when he emerges into the fresh air, generally shortly after the helmet is removed; and strange as it may seem, on the descent a partially paralyzed diver recovers the use of his limbs again and his circulation becomes normal. Many of them, in the prime of life paralyzed and crippled, unfitted for anything else, continue to drag themselves about at their wearisome work, believing the disease to be indispensable to the vocation.

The generally accepted theory of diver's paralysis is that the various vessels of the body are contracted and the blood is driven from the central intestines, causing congestion, with or without hemorrhage, minute balls of air expanding and rupturing these vessels, the great danger occurring when the balls develop and last. They consist of azote [nitrogen] dissolving in the blood and becoming free when the pressure is withdrawn, sometimes preventing circulation in the lungs or, blocking it in the nervous system, producing local anæmia. If these balls of azote are large and many, death usually occurs through paralysis of the heart; when small they are carried by the circulation of the blood to the brain and medulla, causing paralysis in one or more of its multitudinous forms. Part of the cure is by immersion and gradual ascending, stopping one minute every five metres.

The character of the phenomena of diver's paralysis may be seen in the following instance:

A scaphander, Michael Sygalos, descended to a depth of fifty-two metres, remaining below fifty minutes and making a very rapid ascent, descending again in an hour and a half to the same depth, where he remained for forty-five minutes, and again made a very rapid ascent, but felt no ill results. In an hour he descended once more to the same depth, where he remained for thirty minutes, making for the third time a very rapid ascent. For a few minutes he felt no ill effects, but as the helmet was removed he was seized with a terrific dizziness and fell unconscious to the deck. Later he revived, feeling a congestion or pressure of blood, as it were, in his legs, preventing him from standing alone. This condition lasted until midnight when he was attacked by complete paralysis, losing all his senses and power of movement save the ability to slightly move his head. He lingered through the hot summer until the middle of August.

Many paralytics are incurable, and death through paroxysms often results, though many are partially and some permanently cured.

One hot day, not long after our talk at the Café, we stood out in one of the *Crête's* whaleboats under a small lug-sail to meet the deposit boat *Panayea*. Close-hauled, she bore down upon us, her rakish rig with big lateen sails and jib straining at every line and spar. On she came, painting two long diverging lines of foaming white on the sparkling blue. She crossed our bows, her great sails flapped, she came into the wind; and as she filled away I climbed aboard, and we stood to the edge of the sponge grounds, which extend from five to twenty miles off the Tripoli coast.

So began my acquaintance with the Greek sponge divers, whose day's work is the season's work and who, for six months of the year, from April to October, labor from sunrise to sunset, generally on a rough sea and under the scorching rays of an African sun.

We scudded by some small *harpun* [harpoon] boats and *gangara* [trawlers], near enough to the former to see their small crews, of from three to five men each, at work. They carefully examined the sea bottom, sometimes to a depth of twenty metres, with a special glass of their own, and pulled up the marketable sponges with harpoons attached to the ends of long poles. The slightly larger gangara—the *gargameleon* of the ancients—slowly trawled for sponges, dragging their destructive nets along the bed of the sea to a depth of seventy-five metres, tearing and accumulating everything in their path. But these methods have practically been abandoned along this coast for the more productive grounds of Cyprus and Crete.

A sponge fleet consists of the five and six ton

machine boats [trehanteria] which carry air-pumping machines and equipment [scaphandra], and which are divided into two classes, according to the quality of their divers' suits. A first-class boat is manned by twenty to twenty-two men, of whom ten are professional divers who descend from twenty-three to thirty fathoms. The second-class boat is manned by from fourteen to sixteen men, of whom five to seven are divers who descend from fifteen to twenty fathoms. As the fleets keep to sea for two months at a time, every four machine boats are attended by one fifty to sixty ton deposit boat [deposita]. Aboard the deposit boat are stored the sponges, food, clothing, and other necessities; they also serve as sleeping quarters for some of the crews of the machine boats. Smaller supply boats [bakietta] communicate with shore, bring supplies from Greece and also men to take the places of those who have died. Some three thousand men work by scaphandra on the African coast.

Attacks by ferocious fish have frightened away the "common" divers, who dive naked with a piece of marble [scandli] and line. They dive with great rapidity, forty-five to over fifty metres, and usually remain below two minutes.

Experts have stayed as long as four. The best divers are from Kalimno and Symi. A few years ago that hideous black creature, the dog-fish, bit a diver in two and desperately wounded several others. One of the most thrilling escapes ever recorded is that of a diver, who, as he descended, holding the scandli in front of him, entered the mouth of a large shark. The scandli being edgewise prevented the huge jaws from closing, and the diver with difficulty wriggled out and was hauled up. The shark, ejecting the scandli, pursued him to the surface, and was seen by those in the boat to leap for his prey as the crew hauled the diver aboard. By careful nursing the wounded man recovered from the long, deep scratches of the monster's teeth on his chest and back. Now virtually the scaphanders alone remain to claim the profits of the industry, the proceeds of which in a single year have amounted to almost a million dollars.

Reaching the grounds, we were transferred to the machine boat *El-Pish*. The greater number of the sponge boats fly the Greek flag, and are manned by Greeks hailing mainly from the islands of Hydra and Ægina, while a few fly the crescent flag of the Ottoman Empire and come from the Turkish islands of Kalimno, Symi, and Khalki in the Archipelago, whose crews are made up of subjugated Greeks from those islands.

During the long, cold winter months the sponge fishers spend most of their time ashore in their island homes. When the first balmy airs of the African spring are wafted across the Mediterranean from the oleander-fringed wadis and oases of the Sahara, the little seaport towns of the sponge fishers bestir themselves, the last boats are put in commission, and the final contracts among owners, captains, and crews are drawn up.

For equipment, provisions, and advance payment of the crews, each captain is required to provide a capital of forty to sixty thousand drachmas—being approximately $12,000, but at present much depreciated. Capitalists advance this money at a rate of from two to three per cent. per month, for the season, which is deducted at once from the capital. The novice receives from three to seven hundred drachmas for the season, the experienced diver from one to three thousand. In some instances the diver shares in the profits, but it more often happens that his season's earnings are less than his advanced pay, in which case he must work out the difference the next year. Should he be injured or disabled, his pay continues on the same basis, and in case of death his heirs receive his money.

After the final haul is made and the sponges are sold, the commission to the Turks, who maintain a war-ship here, is first taken out of the proceeds, a third of the remainder goes to the captain for ship's expenses and equipment, and from the remaining two-thirds must be taken the expense for the provisions. Of the final balance, one and a half shares go to the captain and supervisor each, four shares to each diver, and one to each sailor.

Not only to increase the proceeds, but to come out even on the outfit, the captains are obliged to treat the divers with great severity, and hire overseers who devise most brutal means of forcing them to fish at any cost. On the other hand, the divers give much cause for complaint. They come from all parts of Greece and the Archipelago; many are nondescripts who have never been sailors and are persuaded to go into this for easy gains, failing to realize the dangers of the life; for once they are injured or disabled by their arch enemy, diver's paralysis, they become un-

" The bag of dark, heavy sponges . . . was hauled aboard "

fitted for any other work, and are provided for
by the captains during the winter.

The deck of the *El-Pish*, where I slept, save
for its dirt and confusion, was not unlike that of
the ordinary fishing schooner. At daybreak I
threw off the dew-soaked canvas that served as
my covering at night. A number of sponge
boats disturbed the placid rose surface of the
water; high up in the air several white gull forms
overhead broke the tender blue, mingling their
cries with the voices of the men and the creaking
blocks. The first rays of the sun lit up the
bronzed features of the overseer, as he stopped to
examine the air-pump, in which are three cylin-
drical, leather-lined compartments. Through
these the air, is pumped to the diver below. The
warmth of this air which is often blown from the
heated sands of the Desert, is increased by friction in the compartments, and is obviated by
coolers supplied every half-hour with cold water.
On the deck by his side was a rubber tube which
must resist the pressure of twenty atmospheres,
and is consequently re-enforced on the inside
by coiled wire.

Screwing one end of the tube to the air-pump
and the other to the back of a heavy brass hel-

met, the overseer ordered the two sailors into the main-hatch, to "stand by" the big pump wheels of the machine. On a board placed across the deck sat Basilio Pteroudiz, a diver, preparing for the descent. He had already donned the main garment, which was made of strong, double water-proofed cotton cloth, with an interlayer of rubber; around his neck was a collar of rubber, to which was attached the brass collar of the helmet; at his wrists, which were soaped to aid suction, the garment ended in tightly fitting rubber wristbands, and under his garment he wore heavy woollen underwear and socks. The buoyancy of the suit when inflated necessitated the addition of a seventeen pound lead weight attached to each shoe, while about his chest and back were fastened a ten and a seven pound weight respectively.

With assistance he staggered to the forward rail, where a ladder hung by which the divers descend to the water. A sign from the overseer and the men gave way at the pumps, a sailor seized the helmet with its four glass windows, placed it over the head of Pteroudiz, screwed and bolted it to the brass collar. The suit at once became inflated as far as the waist, where a rope was fastened. This with the tube was paid out, and taking a net sponge bag he descended over the side. Even with the extra hundred and seventy-five pounds of equipment it was some seconds before he was able to sink. The rope was held by the overseer, serving not only as a safeguard but also as a means of communication. From time to time the overseer consulted the *manometrom* in the machine, which indicated the pressure of the air in the diver's suit, consequently his depth.

I followed his sinking form, as the last glint of his shining helmet, radiating shafts of reflected light in all directions, disappeared into the oblivion of the mysterious depths. Crawling along the bottom, taking care not to wrench the weights from his feet, which would cause him to turn head downward, he searched among the wonders and beauties of the semitropical sea garden, and when he found a colony of the reddish-brown Tripoli sponge, signalled to the overseer, whereupon the spot was buoyed. Discarding among others the few black and worthless male sponges, he selected only the marketable sponges, the best of which he gathered from the rocks. Way above and over him, seen through the luminous half-lights of the sunlit sea water, the fishlike shape of the *El-Pish* rocked on the surface; and as he sought new spots she followed him, her four huge finlike sweeps stirring and churning the water as though breaking and scattering myriads of jewelled braids. Sometimes the shadowy form of a huge shark or dog-fish glided dangerously near him, notwithstanding the repeated piping of the air whistle on deck—though as yet their attacks have been confined to the common diver.

In the helmet to the right and behind the head was a valve, against which he pressed his head from time to time in order to expel the expired air, which rose to the surface like magnified wobbling globules of quicksilver, assisting those above in locating his position. The descent generally takes about two minutes, the diver staying down occasionally as long as fifty, and sometimes reaching a depth of over sixty metres, absolutely disregarding the limit of thirty-eight metres set by the laws of the Greek Navy Department. About two minutes are occupied in pulling him up by rope, but usually he buoys himself to the surface in less than a minute, ascending more rapidly than the rope can be hauled in; and to this cause in particular can be attributed diver's paralysis and other common injuries.

Suddenly Pteroudiz made his appearance at the surface, the water rolling off his helmet and shoulders as from some great amphibious creature; and the bag of dark, heavy sponges, dripping and streaming with ooze and sea water, was hauled aboard. No sooner had he appeared on deck and removed his helmet than another diver, dressed and waiting, at once made his descent, and so it goes on through the hot day. It was not without some persuasion that the captain acquiesced to my request to go down in one of the suits. But at last one day, when five miles out to sea, I donned the suit and the heavy brass helmet was screwed down and locked to the collar. At first it was with great difficulty that I managed to control my heavily weighted feet and walk across the rolling slippery deck, during which experiment the barefooted Greeks gave me a wide path. The sensation as the helmet was locked and the pumps started was one of slight compression only, about the head, to which one at once becomes accustomed. The overseer, despite my signals from the vision of opalescent refracted lights into which I had sunk, refused to pay out sufficient rope to allow me to make bottom. He feared the dangers which attend the novice on too great a depth at the start, and particularly when no preparation pertaining to diet has been made.

Many captains and overseers pay practically no attention to depth and time, compelling the diver to descend again at once if his sponges are too few or of inferior quality. Often no consideration is given the defenceless diver, as, staggering and almost overcome in the depths below, he signals to come up, and if he buoys himself to the surface, he is forced to go down again.

Overseers direct the descents, deciding the divers' time below, and frequently take command when the captains are ashore.

Sometimes the overseers not only secretly fix the pumps so that less pressure is indicated, but instead of using pure vaseline they grease the machines with old lard and oil, which leak into the tube, sending foul air down to the diver. The coolers are so neglected that the water becomes unbearably hot to the touch, and the air forced down even hotter. The suit is sometimes neglected and twice in the year preceding my visit the helmet became detached while the diver was below. One of the men was saved and the other drowned.

And so, it is not strange that divers often bribe their overseers in order to secure leniency, and even at the moment of descent make agreements by signs to spare their lives.

As soon as the sponges are brought aboard they are thrown in heaps on deck near the scuppers, where the barefooted sailors tramp and work out the ooze; then strung on lines they are soused over the side and trail overboard some ten hours during the night. To break and separate from them shell-fish and other parasites, they are beaten with heavy sticks on deck or on the reef rocks off Tripoli; and, after being well soaked in the sea again, many are bleached by being immersed in a tub of water containing a certain solution of oxalic acid, from which they emerge a yellowish color, care having been taken to avoid burning them.

Tripoli sponges are inferior to those found in other parts of the Mediterranean, the best quality [those gathered from rocks] is worth from $4.00 to $5.00 per oke [2.82 lbs.]; the second quality [where seaweed abounds], from $3.20 to $4.00 per oke; and the third quality, brought up without intent by the trawlers, from $2.40 to $4.00. Male sponges, which do not abound on the Tripoli coast, are worthless.

Notwithstanding the importance of the sponge industry the season after I left Tripoli the following was received from Mr. Riley:

A short time since the Governor General issued orders that all machine boats had three days to get their provisions and clear out of Tripoli Harbor and Tripoli Port. This upset things a bit and meant ruin to some and thousands of £'s loss to others, so I saw his Excellency, and in two hours had fixed it up, at least until he wired to Constantinople. Afterward I saw him again and the thing is fixed up for this season at least, and no bothering through the Consulates.

Often great strings of sponges bleaching and drying in the sun cover large portions of the standing rigging of deposit boats when in port. When dry they are worked up in sand, then packed in boxes ready for shipment; a third to a quarter of the crop is sold direct from Tripoli, mainly to England and to France and Italy; the bulk of the crop, unbleached and unprepared, is taken at the close of the season to the islands from which the boats came, where long experience, manipulation, and cheap labor prepare them for the European market.

At sundown, after the last descent had been made and the sponges put over the side, the ma-

A deposit boat

Great strings of sponges cover . . portions of the standing rigging"

chine was housed and the crew boarded the *Panayea.* The smoke from her galley stove drifted lazily toward the distant low-lying coast of Africa, where was just visible the long palm fringe of the oasis of Tripoli. Until dark, the men lounged around the deck, an occasional group at cards, but most of them absorbed in smoking or conversation.

The glittering eyes and bronzed faces of the crew reflected the light from a lantern and the glow of the galley stove, near which, squatting on the deck, spare boxes, or spars, we ate the evening meal, the only one of the day allowed to divers on account of the character of their work; but the sailors fare better, having at noon a meal of cheese, olives, herring, and rice. To-night we sat down to sun-dried goat's flesh, hardtack, a hot dish of lentils, and a pint of wine each.

In less than an hour the crew had turned in for the night—on deck or below, as the case might be. A few paralyzed divers had dragged themselves, or been assisted, to the unspeakably foul-smelling, congested quarters below, where between the narrow bunks the spaces were filled with provisions, clothes, water-casks, fuel, and sick men.

At the end of the season, when the wind sweeps down from the north, and the jagged reef-lined coast of Tripoli is lashed into foam, these men of the sea, who have not already weighed anchor for unknown ports, set sail for their island homes, carrying with them the season's haul, though a few remain, going out when the weather permits, or fishing in certain protected parts of the Archipelago.

I was alone with the watch on deck. Through the criss-cross of the rigging and spars I could see his dim moonlit form as he "gave a spoke" at the wheel now and again. Over the side the phosphorescence mingled in the quiet water with the silver star dust of the blue night. I gazed down into the dark, mysterious, and seemingly bottomless sea, where I, too, had felt the first suffocation and tight congestion, that strange sense of entire isolation and chance—then the depth and wonder of it all.

So it is with some of the men who go down to the sea in ships.

CHAPTER EIGHT

THE ESPARTO PICKERS

SUNRISE shot over the limestone range of the Tripoli hills. Back of them and to the south canoned out by numerous wadis the plateau lands of the Sahara stretched away. Northward forty to ninety miles to the sea ran a tract of country sprinkled with oases. About these and along the river courses where Arabs, Berbers, and Blacks cultivate the arid wastes, at harvest time golden grains wave under the hot Desert winds, and here and there green patches of olive groves darken the clayey, sandy soil. A night mist still hung tenaciously in the valleys and over the low foot-hills along which I rode, and the heavy dew-bejewelled blades of esparto grass [1] drenched hoof and fetlock as my horse scattered myriads of water diamonds from its wiry clumps.

---

[1] Esparto—a Spanish name given two or three kinds of grass, more particularly to the *marcrochloa tenacissima* indigenous to Southern Europe and North Africa.

Suddenly from over the brow of a dune a strange, bulky apparition lifted indistinctly from the great solitudes. Then another and still others of these gray spectres moved silently toward us through the mist film, and a caravan of heavily loaded camels squdged silently by, their great incongruous shapes almost lost beneath the huge bundles of esparto grass which were thrown across their humps.

As the night mists dispelled before the heat not a tree or a shrub broke the monotonous yet imposing harmony of the landscape. My eye wandered over mile upon mile of an immense plain covered by halfa,[1] nothing but halfa, over which the soft, hot breeze of the gibli played in lazy wantonness, rolling, ever rolling in long billows its undulating tops.

So from Portugal and Spain, along the sandy regions of the Atlas, as they range through the western half of Northern Africa until they finally dwindle away into the Desert sands of Tripoli, at intervals great seas of this waving broomlike weed grow at the bases of the mountains and on the plateau lands. While in Spain and the Barbary States it is an object of commercial enter-

[1] By Arabs esparto grass is called *halfa* or *alfa*.

prise, in Tripoli the industry is unique in its importance and has enough of the unusual and of the element of danger to make it picturesque in its setting, from when the grass is gathered by the Arabs of the wadan to the time when husky Blacks hook the great bales aboard vessels which bear it away to England for the manufacture of paper.

In the distance the rude shacks of some esparto pickers appeared, looking more like mounds of earth than habitations. About them some hobbled camels browsed on the dryness. I drew rein before one of the shacks, while some of the family ventured forth. A boy, first with one dirty hand, then with the other, compressed a moldable mass of something into a hard lump, which my head Arab tried to convince me was a camel's milk cheese. That it bore the hallmark of the maker there was no doubt. Not far off were the bobbing heads of the esparto pickers. Standing leg-high amid the waving halfa they paused in their work to view me curiously.

On close approach one finds the grass, which is perennial and bears a small flower, growing quite sparsely and in separate clumps; the strong stems, tough and fibrous, radiate from the large tap-root of each plant. Here the hired picker puts in a long day's work for starvation wages of perhaps twenty cents a day. When he has picked a quantity of grass he ties it up in bundles with bits of esparto rope, ready to be packed into large nets.

Despite the fact that the esparto is considered nonreproductive and is incapable of cultivation, I noticed that the Arabs pulled it up, root and all. This is the custom among the esparto pickers in Tripoli, and was so in Tunis and Algeria until the French put a stop to this disastrous method of gathering. Now they require it to be cut, and thus the great esparto districts of Oran, Bougie, Philippeville, and Oued Laya owe their preservation to the foresight of the French colonial government.

Under the moonlight of early morning these Arabs began the day's work. One or two had discarded their woollen baracans as the early chill wore off, and had put on the fantastic broad-brimmed esparto hats of the Sahel, as a protection against the intense heat which had already hushed down on the landscape. I knew that later the majority of them would again throw on the woollen garment, which in this sun-scorched land is worn to keep out the heat as well as the chill. Sandals woven from esparto grass or the broad-soled Desert slippers protected their feet from being scorched and cracked by the sun-baked ground. But the heat and the chill are the least dangers which beset the esparto picker.

With careless ease he gathers the longest of the wiry stems from the most matured clumps. Suddenly with a catlike spring he jumps aside and eludes the thrust of his arch enemy, the deadly viper, whose nest he has disturbed in a tuft of matted halfa grass. But even the sharp eye of the Arab sometimes fails to discern the viper's lair, and he plunges his bare arm into the very nest of this poisonous reptile, only to withdraw it stung and bleeding from the fangs which have buried themselves in his flesh.

In the halfa clumps as well as in crevices under stones lurks another enemy, the great rock scorpion of Northern Africa—a noxious creature sometimes ten inches in length. Its peculiar aversion to light and desire for warmth make it a much-feared night visitor.

"Arise, let us make morning," sounds over the

camp, and the esparto picker not infrequently shakes out of his baracan a scorpion or two. Perhaps he neglects to dislodge one from his broad-soled Desert slippers, and, thus cornered, the scorpion with the lash of his venomous tail attacks the intruder.

The consequences depend greatly upon the size of the scorpion and the constitution of the victim. While the sting is not necessarily fatal, yet the Arabs' sole idea of treatment, so far as I could ascertain, was either to cut off the injured part at once or bandage it tightly above the wound. Then far back on the throbbing Desert the poisoned man is left alone with his wild delirium and burning thirst. In many cases the corpse is soon cast out to the vultures and carrion crows, whose shadows likely enough have already for hours been passing to and fro over the body.

In the shadows of the shacks the women and children not employed in gathering were braiding ropes and making them into immense coarse-meshed nets. Each net when stuffed with halfa contains enough for a single camel load, and this unwieldy bulky mass, often four feet wide and twelve in length, is balanced across the camel's hump and secured with lashings which are fastened fore and aft under the camel's neck and tail.

Summer is the close season, but halfa may be gathered during the entire year. It is extremely difficult to dry if picked green, and should not be gathered until the rainy season—November to March—has passed and the hot Desert breezes have thoroughly dried out its moisture Frequently, however, it is collected green by the Arabs, who then dry it slightly before taking it to market, and in seasons of close competition the dealers themselves have been known to buy it green.

When the time is ripe for transporting the esparto to the seaports of Bengazi, Khoms, Zleiten and Tripoli, a caravan is organized and takes up the march of from two to four days as the camel journeys. In irregular single file, such as the one which passed me in the early morning, it creeps its way over the Desert. Perhaps beside the huge camels a donkey with a smaller load of halfa or water-filled goat-skins trudges patiently along, in the vanguard a big white wolfhound, while the Arabs on foot distribute themselves the length of the caravan. Their ever-ready long flint-lock guns or broadswords are slung loosely across their backs, and their senses are ever on the alert for Desert thieves who may lurk in the shadows or lie buried in the sand beside the trail.

Snap!! Over in the shadow of a dune a flint-lock has flashed in the pan, but it is warning enough. Bang! Bang! red shafts of light like lurid meteors light up in fitful glares the esparto pickers as amidst the confusion some bunch the animals, while others repel the attack. But the enemy, as is his custom, has withdrawn as suddenly as he appeared. A wounded esparto picker is lifted on to a camel; a bunch of halfa lying on the Desert a short distance off tells the tale of a successful raid, in which the profits of the cargo have been wiped away in a moment by the stampeding to the enemy of a valuable camel; but Allah wills! and the garfla takes up the march, soon to pass along the hard-packed caravan road through the palm groves of the oasis of Tripoli to the Suk-el-Halfa [Halfa Market] without the town.

A cursory glance at the Suk-el-Halfa will impress even the stranger with the importance of the esparto trade, and a few words with any Tripolitan merchant will reveal the fact that not only is it Tripoli's leading export, but in years of little

rain and scant harvest, with practically the ex-
tinction of the trans-Saharan caravan trade, it is
the only natural resource which the Arab peasant
can fall back upon. In years of full harvest little
halfa, comparatively speaking, is brought into
market, for Hadji Mohamed, having reaped his
wheat and barley, has not only made provision
for his simple wants for the year, but has even
brought back from the town bazaars silver ornaments for his women. Consequently necessity
does not drive him to the tedious process of halfa
gathering, with all its attendant risks and the
long journeys to the coast on camel back, so often
unproductive of satisfactory results.

Esparto is not an agricultural product, and it
seems fitting that the leading export of that nomadic people should be a product of their own
arid land, wild and incapable of cultivation.
Since 1868, when the first shipload of esparto was
sent to England, vessels have borne away thousands of tons yearly to that country. You or I pick
up a heavy-looking novel, perchance, and marvel
at its lightness, and the reader of some London
newspaper peruses its columns and then casts
aside the finished product of the esparto pickers.

In 1901, which was an average year, 215,155

camel loads came into the coast towns; nearly 134,000 passed through the gateway to the Suk-el-Halfa, the total export of the country amounting to about 33,000 tons. That from the town of Tripoli, 16,690 tons, brought £75,500, which was over a fourth of the amount of Tripoli's total exports.

Not ten minutes' trudge through the sand from the heavy battlements which surround Tripoli is the big square-walled enclosure of perhaps three acres—the Suk-el-Halfa. The scenes of this great suk have left an indelible impress on my memory. I but close my eyes and see that great panorama of the heat, the sweat, and the toil float across the horizon of my imagination like some vivid mirage of that far-away Desert land.

One day I loafed across the Suk-el-Thalat and followed in the shadow of the wall, lagging after some esparto camels to the arched gateway of the Suk-el-Halfa. Here the caravan halted and the leader was accosted by an Arab guard. A short parley, and the guns of the drivers were handed over, and the leader tucked the greasy receipt in a leathern money pouch beneath his baracan. Each camel entirely blocked the gateway as with his load of grass he passed through. Following

ın their wake through the shady portal I entered
the sun-flooded suk. My first impression was
of a great sea of yellow-gray espartò bales, resembling a vast herd of half-submerged hippo-
potami; among them the cotton garments of the
negroes flecked white, each dotted by the ebony
head of its wearer, and over the glaring white
walls which shut in the scene the arches of some
neighboring buildings seemed to peer like so
many curious monster eyes.

Here and there great bales poked their noses
above the rest, and once in a while one would rise
or lower as a camel arose or was unloaded. In
this great weighing yard of the Suk-el-Halfa,
called by the natives *rahbah*, a simple though
effective system was evident. Across its centre
the suk was divided by a fence in which breaks
occurred at intervals. At these openings big
primitive scales had been erected, the number of
these depending on the number of buyers; this
year there were four. These lever-scales are put
up at auction, and public weighers, who are generally Arabs, weigh up the nets of esparto and re-
ceive a certain amount per hundred-weight. On
one side of the fence is the unweighed, on the
other the weighed, esparto.

Each picker as he enters deposits his esparto in one lot, which is auctioned off unweighed to the highest bidder. Prices fluctuate, due to the competition of the buyers, but the year I was in Tripoli six francs per hundred kilos was a fair price for the raw material. When the bidding opens in the early spring, the competition among the buyers is very keen, reaching sometimes as high as £3-8s-6d a ton. But it sometimes happens that there is not a corresponding increase in its value in England, and the buyers at times sell at a loss.

From the topmost bale of a pile of heat-soaked halfa near one of the scales I watched the day's work. These scales were huge levers. Through a loop of coarse rope suspended from the cross point of two rough-hewn beams, a third hung lazily balanced. At the larger end a chain and tackle containing a scale dangled to the ground. Near by the flapping broad-brimmed hat and officious manner of an Arab at once stamped him as one in authority, a public weigher. By word and gesture he would order a bale rolled out from the heap where the owner had deposited it.

It was noosed in the tackle; a yell from the weigher, and a number of strapping Blacks

Weighing esparto grass in the Suk-el-Halfa

sprang from below me like so many leopard cats upon the other more slender end of the beam. They held for a minute suspended in the air, others hung to their legs, the great beam trembled, then the monster bale at the other end slowly began to lift, and its human counterweight sank gradually to the ground.

"Four hundred-weight" called out the overseer with a glance at the scale as he released the tackle. Crush! dropped the huge bale as it sent up a great puff of sand dust, which drifted away in quiet space, powdering the shiny skins of two Blacks. With remarkable strength they grappled the meshes with long iron hooks, whirled and rolled it beneath the scales to the other side of the fence, where another relay bundled it end over end into its place.

One cannot sojourn long in Tripoli without being impressed that it is a land of ancient tradition, a land where even to-day only the mere fringe of modern civilization has touched one or two of her ports, a land of customs, implements, and usage of a time long before the Israelites shook the dust of Egypt from their feet.

But somehow of all the primitive native devices none interested me more than the great rough-hewn levers in the Suk-el-Halfa. Many a time I diverged from my objective point to watch the great beams lift and dip on their fulcra. The timber had come, perchance, from the neighboring oasis, but the idea—? Could it have travelled through the long reaches of centuries from the times when men first had occasion to lift great weights? I venture an opinion. Could this be a modification of the device by which the ancient Semites and Ethiopians raised, tier upon tier, the great blocks of the Pyramids of Egypt? Simply constructed, easily shifted, admitting revolving the weight when once lifted through an arc of almost 170°, it might well have been adapted to such a use.

Now that the esparto is weighed the Arab from whom it was bought must have his drivers load it again on to their camels and deliver it into the private esparto yard of the buyer. As each driver enters a private yard, a clerk checks and countersigns the ticket given him in the Suk-el-Halfa; then, having deposited their nets in one heap, with unloaded camels they present their tickets to the cashier and are paid. Along the outskirts of the halfa piles I watched them load up the groaning camels.

Always remonstrating, an occasional beast more defiant than the rest refused to lie down to be loaded. Near me one vicious brute had twice shaken off his heavy burden, and now a third time had prematurely lurched to his feet. It finally required the combined efforts of five men to land the unwieldy net of esparto securely across his hump. My sympathies were with the camel.

It was shortly after one siesta time that I accompanied Signor Cortugna to one of the private esparto yards, of which he was manager. As we turned into the main street of Tripoli, which leads through an outer gate, a man, breathless and excited, dodged and jostled through the leisurely moving crowd, approached Signor Cortugna, and addressed him in Arabic. Signor Cortugna hailed from their stand, near the market gate, one of the quaint little rigs, several of which Tripoli boasts. "Step in," he said; "the Arab informed me of an accident to one of my men." We rattled and bumped over the caravan road to the esparto yard.

We passed through the gate and were joined by the foreman, who led the way through lanes of loose halfa to a long inclined structure, over

which from sunrise to sunset during baling periods an endless traveller with its ceaseless noise
conveyed the sorted esparto to the upper floor of
a two-story building.

Now a deathless silence hung over the scene,
which but an hour ago was alive with the drone
of industry. The foreman stopped at a pit at
the base of the traveller in which a Black constantly watches and controls the endless chain.
A few remnants of cloth left in the cogs were
least among the evidences which told of a lapse
of vigilance or a moment's dozing on the part of
the lone watcher in the heat and din of the narrow pit.

Followed by several Blacks we turned away
from the sickening sight. A woman's moan
floated out from a distant part of the yard; as it
rose and fell other women added their wails to
the crescendo in a great pitiful cry to Allah for
the dead, as the good and the bad angels con-
tested for the soul. In a low-lying shed, an old
sack for a shroud, lay what remained of the poor
fellow.

We were not Mohammedans, and Signor Cortugna paused respectfully at the entrance. The
voices hushed, the women from under their col-

ored striped baracans and some of the half-naked men glared savagely.

It is the law of the country to bury the dead by sundown. As the big piles of halfa cast lengthening shadows across the yard, the orange glow of the sunlight played over four dignified figures who strode away with the bier of their tribesman, on to his shallow grave by their village in the oasis. So majestic was their mien, so classic were the graceful folds of their tattered garments, that visions of some ancient Greek borne to his funeral pyre ranged across my vision, and the guttural unintelligible funeral chant sang to my ears:

> "Let us begin and carry up this corpse
>   Singing together.
> Leave we the common crofts, the vulgar thorps,
>   Each in its tether.
> Sleeping safe on the bosom of the plain,
>   Cared for till cock-crow:
> Look out if yonder be not day again,
>   Rimming the rock-row."

It was a weird scene full of barbaric pathos; but rattle, rattle, and the endless chain of the great traveller again revolved with its cold metallic clink, and again some hundred Blacks took up their work. Not the chocolate-colored hybrid of our land, but great powerful savages these, with white, glistening teeth and cheeks scarred with the marks of their tribe or their servitude; men with skins of ebony as polished as patent leather, down which rolled great beads of perspiration. Any day they might forsake their palm-thatched zerebas in the oasis for the jungles of the Sudan from whence they came.

The simple white cotton clothes predominated, but many wore nondescript rags and garments of colored stripes which, with the bright notes of the red fezzes spotting here and there among the esparto hats, served to enhance the color setting of the scene.

From the great heaps of loose esparto where the Arab pickers had deposited it, some of the Blacks with crude short-handled forks pitched it into high windrows. Along these, in irregular order, others sorted it into three qualities—hand-picked, average, and third, the qualities depending on the length and condition of the grass; at the same time all roots, stones, and foreign substances were discarded. Then the grass which had been thoroughly dried was ready for baling. My use of sketch-book and camera caused some of the sorters to show an ugly disposition, and even after I was joined by Signor Cortugna, who

" Strode away with the bier of their tribesman "

motioned them to get about their work, their vengeful eyes leered maliciously as they paused again at my approach.

In the yards as in the fields the esparto workers are in danger of the scorpion and the viper. "Their bite seldom proves fatal," explained Signor Cortugna, "for we have medicine and treatment ready at hand. But I have never seen one of my Blacks kill a scorpion, for these fellows, like the Arabs, say, 'There is a compact between us, and if we do not kill them they will not kill us.' I have seen an Arab take a scorpion as I would take a cigarette, but then they know how to hold them, and I notice they always pick them up after they have struck at something. This is not a land of plenty and there are few things that the Arab does not put to some use, and so with brother scorpion—he sometimes eats him.

"But we must move along if we would see our new Manchester-built hydraulic presses baling up the grass," and we went up the traveller on a pile of halfa, stepping out on the upper floor of the well-built two-storied building. This had superseded some sheds in a corner of the yard under which were discarded old hand-presses. Here the thoroughly sorted and cured halfa had been deposited and was being pitched into a deep twelve-foot pit at one end of the loft, where an Arab and two Blacks grunted and bobbed in unison as they trod down the grass into a big case. When it was full, at a given signal they drew up their legs and hung suspended, while the case below swung its cargo of esparto under one of the heavy presses.

Down came a pressure of six hundred tons, mashing the grass into a hard-packed bale of six and a quarter hundred-weight. While the great jaws of the machine held it at this tension, strong steel bands were quickly strapped about it; then, rolled off and weighed, it lay ready for shipment.

Work in the esparto yards begins at six in the morning and ends at six at night, with a midday rest; but during Ramadan, when all Mohammedans fast through the day, the Blacks prefer to work from six until five without let or sup. And now, as the lurid sun disk painted red the interstices of the tracery of the date-palms which feathered over the neighboring walls, the rattle of the great baling press ceased, and down the long windrows the workers seemed to be converging in a human vortex toward one point—

the quarters of the cashier. Here the clerks and foremen, who received from two shillings and sixpence to four shillings a day, had already been paid, and some of the pressmen their fifteen and eighteen pence.

I halted on the outskirts of this virile crowd. They seemed to surcharge the very atmosphere with a sense of healthy animalism and good nature, under all of which I well knew lay the fierce and cruel nature of the savage. One by one they were rapidly paid off, great burly carriers collected each his ten pence, and at last a lone sorter tucked into a bit of lizard skin his meagre eight pence, then hurried on out through the gate.

I watched the gray herd patter through its cloud of sand dust until it lost itself toward the oasis in the dusk of the coming night. I knew that it would wind a short half-mile through the shadows of the palm groves, and empty into its native village—then each man to his own compound which enclosed his zerebas. Here little balls of ebony with ivory settings would tumble laughingly to greet him. The aroma of the cooscoos would make his broad, flat nostrils dilate as he neared his hut and his wives—black wenches these, with the heavy crescents of silver sagging from their ears, and perchance a piece of red coral shoved through a nostril.

While most of the tribe work in the esparto yards, many find employment in and about the town. They live after the manner of the life in the interior from whence they had drifted across the Great Desert. Under a marabout they conform to their tribal laws and customs.

But a few days previous, accompanied by my man Bringali, a hybrid native of Sudanese and Arab stock, I had wandered along the paths of their village, hard packed by the tread of many feet, and had ventured here and there a peep into a compound. Discretion prevented me from seeking a crawling entrance to their primitive dwellings. I well knew that jealous eyes were peering out from the small, dark openings of the hive-shaped, palm-thatched huts, and vicious dogs with an undeveloped sense of discrimination lurked in unexpected places. It is not the safest thing for a stranger to enter their village alone, as can be attested to by a German, who recently nearly paid with his life the penalty of idle curiosity.

I parted from Signor Cortugna near where the mosque of Sidi Hamet backs into the bazaars, and turned down the Arbar-Arsāt to my lokanda. In the quiet of the African night, from under the great date-palms far out beyond the town, the hoarse bark of a wolfhound drifted in, and once a soft Desert wind wafted from the negro village, the faint, distant sounds of the barbaric clink of steel cymbals, of the thrumming gimbreh, and, above all, the hoarse, wild shouts of wilder men, and I knew that the hoodoo and dance were on. Then I fell asleep, to dream of great fires which cast gaunt, fluttering shadows of whirling, frenzied savages into the darkness of the palm groves.

A dark spot on the horizon, a graduated fume of trailing smoke, and the incoming steamer for the time being furnished an animated topic of conversation among Tripoli's little business and social world, isolated as it is far south from the highways of the Mediterranean. Not until she drops anchor off the esparto jetty and her mission is known does Tripoli settle back to its lakoom and coffee.

The entire halfa crop is carried in British bottoms to the United Kingdom. So far as I could ascertain only one bark had ever cleared for the United States, and that for New York. Within

the remembrance of Mr. Vice-Consul Dickson
of Great Britain only a bark and a sloop from
America have ever made port here. The sloop
brought petroleum.

Before the esparto is shipped from the yards
all dampness must be thoroughly dried out, and
often when it is held over through the rainy season, is reopened for that purpose. Not only does
dampness cause the halfa to rot, but increases
the danger of spontaneous combustion, as was
the case in the cargo of the *Ben Ledi* of North
Shields, which, under full steam from Zleiten,
suddenly made her appearance off Tripoli and
signalled for assistance, which was rendered by
the Turks.

The heavy bales are transported from the
yards on two-wheeled carts drawn by horses, and
then dumped on the stone jetty, which is suffering greatly from the action of the sea waves and
the inaction of the Turkish authorities. Here
government dues of twenty paras [two cents] a
bale are levied, as the wharf is government
property.

Often I have sat on the hard-packed bales
which lined the jetty and watched Arab and
Black stevedores hook the cumbersome weights

aboard ponderous lighters which had been warped alongside.

Transporting from the shore to steamer under sunny skies and on summer seas has a certain monotony. But when the wind and the storm rip across the Mediterranean from the north, and whip the great yeasty combers across the reef rocks of Tripoli, it ill becomes the lubber or man of little nerve to make venturesome trips in the heavily loaded unwieldy lighters. Occasionally a barge is swamped, which is not particularly disastrous to the stevedores, all of whom can swim like ducks; but when a lighter rolling and lurching turns turtle it is a more serious matter, for then with a sudden lurch the cargo shifts, and without warning the great ponderous lighter turns bottom up, sending hundreds of tons of esparto bales crushing down upon the crew, and fortunate is he who may appear bobbing to the surface.

The steel hooks used by the stevedores are charged up to each vessel on account of the propensity of the natives to steal everything they can carry away. On one occasion they knocked off or unscrewed all the brasses which locked the ports of a converted passenger steamer. These trinkets proved expensive luxuries, and a few days afterward found all concerned imprisoned within the grim walls of the Castle of the Bashaws.

A striking instance of a man hanging himself by his own rope was that of a stevedore who, down in the dark hold of an esparto vessel, came across a short length of chain. Stripping himself to the waist, he wound the steely links round and round his black body, and, donning his shirt again, appeared on deck and started to descend over the side of the lighter. Splash! Men ran to the side of the rolling half-emptied barge—a column of spray and some bubbles, that was all. When they found him he lay anchored securely by his prize down among the sponges and sea-coral.

Forty-five years ago the trade of Tripoli was diminishing, chiefly owing to the suppression of the slave trade with the interior by which the Turkish markets were supplied. This was a lucrative form of investment to the Arab merchants and others; but as the great caravans with their black, human merchandise grew scarcer and scarcer, there sprang up a larger, more important traffic between the Sudan and Tripoli, in which

A Black sheik

Manchester goods were bartered for gold, ivory, and feathers. But the profits of this soon began to leak out by the way of the new water routes from the Sudan to the east and west coasts.

Already the esparto trade had come to the front and to-day it is Tripoli's leading export. But back in the jebel the halfa picker still with ruthless short-sightedness tears and rips it root and all from the sandy wastes. Each successive year now entails longer journeys to the coast, with increased labor and cost of transportation. Each year brings smaller returns, three pounds per ton being the selling price in England as compared with twelve pounds of former times.

A decreasing demand for esparto grass has followed the introduction of wood pulp into England from North America and Norway, naturally resulting in a decreased value in the English market. And many pickers have preferred to leave the gathered grass to the sun and the sand-storm to transporting it at little profit and, perhaps, loss. Not many years hence will, in all likelihood, see the passing of the esparto trade of Tripoli, of a labor big and primitive, of swarthy Arabs, heavily burdened camels, and sweating Black men. A few camel loads of halfa will now and again be brought into Tripoli, Misurata, and other coast towns, to be used in the weft of mats, and for shoes, hats, and cordage; and, perchance, the traveller may now and then meet one or two lone esparto pickers, as with empty nets thrown over the camels' humps in front of them, they lurch, lurch, homeward to the plateau lands of the jebel where the wild grass and the sand lily nod to the Desert breezes of the South.

CHAPTER NINE

THE CARAVAN TRADE

STRAGGLING down here and there into the Desert from some of the important towns of the North African coast, go the trade routes of the caravans. But it is the town of Tripoli, low-lying and white, shimmering under the hot African sun in her setting of palm gardens, which is the nearest coast port north of the Sudan; consequently it has become the natural gateway to the Sahara, the northern focus of the three great caravan routes which stretch away south. The sun-scorched surface of the Sahara with its sand-hills and oases, mountain ranges and plateaus, is greater in area by some half million miles than the United States and Alaska combined, and is peopled by some three to four millions of Berbers, Arabs, and Blacks, with a few Turkish garrisons in the north. By way of Ghadāmes, Ghāt, and Murzuk, through the Fezzan to Lake Chad, go the caravan trails, and then far away south again, south to that country called the Sudan, Land of the Blacks. Here its teeming millions form the great negro states of Bambara, Timbuktu, and Hausaland in the west; Bornu and Baghermi around Lake Chad; Wadi, Darfur, and Kordufan in the east, extending from Abyssinia to the Gulf of Guinea.

Of these trails, their trade, and the men who escort the heavily loaded caravans little enough has been said; still less of the innumerable dangers which constantly beset them as they creep their way across the burning desolate wastes, on their long journeys to the great marts of the Sudan,—Timbuktu, Kano, Kanem, Kuka, Bornu, and Wadi.

South-west from Tripoli, twenty days as the camel travels, on the direct route from Tripoli to Timbuktu, lies the little sun-baked town of Ghadāmes, which has figured largely in the history of the caravan trade with the interior. From Ghadāmes also runs the route to the Sudan by way of Ghāt; so, by reason of her location, Ghadāmes erected fondūks and became a stopping place for caravans, and her merchants, pioneers of the caravan trade.

Many years ago they established themselves in

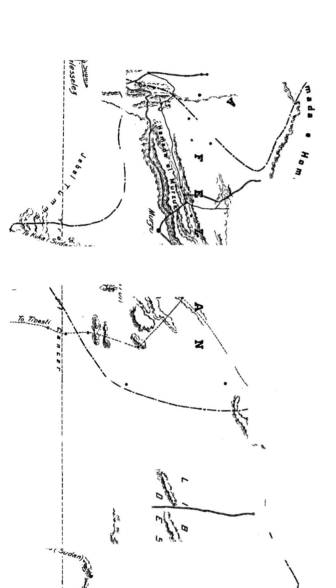

Gorba I

▷ TRIPOLI...n..n.

Gulf of Sidra

Bengay

Derna

the town of Tripoli, with agents at Ghāt and the big trading posts in the far Sudan. To these caravans conveyed periodically large consignments of goods which were exchanged for ivory, ostrich feathers, and gold-dust, to be sold in Tripoli, and eventually, in the form of finished products, to enhance the wealth and display of Europe. Through their superior intelligence and honesty the merchants of Ghadāmes enjoyed for many years the monopoly of the trade which they had created.

But the Tripoli merchants could not indefinitely withhold their hands from a trade within their grasp and upon which the commercial prosperity of their own city depended. However, it was not until some thirty years ago that they seriously entered into competition with the Ghadāmsene. At times large profits are reaped, but frequently enormous losses are entailed—not so much through the rise and fall of the European market as through the dangers *en route*, in which attacks and pillage by Desert robbers, and reprisals to make good losses incurred by tribal warfare, play no small part.

The merchants who fit out a garfla must stand all losses; consequently great care is given to the selection of both the camels which carry the valuable merchandise and the men who accompany them. The respect paid to the adventurous caravancer is no small criterion of the fatigues and dangers which attend the traveller. Caravans vary in size, from that of some lone nomadic trader or esparto picker, who trudges beside his few camels on his way to some local market, to the great trans-Saharan trade caravans with thousands of camels, not to mention donkeys, goats, sheep, and dogs. Such a caravan is rarely met with; it takes a year or more to outfit; thousands of dollars are invested by Arabs and Jewish merchants. Its numerical strength is increased by smaller caravans, whose sheiks, believing in the safety of numbers, often delay their own departure for months.

Moving south from Tripoli, it must cover some fifteen hundred miles of arid Desert before it reaches one of the important marts of the Sudan.

After numerous stops and leaving many animals and some men to the vultures, the caravan, if fortunate, reaches its destination. In its heavy loads are packed the heterogeneous goods generally taken, consisting of cotton and wool, cloth, waste silk, yarn, box rings, beads, amber, paper, sugar, drugs, and tea, of which British cotton goods form more than fifty per cent. of the value. Besides these it carries some native products. This cargo is bartered for the products of the Sudan: skins, ivory, ostrich feathers, guinea corn, and gold-dust. Every autumn caravans also arrive from the interior and return with dried dates; for, among the tribes of the Fezzan, Tripoli dates form the chief article of diet, and in the oases of the Desert, dates chopped with straw are used as fodder. A year, perhaps, after its arrival it begins the return voyage, with a cargo likely enough amounting to nearly a million dollars in value; and it is a gamble whether it ever reaches Tripoli.

The tall, swift, riding camel known as the mehari is seldom met with in Northern Tripoli. The finest male draught camels, the *jamal* costing from $50 to $60 apiece, with a carrying capacity of about three hundred-weight, are used for transport. From consumption or the effects of the long strain scores often die by the way, and many others at the end of the "voyage." The wages of the men for conducting a return cargo are sometimes as high as five thousand dollars. Not only must the garfla sheiks have

great courage and endurance, but must be trust-
worthy and shrewd traders, diplomats of no
small calibre. Many of the sultans and chiefs,
particularly the Tuaregs, through whose terri-
tories lie the garfla routes, exact not only homage but tribute from the garfla sheiks. To bring
this tribute within a reasonable sum and secure
a safe conduct requires extraordinary skill and
tact. The opportunities for dishonesty afforded
the garfla men are many, and occasionally men
and goods are never heard from again.

Preliminary to making up an outfit for travelling in the Tripolitan Sahara, a firman [pass-
port] from the Porte at Constantinople is considered necessary; but this, if eventually obtained, takes time, even years.

The influence of friends and the courtesy of
Redjed Pasha circumvented this difficulty, and
the privilege to travel *sans firman* was rather re-
luctantly extended to me by his Excellency, after
I had told him the exact ground I wished to
cover. This was not by any means easily secured,
owing in part to the indiscretion of the last European traveller, a German who had abused this
privilege two years before This man had di-

verged from the route over which he had asked permission to travel, which breach of faith led him into serious difficulty. It reached the ears of Redjed Pasha, who declared he would not again allow a foreigner to travel beyond the oasis of Tripoli.

The next thing was to secure that great essential to the traveller in Oriental countries—a reliable dragoman. A dragoman generally fills the position of head servant and guide, superintending all meals, and to a great extent, making arrangements at fondūks, and is directly responsible to his employer for the character and good behavior of the other men. Many Arabs there were in the town who would gladly have risked the dangers of the Desert as dragomans, but as my object was to obtain information of Desert life, a man who could act also as an interpreter was indispensable: and Muraiche, an Arab about sixty years old, proved to be the only available man. It is true that he had an unsavory record; and I was so warned by members of the little English colony there. But his broken English and *lingua Franca* were valuable assets; besides, forewarned is forearmed, so it came about that Muraiche became my dragoman.

He soon picked two other men. One, by the name of Ali, was an Arab of the lower class. He was a supple, wiry fellow and, on the whole, willing and good-tempered. The other, Mohammed by name, was of mixed Arab and Berber stock, heavy and muscular—and predisposed to rest.

One morning found us at Mohtar Haarnsh's, the horse trader, whose stable faces the Suk-el-Thalet. Mohtar was the embodiment of all that a horse trader should be, with a little more thrown in, for, like his twin brother, he had six fingers on his left hand.

A number of horses were brought out and run up and down the sand stretch of the Suk. Mohtar's boy, at my request, mounted one and was forthwith deposited in the sand. I finally selected two horses and a large, fast-walking pack donkey; then, proceeding to Riley's house, a contract was drawn up and the men and animals hired. Before I left Tripoli—taking Muraiche with me—I deposited all my money in my friend's safe. I advanced Muraiche half his wages, telling him to carry enough with him to meet our expenses and for me to borrow in case of need.

A caravan was to start on the morrow at the

first hour [sunset], and at an appointed time I rode down the Suk-el-Turc, through the Castle Gate, and headed for the Fondūk-el-Burka, where the camels were being loaded.

Groaning, grunting, wheezing, and bubbling, the last camel of the caravan was loaded. His driver, a Black from Hausaland, took an extra hitch in a rope; in silhouette against the lurid after-glow the camel moved through the Tripoli fon-dūk gate, resembling a hair mattress on stilts.

With my own Arabs I brought up the rear. Another long shadow merged itself into those of my horses and men, and a keen-eyed, well-armed Arab, Rais Mohamed Ga-wah-je, leader of the caravan, b'slaamed to my Arabs and rode on. No fiery barb carried this man of the Desert, but a little pattering donkey. Soon he was lost among the camels and dust.

Passing through the suburb of Sciara-el-Sciut we were well into the oasis of Tripoli, a five-mile tongue of date-palms along the coast at the edge of the Desert. Under their protecting shade lie gardens and wells by which they are irrigated. In this oasis lies the town of Tripoli. It is be-yond this oasis that the Turks object to any stranger passing lest he may be robbed or killed by scattered tribes which the Turkish garrisons cannot well control—or become too interested in the country. Safety over part of my route was doubly secure, for Hadji Mufta, a Tripoline acquaintance, had spoken to his friend, Rais Ga-wah-je, and I was assured of all the hospitality and protection which these nomads could offer—that is, after we had broken bread together. Mohamed Ga-wah-je was among the most trusted of these leaders, having at times conveyed large sums of money along the dangerous coast routes to Bengazi, and it was a common thing for him to carry £1,000 or more in gold for Mr. Arbib, Nahoum, and other leading Tripoli esparto merchants for their branch houses in Khoms and Zleiten.

So one August night I found myself a part of a Saharan caravan, one of the vertebræ of a monster sand snake which wormed its way through the oasis of Tripoli toward the Great Desert. The distorted shape of the moon bulged over the horizon through a silent forest of palm groves; the transitional moment between twilight and moonlight passed, the heavy dew had already begun to cool the night, and the garfla had struck its gait.

THE CARAVAN TRADE

Across the moonlit roadway stretched the long shadows of the date-palms lifting and wriggling themselves over the great dun-colored camels and their heavy loads, over little trudging donkeys, goats, and sheep, over the swarthy figures of men, some heavy covered in their gray or white baracans, some half naked, a law unto themselves, its power vested in their crooked knives, knobbed clubs, and long flint-locks whose silvered trimmings caught the moon glint, as in the distance they scintillated away like scattered fireflies.

Silently the great snake moved on, save as some hungry camel snatched at the cactus hedge and gurgled a defiant protest as its driver belabored it about the head; or as the oboes and tom-toms in barbaric strains broke the stillness of the night. Then, to ease the march or soothe the restless animals, the garfla men from time to time would take up the wild peculiar chant, with its emphasized second beat, and the songs of brave deeds in love or war would echo through the palm groves far off on the Desert sands. We passed Malāha, a chott [dried lake] where salt is obtained. About midnight the garfla halted.

"Fondūk-el-Tajura," remarked one of our men. Here we made our first halt.

Serving as places of rest and protection, and in some cases supply depots, the importance of the fondūk to caravans and the trade is inestimable. These are usually rectangular enclosures with arcades along the sides and open in the centre, surrounded by the palm and olive gardens of the keeper, who may supply fresh fruits, vegetables, and other domestic products. There is one entrance protected by heavy doors, which are barred at night. Usually, either town or country caravansaries occur so frequently on the trails that long, forced marches are seldom necessary. About four cents per head is charged for camels and a nominal price for goats and sheep: at fondūks green fodder and other supplies may generally be obtained.

Fondūk-el-Tajura was typical of those found throughout North Africa. The impatient beasts, hungry and eager to seek relief from their heavy loads, tried to jam through the single portal wide enough for but one camel and its burden. All was dust and confusion. Midst yells, curses, and "hike, hikes," their drivers sought to extricate the animals or save the goods from being

Fondūk-el-Tajura

Muraiche entering, leading the author's horse

ripped from the loads. The inside of the fondūk was a square open enclosure bordered by a covered arcade as a protection for the men in the rainy season. When all were in, the heavy doors were closed and barred against marauders. All about me the great beasts were dropping to the earth, remonstrating and groaning as vigorously as when they were loaded. The packs taken off, their saddles were carefully removed and scoured with sand, for the hump must be kept clean, healthy, and free from saddle sores.

The camels were soon given their green fodder, which at fondūks generally consists of fōoa [madder-top roots] or barley, the ksūb [guinea corn], or bishna [millet], while that cheapest and almost indispensable food, the date, finds its way to the mouths of men and beasts. The mainstay of the caravan men is dried dates and bread made with guinea corn.

On long voyages the day's fare is often consumed on the march, and halts at such times are made only to rest and feed the camels. At fondūks or oases longer stops are made; there groups of men may be seen squatting about a big wooden bowl of bazine or coos-coos, their national dishes, made chiefly of cereals.

The quick-moving form of Ga-wah-je appeared here and there with the manner of a man used to command, and after he had brought out of the confusion an informal order, I had an opportunity to meet my host. Under the portal of the fondūk a charcoal fire glowed red in an earthen Arab stove. About it in the candle-light we seated ourselves—Rais Ga-wah-je, the fondūk keeper, my dragoman Muraiche, and myself. To Ga-wah-je my dragoman presented my gifts, seven okes of sugar cones and fifteen pounds of green tea. Some of the tea was immediately brewed and mixed half with sugar and a touch of mint. We drank the syrupy liquid and broke bread together—then Ga-wah-je bade me welcome.

From my bed on a single stone seat at the side of the entrance I looked through an open door across the passageway to the only room of the place, used as a prayer chamber, in which was the kibleh. In the dim light of an oil lamp the indistinct forms of several devout Moslems knelt or prostrated themselves before Allah, low-droning their prayers. Out in the fondūk enclosure all was quiet save for the peaceful chewing of cuds, or an occasional sound as a camel swallowed or a cricket chirped. The moon-beams shooting their silvery shafts lit up portions of the farther wall. The soft breath of the silent night blew gently from the south through the feathered tops of the date-palms, and pulling my blanket over me I fell asleep.

A low cry from outside the fondūk awakened us, and pandemonium broke loose among the dogs. Cautiously drawing aside a small panel covering a peep-hole, the keeper, after a brief conversation, satisfied himself that all was well, and as the heavy doors swung open, another caravan entered. The first beasts came through like a maelstrom. Half awake in the semidarkness I dodged the swing of a long neck as one of the vicious brutes attempted to bite me in passing, while several Arabs dragged aside a badly crushed comrade.

Invariably the Desert thief lurks about the fondūks in the small hours of the morning, watching an opportunity to prey on any belated traveller as he approaches, or to rob the fondūk. With the help of a companion he scales the wall outside, and by a rope drops noiselessly down in some dark corner of the square enclosure, or, near a corner, he scrapes a hole in the wall large enough for him to pass through. This is not difficult. A quart or two of vinegar occasionally applied not only assists in disintegrating the wall of sun-dried bricks, but renders his work noise-less as he digs with his knife. Inside, he sneaks among the garfla, keeping always in the shadow, stealing here a baracan, there a gun or whatever it may be, and frequently, unobserved, retreats as he entered.

After a scant three hours' sleep a lantern flashed in my face, Ga-wah-je passed, and the fondūk was soon astir. The camels once more took up their heavy burdens and passed out. The last to leave was Ga-wah-je. At the en-trance he and the keeper kept tally of his ani-mals, after which he paid the fondūk fee of ten paras [one cent] per head for camels and don-keys, and a nominal sum for goats and sheep. The charge for my horses was twenty paras apiece.

The gardens were soon left behind, and the lanelike roads lost themselves in the sand which carpeted the palm groves through which we now travelled. The night dew which nourishes the scattered Desert plant life lay heavy jewelled on bent blades of rank grass and sand lilies. The date-palms through violet ground mists showed indistinct and softened against the brilliant rose dawn of day. They ended, and suddenly in the orange-gold of the morning sunlight the sand billows of the mighty Sahara rolled away south over the horizon.

For days we travelled over these hills of sand, sometimes over endless level reaches, through districts of clayey, sandy soil, over which Desert grasses undulated softly in the hot wind; there the trail was hard packed and easily discernible. Once I looked across a valley to where the trails seemed to tumble over a distant hillside, like a series of cascades losing themselves in the ocean of sand below. Where it descended into the dried river beds, the tread of generations of camels had worn ravines ten or twelve feet deep. These interlaced like the paths of a maze, and passing through them with a caravan was like a constant game of hide-and-seek, for every man, camel, and donkey took his own course. During the greater part of the year these river beds are veritable ovens of heat, but in winter they become raging torrents in which men and animals frequently lose their lives. In the sandy areas the trails are often mere directions, and the only guides are the sun and the stars, for the passing sand-storm not only quickly obliterates all tracks, but sometimes a single one changes the topography of the landscape.

During the season of the warm rains, which sink into the porous surface until they are arrested at no great depth, vast subterranean sheets of water are formed, which could almost anywhere be brought to the surface by sinking artesian wells. Many streams flow inland, where they are lost in the sand of the salt lakes. At this time whole sections of the parched Desert seem almost over night to have been changed to another land. Mountains and valleys blossom, and the banks of the wadis seem afire with the flaming oleander. By these streams or springs are the oases where date-palms and gardens are planted, and Arab houses, fondūks, or towns are built which determine the course of the caravan routes. At intervals are wells for the use of caravans, and a great danger lies in missing these wells. One very hot summer some men nearly reached the gardens of Tripoli, but could go no farther. When found they could only say, "Ma! ma!" [water! water!]. It was given them; they drank and died straightway.

THE CARAVAN TRADE

I watched our garfla wind around or zigzag over the sand-hills, breaking and linking itself together again as it crawled its slow pace of three miles an hour. It marched in irregular order characteristic of the Arabs, stringing out for miles, but closing in together for protection against attack as night approached. The Arab usually refrains from riding the baggage camel, for every pound of weight and its adjustment on these great beasts must be considered; and even an Arab has to ride a jemal but an hour or two to appreciate the luxury of walking.

Through the most dangerous districts the men were distributed the length of the caravan with a strong rear-guard—for it is from this point that an attack by an enemy is most feared. As the sun gets high, most of the men muffle themselves in their heavy woollen baracans to keep out the heat, and transfer their long flint-locks from across their shoulders to the packs of the animals. Between eleven and three o'clock occurs the midday rest. Tents are rarely, if ever, carried by the garflas: in fact, I have never seen men of a trade caravan carry tents. Instead they use that ever-available garment—the baracan. This answers all their immediate needs in

the way of clothing and trunk. In its loose folds
the native carries anything from his shoes to his
coarse staple food, barley bread. At one caravansary I found Mohammed rinsing my dishes
in some stagnant water and carefully wiping them
on his baracan, which bore all the hall-marks of
a family heirloom. In winter the baracan is a
protection against the chilling winds, in summer
against the intense heat. When the midday halt
is made, the men cast off the loads from either
side of the recumbent camels and with their
baracans construct improvised tents propped up
with stick, club, or gun. Under these in the suffocating heat their owners snatch what is sometimes the only rest of the day, for they often ·
travel twenty hours out of the twenty-four.

Passing caravans were scarce. A dust cloud
would appear in the distance, grow large, and
a caravan of Bedawi, those nomads of the Desert, in all their barbaric paraphernalia would
pass by, erstwhile eying us suspiciously with
unslung guns, holding in leash or calling to their
savage wolf hounds in order to avoid a mix-up
with our garfla dogs. For many of their tribal
wars and feuds have started under less provo-
cation than a dog fight.

Trade caravan resting in the heat of the day

CHAPTER TEN

PROBABLY none among the country people and the Desert tribes arouse the interest of the Occidental mind more than the Bedawi. From time immemorial they have lived in tents in the Desert, subsisting principally by the robbery of caravans on the road to Mecca; but to-day Tripoli Bedawi, although given somewhat to agriculture, are really tribes of petty, wandering merchants, trading articles of their own manufacture which they carry from place to place. These consist principally of dark cloth for baracans and thick webs of goat's hair for tent covers, also loose woven baskets and plates of raffia weave.

Like the Jews they still retain many customs described in sacred history, and are in almost every way the same kind of people we find mentioned in the earliest times of the Old Testament. Owing to their constant exposure to the sun they are much darker than the Moors.

In the spring of the year the Bedawi approach Tripoli, pitch their tents on the plain or sometimes in the oasis itself. There they sow their corn, wait until they can reap it, and then disappear until the year following. During their stay in the oases and vicinity the women weave and sell their work. When the fine weather and corn fail them in one place they immediately travel on to a more fertile spot with their families, horses, and cattle. A family of distinction among them will pitch four or five tents, which present a most striking picture with their varied shapes sometimes against a background of date-palms. The women wear the same kind of a coarse brown baracan as the men. They put it on by joining the two upper corners with a wooden or iron bodkin, afterward folding the rest gracefully about their figures. They plait their hair, cutting it straight above the eyebrow, and many of the black-eyed, white-teethed girls are pretty in their wild, picturesque way. The women do practically all the labor of the camp: fetching wood and drawing water; pitching and striking tents; milking the she goats and camels, and preparing food. They are divided into a prodigious number of tribes, distinguished by the names of their sheiks. Each tribe forms a village and each family has a tent or portable hut. In Tripoli each sheik is answerable to the Turkish Pasha for the actions of each individual of his tribe. One evening I saw some dozen male members of a tribe driven in to the Castle Prisons by a Turkish guard. The arms of all of them were securely bound behind with a single piece of rope, and their arrest was due to the Turkish suspicion which had centred about one of them.

The Bedawi, unlike the Moors, frequently visit one another's domiciles, taking their children with them, but the life of these wandering Desert waifs, at the best, is a hard one. The women soon become wrinkled and leather-skinned, and the men are old almost before they have had a chance to be young.

Sometimes I would ride forward with my dragoman, anticipating a longer rest by making a fondūk several hours ahead of the slowly moving garfla. On one of these occasions, as we ascended a sand-hill, the advance guard of a homeward-bound caravan suddenly loomed up before us. Eleven months before, they had started from the great trade mart of Kano, the first caravan to arrive from there for two years, owing to the general insecurity of the roads. Three months they had held over at Zinder and à month at both Aïr and Ghāt. It took us all the afternoon to ride by the twelve hundred and twenty camels. They carried a thousand loads of Sudan skins from the famous dye pits of Kano, destined to find their way to New York for the manufacture of gloves and shoes; two hundred loads of ostrich feathers, and ten loads of ivory, besides odd lots of rhinoceros horn, gum-arabic, and wax, valued altogether at over two hundred thousand dollars. Ostrich eggs, worked leather and basket, work dangled from the loads. Here and there a leopard or cheetah skin, shot on the way, was thrown across a pack or hung from the shoulders of some big negro. Black women there were, too, slaves, perhaps, or concubines for some of the rich Moors or Turks. As the garfla neared Tripoli, runners would be sent ahead, and there would be great rejoicing among the men who had waited several years for the return of their goods. I well remember one day in mid August: the mercury stood at 155° in the sun. I do not know what it registered in the shade, for there was none, save our own shadows. As the sun wore round behind us, I shifted the broad band of my woollen cholera belt to my back and cast my own shadow to protect as far as possible the neck and head of my horse, for the poor beast was suffering terribly from the heat.

All day we rode in this furnace and the brave fellows trudged barefooted in the scorching sand. At intervals I heard a rumble like distant thunder, which proved to be only the soughing of the gibli through the vent in the top of my sun helmet. Strange as is the fascination of the Desert, yet one feels its monotony keenly; he notices with avaricious interest anything which will relieve him from the intense heat overhead and the everlasting wriggling heat waves of the sun glare underneath. So for hours at a time I watched the formation of camel footprints in the sand; watched them scuff through and destroy the beautiful point-lace patterns of the lizard tracks left by their frightened designers. As the afternoon wore on I would doze in my saddle, to wake up with a jump as I jammed against a camel, or the muzzled mouth of a "biter" swung sharply against my head.

Tall, sun-tanned Arabs and big negroes black as ebony formed the escort of the garfla. Many of the latter first saw Tripoli when they were driven up from the Sudan under the crack of the slave whip. Rarely complaining in the intense heat, they moved forward, long guns slung across their backs and often native fans in their hands. Usually the men go barefooted: sometimes over stretches of soft sand they wear broadsoled Desert slippers, and on rocky ground sandals are worn. Most of the Blacks have their tribal marks, a certain number of deep slashes across the cheeks and temples, made by their parents with sharp stones when they were chil dren. As one Black trudged along beside me, his splendid calf muscles played underneath three stripes cut in the black skin.

Early one morning I had ridden some miles in advance of the garfla. Save for the soft scuff of my horse's hoofs and the stretching of my leather trappings, a great silence hung over the untrammelled sand hillocks, and their blue-pervaded mysterious shadows lengthened. A rounded top here and there broke the silver moon as it mellowed toward the horizon. Suddenly my horse shied, nearly unseating me. Instinctively I searched the sky-line of hilltops. Had it not been for the black spot of a head I might not

" A homeward-bound garfla suddenly loomed up before us "

have noticed the gray baracaned figure of a Desert thief who, in his sleep, rolled out of his sandy lair. Startled, he sat bolt upright, and for a second stared blankly at me. He reached for his long gun which lay by his side, but I covered him with my revolver and there he sat until out of range and sight. The fellow had been left by his comrades, who were probably in the vicinity. This trick of burrowing under the sand beside the course of an on-coming garfla is often resorted to. As the garfla passes, the thieves rise out of the earth, make a quick onslaught, then rapidly retire, taking with them what booty they can lay their hands on and frequently stampeding some of the camels.

Occasionally these vultures also resort to the tactics of a sneak thief, and choose a time at night when a fast-moving caravan overtakes a slower one. During the confusion caused by the mixing up of men and animals in passing, the thief falls in from the rear and naturally is taken by either party to be a member of the other garfla. Then, pilfering anything he can seize from the loads, he falls back to the rear and drops out of sight behind a sand-hill.

Lightly blowing in the face of the south-bound

garflas, there springs from the south-east a gentle wind, the gibli, which playfully spins little eddying whiffs of sand into miniature whirlwinds. In this manner it may blow for days, evaporating the water in the goat-skin bags and sometimes terminating in a sand-storm. Then, when the camels, craning their long necks, sniff high in the air and utter a peculiar cry, the garfla men know well the ominous signs; far off on the horizon, creeping higher and higher, the sky of blue retreats before a sky of brass.

To the hoarse cries and curses of the men as they try to hobble the fore legs of the excited camels are added the uncanny guttural groanings of the jamal, the braying of the asses, and the pitiful bleating of the goats and sheep. High in the air great flames of sand reach out, then the lurid sand cloud, completely covering the sky, comes down upon the garfla. In the confusion some of the water bags are broken and the precious liquid disappears in the sand. Turning tail and driving down before the blast go some of the unhobbled camels, maybe carrying a driver with them, never to be heard from again.

In the deep yellow gloom the garfla, back to the storm, lies huddled together; the men, wrapped up completely in their baracans, hug close to the goat-skins of water. The whole air is surcharged with suffocating heat and fine powdered sand dust, which finds its way even as far as Malta and Sicily. It penetrates everywhere, inflames the eyes and cracks the skin of the already parched tongues and throats of the garfla men. The torment at times is indescribable, and some poor fellow, like the camels, will run maddened into the hurricane.

The sand-storm lasts from a few hours to six or seven days, and during it the men lie thus, occasionally digging themselves to the surface as they become partially covered with sand. Frequently all the remaining water dries up. At such times camels are often sacrificed for the sake of the greenish water which may be obtained from the honeycomb cells of the reticulum, a mature camel yielding about five or six quarts: and, strange as it may seem, this water is cooler than that carried in the goat-skins. The storm over, the surviving garfla of emaciated men and animals staggers on to the nearest oasis or town, over plains which before were sand-hills, and sand-hills which are now plains.

The first stop of any length made by the

south-bound garflas is at Murzuk with its eleven thousand inhabitants, that desolate capital of the Fezzan—Murzuk, the horror of Turkish exiles, where a man is fortunate if the deadly climate takes away only his senses of smell and taste. Here a thorough rest is given to camels and men. Fresh supplies are obtained, the gaps in the ranks filled out, and again the wearisome march is resumed. Some fifteen hundred miles south of the coast they pass over the undefined boundary line of Tripoli through the dangerous country of the Tuaregs and the Damerghus.

From time immemorial slaves suffering inconceivable torments have been brought across the Sahara from the Sudan, for those regions extending from Abyssinia to the Gulf of Guinea have furnished an almost inexhaustible supply. Particularly from the Central Sudan has the Arab slave-trader gathered in his human harvest to the chief depots of Timbuktu in the west and Kuka in the east.

You will find an occasional Arab who will tell you of a route known only to the Senusi, that large fraternity of Moslems located in Tripolitania, who make proselyting wars and expeditions from Wadai to their capital. Along this

route it is said that never less than fifteen caravans cross the Desert every year, which bring
about ten thousand slaves alive to tell the tale;
and they estimate that forty thousand victims fall
on the march. Once on the secret route you
cannot lose your way, for it is lined with human
bones. Many of these slaves were formerly em-
barked for Turkey, and there seems to be little
doubt that slaves are still secretly conveyed to
Canea and Salonica, Constantinople and Smyrna.

The only habitation of many small oases is a
fondūk. Arriving late one night at one of these
we found the place already so crowded that when
our garfla was in, men and animals were literally jammed together. The filth and vermin of
the place, not to mention the sickening odors,
disturbed not the sons of Allah; but for a number of reasons I had objections to spending the
night in such close quarters, preferring to risk
the external annoyance of thieves. Muraiche,
with much suavity, held a lengthy conversation
with the keeper, who shifted the little blossom
which he wore tucked at the top of his ear to the
other side of his head and moved thoughtfully
away. Muraiche informed me that he had con-
fided to him that I was the Consul of Cordova,

and that he had asked permission for us to sleep under the olive-trees within the mud walls of his garden—which was no small favor to be granted to strangers. The keeper was sufficiently impressed with the old rascal's yarn, spread mats for us under the trees, and later brought us some fruit and eggs, then returned to the fondūk and the great doors were bolted.

Well knowing that not one of my men would stay awake during his watch, I slept lightly. Toward midnight the creak of my pannier aroused me. Turning my head cautiously I distinguished a large wolf-dog ın the dim moonlight; under the shadow of a near-by pomegranate-tree, I made out the form of a Desert thief quietly directing the dog in his plundering. Jumping to my feet and giving Mohammed [whose watch it was] a hearty kick to arouse him, I ran after the retreating marauders, who disappeared among the rushes of a neighboring marsh. Knowing better than to enter their lair, I returned to camp, to find Mohammed bemoaning the loss of a pair of broad-soled Desert slippers. To make up much-needed rest I delayed my start next morning to some five hours behind the garfla.

Muraiche and men descending a desert defile

DESERT INCIDENTS

As the sun rose high, I found Hadji Ali, an old caravaneer, seated outside the fondūk adjusting a new flint in his pistol. This done, he gazed long at the weapon, and his wrinkled, scarred old face softened as when a man looks upon a thing he loves. Many journeys across the Sahara with the garfla had sapped his wiry arms of their youthful strength, and the ugly scar over his left eye was a trophy of his last voyage three years before, which had nearly landed him in the fields of the blessed. This was the story:

"You must know, Arfi, that we were a garfla thirteen thousand camels strong, proceeding north to Tripoli from Kano, which was many months behind us. The escort and transport were principally men of Aïr and their animals. Three years before, Sadek, one of their chiefs, was slain by Moussa, a brother of the Sultan of Damerghu. Two years after, the slayer in turn was killed by the men of Aïr.

"As we entered the country of the Damerghus our guards were doubly watchful and our camels tied one to the other. All through the wild country, when in camp, we formed a square with the animals, the men and guards being inside. We were strong and did not intend to pay either tribute or homage for passing through the territory. It was at the end of the dry months, and some of the wells contained no water. We were all weak and suffering and a number of our men had the sleeping-sickness. We made haste to reach the wells of Farok, not two days' journey from Damerghu itself. We had almost reached them when narrow ravines obliged us to fall one behind the other. Suddenly from ambush the men of Damerghu furiously attacked us in great numbers. The character of the country prevented us from bringing our men together. We fought hard and well, but—Allah willed. Two hundred and ten were killed on both sides, among whom were twelve Tripolitans, some of them being among the most famous garfla leaders in Tripoli. Twelve thousand camel loads of guinea corn destined for Aïr, one thousand camel loads of ostrich feathers, ivory, Sudan skins, and mixed goods, with the entire transport, fell into the hands of the Damerghus.

"Near the end of the fight, Arfi, a big man broke through my guard with his two-edged sword. It was night when I came to myself and I had been stripped of everything. With great effort I reached the wells of Farok. Near where

I fell I found half buried in the sand my pistol with its charge unfired—but that is another story."

The total value of these goods lost, including the animals of burden, amounted to more than $800,000; and the wells of Farok, where the capture occurred, lie in an air-line about nineteen hundred and five kilometres south-west of Tripoli.

The opening of new routes southward and deflection of trade in that direction still lessen the prospect of inducing it to return to the shores of Tripoli, and except as regards Wadai and part of the Sudan the bulk of the trade may be said to be lost to Tripoli. Tribal feuds on caravan routes unexpectedly change the aspects and disconcert traders.

Long before the royal caravan of the Queen of Sheba, with its heavy embroidered trappings, brought gifts to Solomon; long before that Semitic nomad, Abraham, came out of Ur, caravans had crept their patient, steady way across the hot sands and deserts of the East. But the days of the Tripoli caravan trade are numbered, and the single wire of telegraph line which has already found its way to Murzuk is but a forerunner to herald the coming of the iron horse into the land of the garfla.

CHAPTER ELEVEN

CAMEL TRAILS

OFTEN in the narrow streets and open suks of many North African towns I had met the great lumbering jemal, but it was not until I had eaten in his shadow, slept by him in fondūks, and travelled with him day by day along the caravan trails of the northern Sahara, that I began to understand and fully appreciate this incongruous model of ugly usefulness.

Through a sweep of saffron sky the glowing sun spilled an aureola of golden light over the heat-swept sand of the northern Sahara. Before me, as I rode, the sand ripples were broken only by big heart-shaped footprints of a solitary camel —then beyond the rounding sand hillocks the great beast silhouetted his gaunt shape against the afterglow, dignified, patient, defiant, imperturbable, a creature of the vast wastes; revered, valued, and ill-treated by the Oriental; misunderstood and surrounded with mystery by the

Occidental; to me an epitome of the deserts and their inhabitants.

Down through the countless ages the silent, cushioned tread of the camel has kept pace with the peoples of the East, and for æons, so far as history or Arab tradition is concerned, he has furnished these nomads with food, shelter, clothing, and transportation; has printed his way across the trackless deserts, and left his bones white-bleached beside the sand-blown trails, guidons for future garflas.

With the advent of human history comes the camel as a domesticated animal. Before the Genesiacal scribe had closed his book, we find camels a main apportionment to the children of men, and even to-day the Arab's wealth is counted in camels.

To the far-off sunken districts of Turkestan in Central Asia is attributed his original habitation, over which he roamed in uncontrolled freedom.

Broadly speaking, there are two kinds of camels—the double-humped Bactrian and the single-humped Arabian. The Bactrian threads its way over Asia east of the Euphrates and the Persian Gulf, clear across to China, and as far as the colder mountainous regions of northern

Mongolia; the Arabian picks his trail westward across the heat-soaked rocks and sand reaches of the Arabian and African deserts.

Not long after my arrival in Tripoli, I took with me my man Bringali, and together we journeyed to a fondūk on the edge of the town.

"O camel driver!" spoke Bringali, as he addressed a muffled figure squatting in the shadow of the wall, "have you two good camels?"

"To thy eye, O merchant!" [judge for thyself], replied Mahmood, the driver, as unrolling himself out of his baracan, he led the way across the fondūk to where two heavily built draught camels lazily chewed their cuds and with their short tufted tails flicked the flies from their rumps.

One was a moth-eaten looking beast, for it was moulting time, and the owner plucked here and there a handful of the soft hair from its shaggy hide. The other was closely sheared, as is customary when the hottest weather approaches. After some bartering I hired them and the driver for the afternoon for sixty cents. They were draught camels, "baggagers," as Tommy Atkins calls them down in Egypt. The Arab calls him just plain "jemal."

While there are many different breeds of cam-

els, the most distinctive of the Arabians are the
heavy, slow-moving jemal and his cousin, the
mehari, a tall, lightly built, swifter, and more
elegant creature, used almost exclusively for riding, known as the riding or running camel.
Much confusion has existed as to the word dromedary, which many have considered a distinction
between the Arabian and Bactrian camels; *i. e.*,
the one and two humped. Dromedary is not
a distinction of species, however, but of breed.
The name, though generally applied to the finely
bred Arabian, may be applied to an equivalent
breed of Bactrian. The word dromedary is undoubtedly, in the root at least, derived from the
Greek *dromas* [running], finding its suffix, perhaps, from the Arabic word *mahari* (mehari),
the name of a swift breed of camels raised by the
tribe of Mahra. This name was given by the
Greeks, about the time of Cyrus or Xerxes, to
certain breeds of swift camels.

One has but to try the experiment of riding
a baggager to realize that there is not only a distinction with a difference, but a distinction with
a vengeance; and any Christian who willingly
substitutes the rump of a jemal for terra firma
deserves all he gets, for even an Arab will often

prefer walking to the lumbar vertebræ of a jemal. My intention was to ride three or four miles into the Desert and back.

"Mount, Arfi," said Bringali, and I straddled a straw-filled sack thrown across the hind quarters of the recumbent jemal, who uttered a fearful protest the whole length of his long throat, turned his head squarely round and looked me full in the face, twitching his mobile upper lip with a half-cynical, half-deprecating curl. The Arabs ride back of the pack-saddle for easier motion and often to be out of reach of the jaws of a biter.

"Up, thou tick of an ass's tail—ar-r-rah!" and with a vicious whack the Arab brought his heavy stick across the beast's jaw. I lurched forward, back, and then forward again; with a final remonstrating grunt, jemal straightened out his numerous joints and was on his feet. We were soon following between mud walls and palm-trees of the oasis of Tripoli to the Desert.

"Hike! hike!" yelled Mahmood, whereupon the brute broke into a lumbering, racking jog. The camel's natural gait, both in walking and running, is said to be a pace, but, so far as I was concerned, it might have been a centrifugal back-action trying to describe an eccentric rotary motion two ways at once on cobblestones.

"*Adda! adda!*" [turn to one side] shrieked the Arab, just in time to save me from collision with a hedge of prickly cactus. The camel, with head and tail outstretched almost horizontally, was now fairly under way. The cushion had slewed to one side, and I gathered my knees up under me and clung desperately to my only support, the tree of the pack-saddle, in order to avoid slipping down the inclined plane of his rump.

Set a section of a North Carolina twelve-rail fence at an angle of forty-five degrees in a farm-wagon, straddle this and have the whole outfit, yourself included, run away with over a rocky New England blueberry pasture, and you will form a mild conception of the sensation of riding a baggage camel in the Sahara.

"*Hot! hot!*" [slower], bellowed Mahmood, puffing along in the distance. Praise be to Allah! the jemal obeyed.

"*Sh, sh!*" [whoa], gurgled the perspiring Mahmood.

The place where I lit was soft sand.

I walked home.

Often in the twilight of early mornings, shortly

after the muezzin's call from the minaret of the neighboring Djema-el-Daruj, I would wind my way with soft-scuffing Arabs through the narrow by-ways of Tripoli to the great sand reach of the Suk-el-Thalat beyond the town walls. In the obscure light, shacks, muffled figures, heaps of produce, and camels humped themselves over the sand stretch like the promontories of a miniature mountain range, and the feathered palms of the oasis to the east were traced in violet against the forthcoming rose of early dawn. Then the sun rose over them and painted out the dim monotone of things in strong contrasts of lights and shades.

Everywhere was the jemal; late arrivals, heavily loaded, carefully threaded their way along; others, relieved of their loads, stood singly or in small groups, or lay resting on the sand, often acquiring most inconceivable and distorted positions, bearing out the remark of a Tripoli friend that the camel with his stiff legs and supple neck was "a combination of serpent and lamp-post."

With every group of camels was at least one caravaneer left to guard them, and he was usually found seated by the guns of his comrades, chatting perhaps, with neighboring caravan men. His camels were hobbled by short ropes tied under the fetlock of the fore legs, or, in the case of the more obstreperous, a fore leg was doubled up, and in this position securely lashed. Now and then the caravaneer rose leisurely and tossed into the centre of the caravan [for the camels are usually facing one another in a ring] some green fodder—bishna or shtell [guinea corn cut green], or other herbage with which they are usually fed in the suks and oases.

To the stranger the greater portion of the Suk might well appear a camel market, but go to that section beyond the esparto jetty, bordering the coast road which leads to Sciara-el-Sciut and Tajura. Here you find a living, dun-colored sea of camels; old and young, male and female, pure breeds and hybrids, well-conditioned and ill-seasoned, ranging in color from the rare black camel through the various values of dun colors and browns to snow white. This is the camel market.

Far back in the Jebel and plateau lands of the Desert the various Arab and Berber tribes breed and raise large herds of camels, pasturing them on the wild esparto grass, mimosa bushes, and the dry camel thorn of the Desert, from all of which the camel derives nutriment, remarkable to me until I once saw a camel devour with relish a piece of dry wood. The principal Tripoli camel raisers are the tribes of Jebel, Sert, Zintan, Orfella, and Weled-Bu-Sef, who, with the small owners, have, it is estimated, brought the total number of camels to four hundred thousand, or one camel to every one and a quarter square miles of the vilayet of Tripoli. From these far-off arid breeding grounds I have passed on the trail herds of camels travelling south toward Murzuk, there to be sold to fill up the gaps in the ranks of the trans-Saharan caravans or other herds being driven north toward the great coast, trade centres, Bengazi and Tripoli, where, in the jemal Suk of Tripoli, they fetch, generally, from ten to thirty dollars per head.

But follow yonder thickset merchant, he with the scarlet haik and six fezes under his tightly wound gold-embroidered turban. He is in search of an exceptional, full-grown male draught camel; one with a weight of close on to twelve hundred pounds; which can stand the strain and carry his goods safely the six to eleven months across the deserts to the Sudan. At

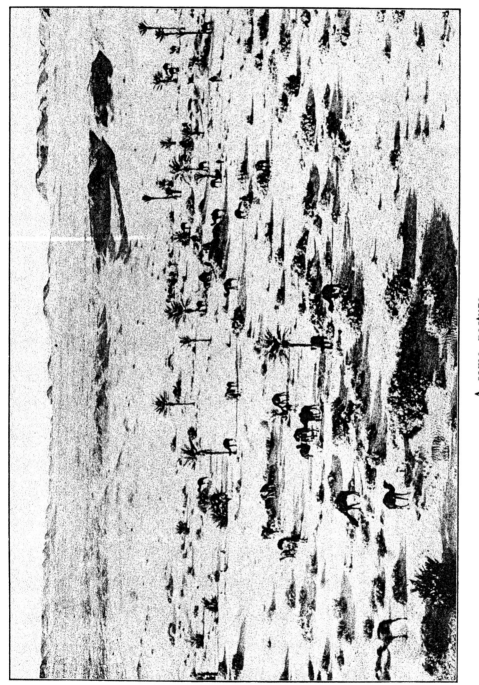

A came pasture

last he stops before a superb-looking beast. The top of its great shoulder is on a level with the Tripoline's turban; he examines the mouth, tail, feet, and skin, and runs his henna-stained fingers through the long woolly hair to the top of its hump, seven feet from the ground; this he finds full and firm.

"Gedash! O brother of many camels, is this one of thy herd?"

"May Allah lengthen thy age, O wealthy one," replied the swarthy man from the wadan; "thou hast truly picked the jewel of my eye."

"Jewel, sayest thou, but one of ill omen, for truly he is darkish in color."

"By the Prophet, throw him into the river and he will rise with a fish in his mouth"; and thus they bartered with all the naïveté and leisure of the Oriental trader, to whom time is invisible, but medjidies may be held in the hand. It was not until the morning waned and they both trod upon their own shadows that the sale was effected to the amount of sixty dollars.

"Baleuk!" came a warning cry as Riley and I steered our way one morning through the narrow channel ways of the Suk.

"That was a close call," said he, as the great

jaws of a biter swung by me with a snap like a steel trap. "In the cold, rainy months of our winter one has to be constantly on one's guard. Only a short time ago I saw a Turkish soldier lose half his face in this very Suk; another had the end of his elbow torn off. Watch the reverse rotary motion of that camel's chew, and the fearful results of the grinding nature of his sharp incisors and canine teeth, in both upper and lower jaw, may be realized, often so mashing the bones that amputation of the limb is necessary."

In passing recumbent camels the stranger need watch the head only, but when on their feet, its "heads and tails," for a camel can be a powerful kicker. Such are the means of defence with which nature has endowed him that one blow of his foot, out and straight behind, will drop most animals to the earth; then, kneeling on his victim and using his strong neck as a leverage, he tears him to pieces with his huge jaws. Biters are often muzzled, as are always camels of caravans bearing guinea corn or barley, to keep them from biting through the sacks. The majority of the camels are by no means naturally vicious, and much of their ugliness is due to the lack of care and brutal treatment of hired drivers. It is said that camels never forget a kindness or an injury.

At times, perhaps from the heat, or without apparent cause, the camel is seized with a terrific frenzy; then look out—for he will attack driver, other camels, or any living thing. But, on the whole, this ancient burden-bearer of man is a dignified, long-suffering, lugubrious anomaly, his joylessness being tersely expressed in the answer to the Arab riddle, "Why has the camel a split lip?"

"Because *once* a camel tried to laugh."

He is not aggressive; his indifference toward man seems almost contemptuous. He is imperturbable and patient beyond precedent, and on the march will continue to stagger on until his last ounce of strength has been exhausted.

Paradoxical as it may seem, he dislikes isolation from man or his own kind. He has an endless repertoire of the most unearthly noises, dominant among which is a sound best likened to blowing bubbles in a basin of water under forced draught and in a minor key.

I well remember one camel which stood apart from the others yawping a solo far out on the plain. Well fed, unhobbled, and unburdened save for his saddle, he had every reason to be happy, but there he stood with mouth agape, belching forth, so far as I could see, just out of pure cussedness. The noise rolled away over the Desert in great volumes of sound—a voice crying in the wilderness.

"The horse," say the town Arabs, "is a gentleman, the camel a boor" Not only has the latter been loaded with literal burdens heavier than he should bear and with the unjust ignominy of a mean disposition, but he has also been saddled, figuratively speaking, with the responsibilities of the vindictive tempers of certain Arabs, because of feeding on his flesh. To me he seems to be, in one respect at least, like his Arab master—a fatalist.

In one corner of the Suk a camel doctor sat beside a forge of hot coals held in a native earthenware stove, occasionally blowing them with his bellows and adjusting the heating irons. Now and then an Arab approaching him with his camel would consult him, perhaps about lameness or ophthalmia. One Hadji came leading a limping camel. As firing was considered the cure, as for many ills, it was first necessary to render the patient powerless. The "doctor" called from the neighboring coffee-booth a number of men; the owner ordered the animal to kneel across a piece of rope stretched on the sand, whereupon the fore legs and a hind leg were securely lashed to his body. Two of the men sat upon his muzzled head; the lame leg, to which a rope had been fastened at the hock joint, was pulled to its full length and the injured tendon seared by the "doctor"

Turning from the distasteful sight, I followed the edge of the sand. Not many yards from the shore the gurgling, groaning sound of a jemal mingling with the swash of the Mediterranean attracted my attention to where two Blacks had forced a half-submerged camel to his knees, where they scrubbed and scoured his hide. This is a common sight off the Tripoli Suk, for camels not only can be made to enter water, thus making excellent fording animals, but are fine swimmers as well.

We continued on toward the town. Its green-topped minarets which spiked the blue sky seemed gradually to telescope below her bastion walls, and we passed under the Outer Gate to lunch and siesta.

Ever and anon there would float in through my window the blatant sound of the jemal, whose defiant, gurgling groan outvied all other noises as it echoed down the narrow street.

One early morning a pandemonium below my window awoke me. "Baleuk! Bur-r-ro!" rose above the din of men and beasts as two drivers battered one another with their camel sticks. It was the old story of a head-on meeting in a narrow way. Finally, by order of a town watchman who happened along, one of the heavily burdened camels was made to lie down, thus enabling the other to squeeze by.

Another time, turning quickly toward my window as a flash of light chased across the walls of my room, I was just in time to see the silvery point of a spear head undulate by the window ledge. As I surmised, it belonged to a mehari-mounted Arab from the south. He was a picturesque figure, this bronzed man of the Desert, in white burnoose, and turban bound with camel's-hair cord, as he lurched along,—a part of the tall, majestic beast he rode. The mehari, or riding camel, was rare in northern Tripoli; so, seizing my sun helmet, I followed on his trail through the town.

His fine breeding was evident at a glance. Compared with the common jemal he was a supple, slender, elegant creature, with shorter tail, smaller ears, and more protruding chest. His dark, heavily lashed eyes in a gracefully formed head seemed lustrous and appealing, and the tawny-colored coat, as soft as that of a jerboa, bore every evidence of care on the part of its owner. Piercing the right nostril a bridle-ring hung to one side of its long, firm lips, which well concealed its teeth. From this ring a single rein flapped loosely under its jaw, passing around the opposite side of its neck to the rider, who was securely ensconced between the horn and cantle of a beautiful leather-worked riding saddle. This was securely fastened over its hump by a belly-girth; the rider, sitting cross-legged athwart the pommel, rested his feet in the hollow of the mehari's neck.

The surging motion of a mehari may at first cause nausea to the rider, but, this condition overcome, one seems to be moving onward as over a long ground-swell at sea, and many consider the mehari less fatiguing over long distances than the horse. Fabled accounts of its speed are a part of Arab tradition. Despite the extremely slender character of its legs below the knee, it is wiry and muscular and can average thirty miles a day under a weight of three hundred pounds of rider and outfit for long distances.

On account of its speed it is often used as a transmitter of important despatches—the telegraph of the Arab. The Bedawi of the Egyptian Sudan still remember Gordon for the fast work of his last memorable ride of four hundred and three miles in nine days, including halts, and Burckhardt gives an account of a mehari doing one hundred and fifteen miles in eleven hours, which included forty minutes occupied in being twice carried across the Nile.

I followed the mehari out beyond the city walls to its owner's camp in the Suk. Here the Arab let go the rein, at which it stopped. "Kh!" [kneel], he ejaculated. "Kh!" at the same time gently striking its right shoulder with his sandalled foot, and dismounted.

My acquaintance with the camel in town and Suk had inspired me with a constantly growing respect and interest long before I struck his trail in the Desert. Many a night I have ridden beside him, seen him pass noiselessly through the palm groves, watched their moonlight shadows wriggle snakelike over his gaunt, dusky form, or, out under the stars in the open Desert, sensed his vague spectre as it merged itself into the tone of night and the sand. I have listened in the darkness to the peaceful chewing of cuds in the Desert fondūks, avoided the mad rush for water at some long-scented pool, or in the heat of day seen his undulating shadow creep along beside that of my horse, and then, from under my sun helmet, have looked up at him slouching along with his great load, ungainly, disproportionate, a connecting link between the ruminant and the pachyderm.

For hours at a time I have ridden before, beside, and behind him, ever fascinated by the study of his strange temperament and stranger structure; a structure which is impressively adapted to his needs, making him like the Arab—a creature of his environment.

His small nostrils, which seem to heighten the benign expression of his ever-twitching upper lip, can be so closed as to keep out the finest sand of the terrific gibli. Protected, too, by their long, heavy lashes are his dark, protruding eyes, overshadowed by their beetling brows which break the fierce rays of the sun glare overhead. On

those parts of his body most subjected to con-
tact with heat and friction great callosities are
formed which act as sort of buffers; the largest
on his chest, one on each elbow and knee, and
two on each hock. View him broadside, and the
contrast in his build fore-and-aft must impress
even the casual observer, for he seems to fall
away behind.

Sometimes, when the monotony of heat and
sand became unbearable, I would sift back
through the caravan until I found Sarābi and
Hallil-ben-Hassam, her one-eyed driver. Sarābi
was a beautiful white *nākat* [she camel]. Hallil,
so it was rumored, had destroyed an eye to avoid
conscription in Egypt; then, wandering across the
Libyan Desert and the wild, dangerous regions
of Barca, he at last, with Sarābi, reached Tripoli.

Mile upon mile I would watch her great nail-
tipped cushioned feet squdge noiselessly, along,
lift and fall, lift and fall, the under sides reflect-
ing the sand, like lighted orange disks glimpsing
in her violet-blue shadow. The hinder ones on
their delicate leg shafts would let into the shadow
a streak of sunlight which reflected on the
heavier, stronger fore legs which seem in all
camels to be bent the wrong way at the knee.

S-c-u-f-f! and now and again a cloud of golden sand dust, always a deeper orange than the surface, would be kicked out from under her, sifting, scintillating away into the brilliant sunshine.

"Hallil," said I, "how much water will a full-grown camel drink?"

"O Father of Glasses" [for I wore spectacles], replied he, lowering the square Arab fan with which he often shaded his eye, "thou askest me something of a riddle. When dwelling in a town or oasis, water thy camel as thou wouldst thy mare, and it will drink but enough for a time; but on the march thy jemal knows well how to make provision for the morrow to the amount of twelve *garaffs* [four quarts], so say those who have sacrificed him on the trail to quench their thirst. But at the end of a journey have a care, for many a jemal dies at the pool on drinking at such times on an empty stomach. After a long march and feeding, Sarābi has drunk well-nigh to forty *jarras* [twenty gallons], and my people say that camels have gone fifteen days without taking fresh water."

"Burro!" shouted Hallil at a jemal which had jammed against Sarābi's load; and he left me in order to adjust her heavy packs.

This was an important matter, for a light load ill balanced is more disastrous to a camel than a well-adjusted heavy one. Where loads are not easily balanced Arabs will use stones or bags of sand as a counterweight. So important is it that the loads do not gall or chafe the shoulders and hump that a careful driver will ever be on the alert to arrange the cushions, often using green fodder when nothing else is available. Sarābi's load had shifted forward, and Hallil proceeded to pull from the open end of the cushions under the pack-saddle great handfuls of straw, which he stuffed into the forward cushions. The wooden frame of the saddle itself is fashioned after the primitive saddles, which were made from the shoulder-blades and bones of animals.

So wonderfully is the camel adapted to his environment that he not only is provided with his own water-bottle, so to speak, but also with his own larder through that strange protuberance of adipose tissue, the hump, which on long journeys is absorbed into his system, so that literally, as the Arabs say, "he feeds on his hump." During months of rest or little exercise the hump increases in size and even flops over and some-

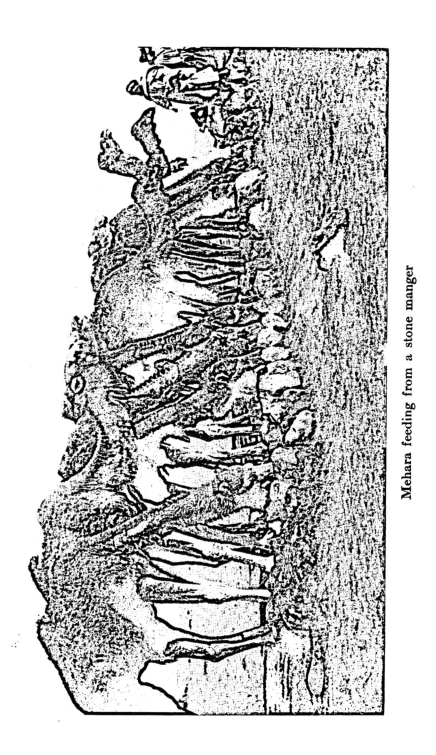

Mehara feeding from a stone manger

times grows so full that the skin on either side is cut and lifted; large pieces of adipose tissue are then sliced off and the skin sewn down again. These pieces are considered a great delicacy by the Arabs.

Beside Sarābi trotted a spindle-legged little bunch of soft, curly wool, as snow white as the mother. Occasionally the little foal, but six weeks old, ventured to sport about some yards away. During a sand-storm the mother shields the young, and during the cold winds of winter two camels will often place the young between them.

There is no doubt but that on the march camels are soothed and cheered by the wild Desert songs of the garfla men, songs undoubtedly induced by the long, monotonous "voyages" and composed to the regular swaying lurch-lurch of the rider or the steady shambling swing of the jemal. Its four heavy steps are said to have given the metre, and the alternations of long and short syllables in the spoken language, the successive pulsations of the metre.

The old Arabian poetry is pervaded with the story and legend of the tending of camels, and words and metaphors based upon him or his life

are in daily use for all manner of strange purposes. Time or death, for instance, is compared
to a drinking camel:

> "Deep was the first draught, deep the next, no stint was
>   there,
> When Time gulped down the great of al-Aswad and of
>   Attab."

While a tribe bereft of its chief by plague is
likened to Death with a herd of camels, to whose
fondūk they must all come home, some sooner,
some later.

> "And to-day they wander a trembling herd, their kinsman
>   Death.
> One speeds away to his rest at eve, one stays till dawn." [1]

And so, "as goes a camel heavy-laden, even-
paced," the "baggager" moves onward, at times
to the song of the march or the wild resonant
note of the oboe and the beat of the gimbreh.

He can carry from three to six hundred
pounds, according to his size, being usually
loaded with about one-third his own weight.

"Look, Sahib!" said Hallil one forenoon, as
he pointed to a far-away distant hill where five
dark spots broke up its soomth surface and slipped

---

[1] From the "Hamasah," an anthology compiled in the ninth century, A. D., by Abu Tammam.

out of sight, to appear again an hour later. Five mehara passed us, the last a black camel. Hallil muttered something under his breath, a curse or a prayer I wot not, then, turning, he looked at me. "'Tis written on the cucumber leaf" [known everywhere] "that a black camel is surely a sign of death." Perhaps I detected a slight satisfaction in the blink of the one eye of this owner of a milk-white camel.

Camels when in caravan are sometimes driven in Indian file, tied headstall to tail, and occasionally, as is practised in some parts of Egypt, by the rope of the nose-ring to tail; the cruel consequence may be easily imagined if the forward camel falls or perhaps stampedes. But usually, particularly in Tripoli, they are driven in droves or string out irregularly over the Desert, which is a more natural and humane way, besides being the most practical.

At times it is necessary to punish a fractious camel; then his driver falls upon him with a large flat club and beats him unmercifully on the neck, just back of the jaw, until the poor beast rolls to the ground and remains motionless.

It has been estimated that one out of every two camels dies before it reaches five years of

age. The camel under man's care would undoubtedly thrive in almost every country, but it
is to the tropics that he seems best adapted.
There, on the long marches, everything must be
sacrificed to his welfare, for on him depends the
success of the caravan or the safe arrival of his
master at the journey's end. Over stony ground
or rocky mountain paths his soft-cushioned feet
become cut and bruised; but it is on slippery
ground or in quicksand that the camel, feeling
himself slide or beginning to sink, loses his head
and flounders about. Sometimes he splits himself
up, or, struggling in the quicksand, breaks a
leg or disjoints a hip. Then the heavy load is
dragged off his back, a crescent blade flashes in
the sunlight, or bang! goes a long flint-lock, and
another victim is added to the unending death roll.

Sometimes, following down the Arbar-Arsāt,
I would turn into a narrow by-way, and, passing
from the hot street, would enter a small, dark
building used as a corn mill. Ensconced in a
dusty seat in a far corner, I would watch Nageeb
plod softly and uncertainly round and round the
pivot of the millstone. A few dim rays sifted
down from the roof through a drapery of cob-
webs on to Nageeb's gaunt, mangy hide and shed

a scant light over his path. But it mattered little to him, for Nageeb was blind, and near to blindness, too, was old Bakri, his master, who now and again emptied corn into the mill and shovelled up that which was ground.

Ten years before the shrill "Lu-lu-lu" cry of welcome of the women and the firing of guns had announced the arrival of a long-looked-for caravan, eleven months' journey from the Sudan and Nageeb, one of the remaining few who had commenced the voyage, exhausted and broken by the long strain, staggered "camelfully" with his load into the Suk-el-Burka. It was his last journey with the garfla, and old Bakri, then in need of a camel, had picked him up in the Suk for a song.

But Nageeb had made the rounds of fifty Ramadans—more than the usual years allotted to camel. Before long, on some Suk day, old Bakri's mill will cease its grinding, and leaving the Arab butcher shops of the Suk-el-Thalet, his bent, turbaned form will bear away a mangy pelt. "Even so!" his cry will be heard about the market. "Even so! The hide of my brown camel for a trifle. In the name of the Prophet, it is excellent."

CHAPTER TWELVE

A NIGHT'S RIDE WITH ARAB BANDITS

MUCH of my travelling was tiresome and monotonous. As a rule, the Turkish and Arab officials were courteous, and the people in both towns and country were rarely deliberately annoying. Most of the people worked at honest labor, and it is not these that the traveller as a rule has to fear, but certain hostile Desert tribes, marauding town and Desert thieves. There is a saying in the Sahara that "unless a man is killed, he lives forever." By Desert law the act of passing through those wastes practically entails forfeiture of goods to whoever can seize them; so highway robbery is not only practised, but is, by a large class, generally conceded to be right.

In Tripoli, as in most semitropical countries, too careful consideration cannot be given to one's mode of diet and dress. Easily digested foods and boiled water are essential to the Occidental traveller. From experience I found that a suit of khaki, a thick flannel shirt, light underwear, and the indispensable flannel cholera belt [to protect the stomach and back from the sun] and sun helmet were the most practical and comfortable clothing. To wear an ordinary straw hat in the Desert would rashly invite sunstroke.

I carried no tent, but frequently needed my blanket at night. Once when camping by a small lake near the coast, my men improvised a tent out of Mohammed's baracan, my sketching umbrella, and the rushes. Under my rug was always spread a piece of palm matting to render less direct the attacks of sand fleas which abound in the oases.

My meals usually consisted of Arab bread, fresh eggs, tea, and fruits. Sometimes we bought these and occasionally chickens from fondūk keepers or Bedawi. When we had occasion to carry a watermelon for half a day on the donkey's pack, the melon became heated through and through by the sun; but, on cutting it open, the slightest breeze, no matter how hot, caused immediate evaporation, and within ten or fifteen minutes the melon would actually seem cool to one's taste. Water was boiled when feasible, and we took as large a stock of it as we could conveniently carry, sometimes in coolers, sometimes in a goat-skin. The wells were occasionally dry or foul, and water contained in earthen jars at fondūks was often stagnant or ill cared for. Mohammed usually acted as cook. Not only our menu but our culinary outfit was a simple affair—a small earthen stove and a few dry palm leaves for fuel. Over this he brewed tea, boiled eggs, and even roasted chicken. Often at evening I would stretch out on my rug and watch the low glow of the embers trace a line of crimson down his profile or a flicker illumine his swarthy face, and cast his big shadow on some tree trunk or fondūk wall. Then, too, I had other than æsthetic reasons for watching him, for chopped horsehair in one's food does not go well in one's insides, and is no more conducive to good health than poisoned ground-glass particles surreptitiously deposited in one's shoes. Many a night I would lie awake, looking up at the silver stars into the far-off silent night, then fall asleep—to sleep lightly, as was my habit when in the open—and lack of sleep more than anything else was the most trying part of my travelling.

A NIGHT'S RIDE WITH ARAB BANDITS

On the mountain slopes we often started coveys of partridges, and out on the sandy Desert great carrion crows would flap across our trail. In some sections lions are found, but I never ran across one. Now and again we would spend a few hours in one of the Desert towns to replenish our supplies. In the low tablelands as we approached the Jebel Nagahza Mountains we came upon some Bedawi shacks, generally guarded by white wolflike dogs. About these habitations the Bedawi plant their gardens, surrounding them by low mud walls. Sometimes a Bedaween family will return to the same spot at certain seasons, year after year, the sheik frequently leaving some male member in charge during the family's peregrinations.

A large onion plant is an important factor in agricultural districts, not as an article of food, for even a goat will not touch it [it is said to be poisonous], but as a sort of Arab "registry of deeds." The country Arabs keep no written record of their real-estate transactions; land is handed from father to son, and its divisions and subdivisions set off by rows of these scattered plants, their great bulbs protruding above the soil.

One day over hot rock wastes of the Jebel Nagahza we rode our exhausted horses fifteen long
hours, trying to cover their heads as much as
possible with our own shadows. Almost every
step was a stumble, for we had little hope of their
surviving the hard, staggering pull over the last
stretch of mountain trail. It was a test not only
of endurance, but of ability—on my part, at least
—to appear unobservant of certain circumstances,
for I had suspected Muraiche, suspected him of
an indefinite something; but the workings of his
wily old Arab mind, its reasons and its purposes,
were to me as mysterious as the great wastes of
the Sahara over which we had been travelling, and
as elusive as the noxious sand lizards which now
and again scurried from beneath our horses' feet.

The long, hot caravan trail at sundown emptied us into the little Arab town of Khoms.
Here we parted with a caravan, forty camels
strong, bound for Misurata, with which we had
travelled for the last three days. Mohammed
and Ali were on foot and drove the big pack
donkey; while Muraiche, like myself, rode an
Arab stallion. His bent old figure, now ahead
of me, now by my side, seemed lost in the folds
of his baracan.

Since sunrise, as we approached Khoms, a change had come over Muraiche; he no longer obeyed my orders with alacrity, and when, several times, it was necessary for me to repeat them sharply he seemed to awaken with a start from deep meditation. This at the time I attributed to the fatigue of our journey and anticipated relaxation, for a rest had been promised at Khoms. Following the custom of the country, I reported to the Turkish governor on our arrival, and saw my men and animals comfortably fixed in a fondūk, with orders to have everything in readiness to start the following afternoon; then spent the night at the house of Mr. Tate, the only Englishman in the place.

This night in mid July and the following night, strangely different, stand out strongly in my memory—perhaps for the contrast with the dusty, monotonous travelling of other days and the sleeping in dirty fondūks; or, perhaps, in contrast with each other. If you would know the pleasure of bathing, of sleeping beneath the snow-white sheets of a bed, travel day after day on the burning, scorching, yellow-red sand of the Sahara; fill your eyes, nose, and ears, your very soul with its fine powdered dust; tie your handkerchief, after the manner of the Tuaregs, across your mouth to prevent evaporation, that your throat may not parch too`much. Travel early and late to make the most of the cool of the morning and evening. Sleep lightly if you are a lone stranger, and do not mind the uncomfortable lump of your pistol-holsters under your arm; they are better in your hands than in the other fellow's. So when, sunburnt, saddle-sore, and tired with long riding and little sleep, you find, what I did, a bath of delicious cold water, brought from an old Roman well still used by the Arabs in Khoms, and a snow-white bed, give praise to Allah. Then let the barbaric noises of a wild Sudanese dance in the distance and the musical chant of the Muezzin melt away with your thoughts into the quiet of the African night.

Bright and early the next morning a Turkish soldier brought to the house an invitation for an audience with the Governor, and I was ushered into his official apartments in company with Muraiche and the Chief of Police, a half-breed Arab-Negro. Our conversation was translated, through two interpreters, from English into Arabic and from Arabic into Turkish, and vice versa.

I explained to his Excellency how I regretted our inability to converse directly with one another. He naïvely replied that it mattered not, as he would look with four eyes instead of two, which I have not the slightest doubt he did while I was in the vicinity of Khoms. Meantime, Turkish coffee was served with the inevitable cigarette, and the customary diplomatic salutations, etc., effervesced back and forth. I still wonder in just what manner and form mine eventually reached him.

On coming out I found our horses at the palace gate, and also a mounted *zabtie* [Turkish guard] who had been assigned to conduct me about the Roman ruins of Lebda, which had formerly occupied the site and neighborhood of Khoms. We rode east from the city out into the plain, passed down a small ravine from whose sides I picked out some fragments of Roman pottery, and soon came to a large depression in the landscape. In the bed of this were reeds, through which a broad, shallow stream meandered to the sea, and into whose waters two half-naked Blacks were casting a net. This depression had once been a splendid Roman harbor, flanked on either side by massive stone quays and majestic buildings. Portions of these still remained, including the ruins of a large Roman palace. But gone is this legacy, scattered over the plain and destroyed by ruthless Arabs and more ruthless Turks. Some sections, too, of the great stone quays remained; but where were the thousands of Mediterranean galleys which once moored to those piles and ring-bolts? Where are the moving, breathing crowds, in Roman toga and Arab baracan, which once thronged those quays in the shadow of their classic architecture and the awnings of the little booths?

Wonderful capitals and other fragments were lying broken and marred about the plain. I smuggled a few fragments of marble details into my saddle-bags unbeknown to the guard, for so opposed are the Turks to a Christian's acquiring or even interesting himself in antiquities that the most beautiful sculptures and relics are often deliberately destroyed. Recently a statue which was taken from Khoms to Tripoli for the gardens of the Turkish Club was first deliberately mutilated by knocking off the head and arms, presumably that it might not attract the covetous eyes of some dog of a Christian.

Had it not been for a casual stroll through the Suk later that afternoon my men might now be recounting a different yarn over their smoking kief and coos-coos. Threading my way among men, animals, shacks, scattered garden produce, grains, and wares which covered the ground in interesting heaps, and pushing through a small crowd which had gathered about me, their curiosity and cupidity aroused by a gold filling in one of my teeth, I stopped for a moment. For there, in the middle of an open space, beside a Marabout's [saint's] tomb Muraiche was engrossed in a low conversation with one of the irregular guards, an Arab in the Turkish employ. Disappearing unobserved to another part of the Suk, I should have thought no more about the matter, but for the fact that when, later in the morning, these two met in my presence, by the Governor's palace, they omitted the customary b'salaams and effusive greetings of Mohammedan acquaintances, and by no word or sound betrayed the least recognition.

Reminding Muraiche of my previous orders to have everything in readiness by two o'clock, I sauntered up to lunch at Mr. Tate's. The route to my next point of destination, the little town of Kussabat, was not only over the rough mountainous range of the Jebel Gharian, but it was considered by the Arabs dangerous on account of thieves. Being under the necessity of making the journey that day, I was anxious to arrive there by sundown. Consequently, when, by half-past two, none of my outfit put -in an appearance, one of the house servants was despatched to learn the reason.

First by wily excuses, and then by an open mutiny, my men delayed the departure until half-past five, when, by threats to appeal to the Turkish Pasha to have them thrown into prison and engage new men, we were finally ready to start.

"But a guard, Arfi?" Twice Muraiche had asked the question, and twice I answered him that the Turkish officials had been notified of my intention to depart at two o'clock. Had they intended to send a guard they would have done so. However, being desirous of conforming to custom, Muraiche was sent to the Governor's palace with instructions to report our departure, but not to ask for a guard, as I personally shared in the common opinion that often the traveller is safer without one.

I watched Muraiche after he rounded the corner and disappeared at a gallop down the narrow street to the palace, from which, immediately reappearing, he set off to a different quarter of the town. Questioned on his return, he replied that an officer had sent him to notify a guard who was to go with us.

"You'll see your way all right, for the full moon ought to be up in about two hours, but *ride last*," were Tate's parting words. It was good advice and had often been given me before. To travellers in North Africa, particularly those among the French colonists of Tunis and Algeria, the saying, "Never allow an Arab to ride behind you," has become an adage, and this night in the Gharian I proved its worth.

We rode to the top of the steep trail, down which the slanting afternoon sunbeams shot by in golden shafts. Back and beyond us these sun shafts sped until, striking the white walls of Khoms, they broke, spilling over them a flood of orange gold, diffusing her surrounding olive groves and date-palms with a golden green, and through the shimmering, sifting gold mist above it all sparkled a scintillating sea of blue. Our course now lay almost due south to the region of the Djebel Gharian, the region I had hoped to enter and pass through by day.

Resting on the site of ancient Lebda, my golden city of Khoms lay nearly an hour's ride behind us, and as yet no guard, to my entire satisfaction. This was short-lived, however, for soon a yell, such as is rarely loosed from the throat of a human being, caused us suddenly to draw rein. Down the steep, rocky incline, where an ordinary horseman could but carefully pick his way, out on to the sandy plateau upon which we had just ridden, riding wild and giving his lithe animal free rein, dashed a guard, and when abreast of us, drew up short out of a full run, after the manner of Arab horsemen.

"B'salaam," to Muraiche, and a nod of the head to me, which was slightly reciprocated; yes, very slightly, for before me was the one man out of all the Arabs I had ever seen that I would have chosen last for a companion that night. There, in the glow of the late afternoon sunlight, the stock of his short carbine resting on his saddle, and the sweat making bright the high lights on his evil brassy-bronze face, sat the worst cutthroat it was ever my fortune to look upon—Muraiche's friend, he of the market-place.

During a short conversation with Muraiche, the guard's peculiar eyes scanned me from the rowels of my spurs to the top of my sun helmet. Evidently the main objects of his searching glance were in my holsters, covered by my jacket; meantime, however, I lost no detail of his weapon, a hammerless magazine rifle of modern make. Then he addressed me in Arabic, but not speaking the language, I turned to Muraiche.

"He tells us to start," the latter replied.

This sudden assumption of leadership came most unexpectedly, his seeming intention being to bring up the rear. Now Arabs, though ignorant, are daring; but like all Orientals, fully respect only one thing, and that is a just and strong hand, which they must feel in order to appreciate. Consequently my course was plain.

"Tell the guard to head the caravan and that if he goes with me, he goes as one of my men." As we got under way the guard rode slowly ahead, meanwhile taking sidelong glances at me out of the corners of his villainous gray-green eyes, filled with all the hatred of the Moslem for the Christian. I realized that never in my life had the assets and liabilities of my *status quo* received such careful auditing.

When the great red lantern of the sun disk had sunk beneath the earth line, from without the deep, mysterious valleys crept the blue-violet mist films of twilight shadows, absorbing and leavening into their darker tones the brighter afterglow, against which moved the dark shapes of horses and men. Suddenly they bunched themselves and the guard dismounted, then Mohammed and Ali went on with the pack donkey.

"The guard's saddle-girth is broken," Muraiche informed me. "But we will fix it and you can ride on very slowly."

"I will wait," was my reply. "But *you* ride on, Muraiche." The girth was soon "fixed," which consisted in a vain effort to cinch it up another hole.

Steeper and more rugged grew the trail, and we entered the range of the Gharian. As daylight dimmed, an uncomfortable darkness hung over the mountains for a short space; then the moon glow appeared in the east, and soon the moon itself lifted its pale, distorted shape above the horizon, and suffused everything with its pale blue-green light, so cool and so satisfying to the eye and mind in contrast to the hot sun glare

" The afterglow . . . against which moved the dark shapes of horses and men "

that, during the day, reflected through to the very brain.

But the dark shadow masses of boulders, parched shrub patches, and shaded slopes—what uncanny things might they not contain? And those gorges, too, which in the day reflected heat like an oven from their red, hot sides? Now they were cold, dank, and foreboding, and a shudder passed over me. Then I reasoned with myself. I was tired, unduly apprehensive; the conditions of heat and long days in the saddle had over-taxed my nerves. I fell to watching the agile bodies of my Arabs on foot, as, tiring of the pace, they dropped back until just in front of me. Mohammed in particular; how the lights and shadows played over his powerful, animal-like form; how subtly his shoulder and calf muscles moved under his sleek, dark skin; how they fascinated me! Willingly through the long journey they had served me, save at Khoms. I started, my dreaming suddenly ended, and almost involuntarily my spurs caused my horse to start ahead. The two men had so imperceptibly lessened their pace that they now had dropped just back of me, one on either side of my horse, and in Mohammed's hand was a wicked-looking knobbed club, which usually he had kept stuck in one of the packs. Each carried a long Arab knife, so Muraiche was ordered to tell the men to keep alongside the donkey.

Down the other side of the moonlit valley a caravan was coming toward us heading for Khoms. Taking a small note-book from my pocket, I wrote: "Should any accident occur to me, thoroughly investigate my men, including the guard," and signed it. Tearing the leaf from the book, and folding it, I watched the great lumbering camels approach us, and dropped a little farther behind, intending to give it to the head man of the caravan for him to bear to the *Muchia* [governor] at Khoms. Then deciding that, under the circumstances, there was not sufficient evidence to thus prejudice the Turkish authorities against my men, I chewed it up and spat it into a patch of sand lilies.

From the distance came the faint report of a gun. Every one of my men heard it, but no comment was made, and we pushed deeper into the mountains. On our left, looking toward the moon, objects were indistinct in the half-tone and shadow, while seen from there, we appeared in the moonlight. Now and again I sensed moving shadows from that direction, but it was some time before I was sure that they were living forms following us, perhaps hyenas, jackals, or some sly cheetah.

As we made sharp turns at times in rounding the mountains, and their sides stood out in silhouette against the sky, I bent low on my horse's neck and watched intently. At one of these turns where the sky cut deep into the mountain side, leaving every irregularity in relief against it, I noticed that men were following us. First, away up on the side, a fezzed head and the barrel of a long Arab flint-lock bobbed against the sky for a second, as, dodging catlike amongst the rocks, their owner rounded the side. Then a second and a third appeared, and I knew we were followed by thieves. This was not comforting, but if we were attacked, the guard's rifle, Muraiche's old-fashioned five-shooter, and my two revolvers would be more than a match for them in point of armament.

One thing puzzled me, however, until later. The manner of these Desert thieves being invariably to attack from the rear, I could not account for their seeming to forge ahead of us. Watching my men, I saw that they, too, were aware of

the thieves; and Muraiche, who had been watching me closely when we occasionally rode abreast,
remarked: "This is a bad country here; I think
robbers are following us."

"Yes, Muraiche; there are men off there. I
have seen three."

"Allah knows, everything is in the hand of
Allah. 'There is neither might nor power save in
Allah, the High, the Mighty.' [1]   La, Arfi, you
must not ride behind; you had better ride first."

"Then I will ride last, Muraiche, for mine are
the best weapons, and I shoot better than any
of you."

After a sharp turn we wound along a valley
side. Just below us the dense foliage of an ancient olive grove shut out every gleam of light
from its black interior, the gnarled old branches
reaching out as though to drag into their depths
any who might come within their grasp, and the
same weird sensations of awe passed over me
which I felt as a boy when I pored over Doré's
illustrations of the wandering Dante and Virgil
in that wonderful, grewsome nether world.

My sensation was complete when, as though
it was the most natural thing in the world for

[1] This saying is used by Moslems when anything alarming occurs.

[252]

a small caravan to leave the trail, dangerous at its best, my guard led and the men proceeded to follow him toward the dark wood, which it was manifestly their purpose to enter.

"Muraiche! Why are the men leaving the trail?" Perhaps he did not hear, for the ground was rough and the stones rattled down the steep bank.

"Muraiche," I called loudly and peremptorily, riding up to him, "tell the men to halt," at the same time drawing one of my pistols and resting it across my saddle. Then I repeated my question.

"The guard says it is shorter," Muraiche replied, still following the guard.

"Then let the guard take it if he chooses. Order the men on to the trail," and we scrambled our horses and donkey up the steep incline.

The guard turned in his saddle for a moment, made a low reply to Muraiche, then descended and disappeared in the darkness. Skirting the wood for half a mile, we passed beyond it. My already well-aroused suspicions of intended treachery on the part of my men were confirmed when, in spite of the fact that the guard had by far the fastest-walking horse of our outfit and had taken a shorter route, there was no sign of him until we had passed a hundred yards beyond the grove and halted.

As he emerged I heard the faint click of his carbine as he pulled the bolt to a full cock, upon which, half turning my horse, I awaited him; as he neared us I saw that he had been running his horse, which was breathing hard and sweating. Then the truth flashed upon me: my men were in league with the thieves who, by a preconcerted arrangement, had gone ahead and hidden in the grove, there to set upon me in the darkness, relying upon my confidence in the guard to follow his lead. Failing in their end, the guard had stopped to parley with them and then made up time. Had their place of ambush not been so evidently dangerous to enter, they might have been successful. Nor would it have been the first time a guard and outfit had returned without the "Arfi," telling a good story of how they were attacked by thieves and escaped, while he was killed.

Now here in front of me that picturesque, venomous-looking devil sat, his rifle full-cocked across the pommel of his saddle, my other men at a little distance to my right, and I a good mark with my white sun helmet—but my revolver resting on my saddle covered the guard.

"Muraiche, tell the guard to uncock his rifle. It might go off by accident." With a sullen look the guard obeyed.

"Now tell him to ride first to protect the goods. Let the men with the pack donkey follow, then you behind them. I'll ride last. If any thieves approach within gunshot, warn them away at once, or I shall fire. You understand?"

"Yes, Arfi," and we strung out in single file. My purpose was to place the guard who possessed the most effective weapon where it was practically of no use against me; for this gave me a screen of the men and animals. The danger from Mohammed and Ali depended entirely upon their ability to close in on me, so while in that position there was nothing to fear from them. As for Muraiche, he was under my direct surveillance, with the advantage all my way, as I rode with drawn weapon.

But I knew the Arab well enough to know that so long as he is not excited or his fanaticism aroused he will not risk his own skin while strategy will serve his ends; and also knew that I had no one to depend upon but myself, and that my safety lay in maintaining, as far as possible, a normal condition of things. So I watched; watched my men in front and watched to the side and behind for signs of the thieves, of whom I caught glimpses now and again. My Arabs' conjunction with these men thwarted, it was but natural that they should communicate with each other to further their plans, and in various ways they sought to do this. While caravan men, when marching through a safe district and many strong, often chant to ease their dreary march or to pacify the camels, in our circumstances the less attention we could draw to ourselves the better. So when Mohammed started to chant in a loud voice by way of giving information, he was ordered to be quiet.

Again, as we rounded a sharp bend, Ali made a break for the brush, but he started a second too soon. I saw him and called his name sharply; he halted and returned to the caravan.

When we passed within gunshot of objects which might conceal a foe I rode abreast of Muraiche, using him to screen myself, knowing well that they would attack only from the side which, from their position, placed us in the full moonlight. And in the narrow ravines, though he growled, I often crowded him close, affording little or no opportunity to the Arabs to single me out for a shot without endangering Muraiche. So we travelled until a thong of one of Mohammed's sandals broke on the rocky ground, and he asked to be allowed to drop behind a little and fix it. Since we were entering a wide open stretch below a long slope of hill, I acceded; but as he fell behind some distance, I called to him to come on, and, when he approached us, turned my attention to the men ahead, feeling a sense of relief that we were now in more open country.

The moon was slightly behind us, high in the heavens now, and cast our shadows diagonally to the right and ahead of us. I watched the shadows of my horse and myself squirm and undulate as they travelled over the ground. As I relaxed from the tension under which I had been for a moment gazing unthinkingly ahead, the movement of another shadow caught my eye—that of an upward-moving arm and knobbed club. There was no time to look first. Instinctively with my right hand I thrust my revolver under my rein arm and turned my head sharply to find, what I had expected, that my weapon was pointing full at the breast of the big fellow Moham-

[257]

med, who, stealing up quietly behind me with sandals removed, had intended to strike.

"Bu-r-r-ro!" [go on] I said. Lowering his club without a sign of embarrassment, he took his place in line, the others apparently having been oblivious to the whole affair

After he left me, and the excitement of the moment had passed, cold chills chased one another up and down my spine. From then on there were no sign of thieves. For four hours I had ridden with my finger on the trigger of my pistol covering my men. For four hours I had sensations which I do not care to experience again.

About one o'clock in the morning, high up on the hilltop we sighted the white walls of Kussabat, and after some hard climbing we came into full view of the silver city, glistening in a bath of silver as Khoms had shone in a flood of gold.

A few words with the town guard, and the great doors of its main gate, the Bab-el-Kussabat, creaked and groaned as they swung open. We entered the city and clattered up the steep, narrow streets, where, from the low housetops on either side, sleeping forms, muffled in baracans, awoke and peered over at us, and big white wolf-hounds craning their necks set pandemonium loose from one end of the town to the other, as they snarled and yelped in our very faces.

Soon we were in a small fondūk with doors heavily bolted. The other occupants were a selected stock of camels, goats, sheep, and fowls taken from the Arabs by the Turks in lieu of taxes; in fact, the fondūk had been converted into a sort of pound. On the roof were a dozen or so of Arabs and Blacks asleep, and I preferred their company in the moonlight to that of my four men under the dark archways. To prevent scheming, I took with me Muraiche, the cause of all the trouble. Some of these Blacks and Arabs raised up out of their sleep to see, probably for the first time, an apparition in khaki and a white helmet. Then we lay down and, thanks to the previous night's rest, I managed to keep awake most of the night. When Muraiche rolled over in his sleep, or a neighboring Black muttered in his savage dreams, I would start from my dozing.

True, I gave my men no baksheesh at the journey's end. I might have had them thrown into the foul Turkish prison of the Castle; but, after all, it was the life of these men of the Desert—they had only tried their little game and failed.

And the stakes? My revolvers and ammunition, the leather of my saddle and riding leggins, and perhaps a gold filling in my teeth. They knew I had no money, for in the presence of Muraiche I had deposited it at Tripoli, and Muraiche himself carried only the necessary funds for the journey. But modern weapons are a prohibited import, save for the Turkish army, and are worth their weight in silver to the Arabs.

Why such a risk for such small stakes? Well, why will the Desert thief risk his life for a baracan, or an Arab scavenger dig up the corpse of a plague victim for the miserable piece of sackcloth that girds his loins?

The next morning by half-past three the fondūk was astir and we breakfasted. While the horses were being saddled and the donkey loaded, I seconded a proposal by Muraiche to look about Kussabat. It was evident that both he and the guard who had accompanied us were disposed to inveigle me into dark and out-of-the-way streets and I soon retraced my footsteps to the fondūk, paid the keeper for the stabling of my animals, and left Kussabat through its other gate.

Descending to a plateau we soon passed the

"The guard left us the next morning"

outskirts of some extensive olive groves. Here the guard left us and we entered the mountains again, often following through gorges which shut out every breath of air and where the heat was stifling. Sometimes we camped in these gorges at night, and the bark of the jackal or the idiotic laugh of a hyena would echo and reverberate from the rocky walls. The day was one of the hottest, for it was now African midsummer and the sun beat down relentlessly on our suffering horses. Beside me on the dapple-gray stallion rode old Muraiche. His hooked nose resembled more than ever a vulture's beak, and his crafty eyes looked out from a bronzed and wrinkled physiognomy. Ahead Mohammed and Ali trudged wearily, ankle-deep in the hot sand over a sun-baked plateau. Noon came and I saw to it that the animals were at once unsaddled and fed; then we ate, and the men prepared to stretch out for their hard-earned siesta. But this was not to be. I meant that by the end of that day's journey they should find themselves more ready to sleep than to scheme.

"Saddle up!" I ordered. My only concern was the horses, and they had already had an hour since eating. However, this unusual curtailing of the mid-day rest was resented by all three, but particularly by Mohammed and Ali.

"They say they will not go!" repeated Muraiche, the sly old fox not caring to openly take the stand himself.

"Then let them stay here in the Desert without water, food, or guns; we will take the pack donkey with us."

The double-faced old rascal would not openly side with the mutinous pair, and the result was, they sullenly saddled up. We did a day and a half's journey in one, but they slept that night; so did I.

CHAPTER THIRTEEN

A DESERT EPISODE

CROWNING the highest crest of some Saharan sand-hills, a lonely castle glistened like a fire opal against the azure of a Desert sky. Over its whitewashed Moorish walls and ramparts the lowering sun splashed in orange gold and dyed a lurid red the crescent flag of the Turk, which hung lazy and lank from its halyards. From the castle a hundred yards away stretched a gentle slope of sand over which two figures passed back and forth, their manner bespeaking the tenseness of their conversation.

Such was the picture framed by the circular rim of a little three-inch mirror [a part of my shaving kit] into which I was looking.

The place called Jefara was a lonely spot. Besides the castle, which garrisoned some sixty Turks, there were but two other habitations. One was the house of the Bey, the Arab governor of the province, from which high walls squared themselves about the seclusion of his seraglio and gardens; the other a small building at the corner of the wall nearest the castle. This served frequently as a lokanda for belated wayfarers, but primarily as a rendezvous where the garrison could exchange their few paras, and the Arabs of the *wadan* their scant earnings, for coffee brewed in little brass utensils and poured into cups of British make. A broad stone seat lined the walls of the single room within, and outside one flanked the entrance on either hand.

Muraiche had, upon our arrival, made arrangements with the Black who ran the place to quarter there for the night, and to provide green fodder from the neighboring oasis for the animals.

By hard travelling the following sunset should find us at the end of our long, tedious journey, back again in the town of Tripoli. This near approach to civilization made me realize that, out of consideration for my friends in Tripoli, certain neglected duties must at last be met face to face, and so the last glow of waning sunlight found me outside the lokanda, belathered, razor in hand, peering into a small pocket mirror

[264]

balanced uncertainly against a bar of the iron window grating.

Some dozen Arabs and Blacks stood about or squatted on the ground, eying me with native curiosity, thinking likely enough that only a fool Christian would shave his beard. One in particular, a nephew of the Bey, engaged me in conversation on the subject. He was dressed in a scarlet burnoose of beautiful texture and wore tucked back of his ear, after the manner of the country, a bouquet of small blossoms.

Again the two figures appeared in the mirror, passed across the crack in its surface, and moved beyond the rim. One, dressed after the manner of a high-class Arab, was the Bey. But my interest lay in the taller of the two men, a Turkish officer in command of the garrison. For it was he who had joined me over my coffee upon my arrival, and had sought in French adroitly to cross-examine me under the guise of a persuasive affability.

I told him I was an American, that we had come from over the range of the Gharian and were headed for Tripoli.

"But your clothes?" he queried, as he eyed suspiciously my suit of khaki.

"I bought them in Malta. We lay over a day and I was pressed for time, so an accommodating tailor on the Strade Reale refitted these from a previous order. You see," I continued jokingly, "my jacket was at first intended for a captain in the British service, and by rights these trousers should now be adorning the legs of an army surgeon." But no trace of a smile lit up his bronzed face.

"Your firman," he demanded. "I will see it."

"The courtesy of your Turkish Pasha at Tripoli has rendered one unnecessary."

"No firman," he ejaculated; "you are travelling through the territory of the Sultan *sans firman*," and abruptly left me.

I was not again aware of his presence until the silver disk reflected the two figures as they strode back and forth behind me. "Gharian firman . . . Tripoli . . ." drifted to my ears, and suspicious glances in my direction left no doubt that I was the subject of their discussion.

Dusk was now settling over the Desert. Muraiche poured from an earthen jar a thin stream of water into my hands, for I washed after the manner of the Arabs; then, leaving me, he entered the lokanda, supposedly to spread my rug and prepare things for the night.

My surprise and indignation were not to be concealed when on entering I found him busily gathering together the outfit. "The Sahib [officer] he order me take the things to the castle," grunted Muraiche.

"Well, the Arfi [master] orders that they be left here." Having seen my orders carried out, I repaired to one of the stone seats outside, where the officer soon joined me.

"You will be my guest at the castle to-night," he proffered.

"Thanks, but I have already made arrangements to stay here."

"La, not here among these Blacks and men of the wadan; it is dangerous."

"I am sure it will be safe enough under the shadow of your castle, and this seems the most comfortable place I have quartered in for three days."

Back in his deep, sinister eyes I caught a look. I had no desire to enter the castle and to stake my safety or convenience on the whims of an erratic Turk. Besides, mere detention in a Turkish fortress would have placed me more or less at the mercies of old six-fingered Mohtar, the Tripoline horse dealer, with whom the contract for my animals expired the following day.

An hour later a Moorish lantern which the Black had hung over the lintel of his doorway cast its uncertain light over the swarthy-visaged men who sat about, engaged in guttural conversation or quietly smoking their long kief pipes. By its light I had jotted down a few notes of the day's journey, and had now settled comfortably back and watched the curling smoke wreaths, like the fumes of so many Aladdin's lamps, twist and curl straight up toward the darkness and the stars.

But in place of the evil "jinnee" again appeared the assiduous Turk.

"Come," said he, standing in front of me, "and we will drink mastica together at my quarters.

"You decline? Then take a promenade and I will show you the castle"

Under the circumstances I was not keen to visit this particular Turkish stronghold at ten o'clock at night, so replied that I was tired from the day's journey and was just about to turn in.

"But just a petite promenade—dix minutes," he urged.

"Monsieur, I wish to be left alone."

Within the flicker of the lamp's rays his manner changed, a red anger flushed over his face, his sinewy hand shot out and seized me strongly by my wrist. "I order you to the castle," he hissed in my face. Some of the Arabs sprang up. My free hand had dropped to my holster, while with a twist I freed my arm.

"Monsieur," I said, springing to my feet, "if this is an invitation to spend the night as your guest at the castle I thank you, but must decline; but if you have orders from Redjed Pasha to that effect, show them to me and I will gladly comply."

"Bah," he jeered, "vous faites mal. When do you leave—in the morning?"

"Perhaps at three, perhaps at four."

"I go with you," he added and disappeared from the arena of lamplight in the direction of the castle.

The Black mounted the stone ledge, unhooked the lantern, and disappeared inside the lokanda. He at once closed the heavy window shutters inside the bars, and when the last one had entered threw over the heavy bolts of the door. The natives, casting off their baracans, spread them along the stone ledge, upon which they immediately stretched themselves for the night. Kicking off my riding leggins I lay down on my rug.

Piff! The Black groped his way to his place, and soon only the heavy animal-like breathing of the sleepers broke the stillness of the darkness.

For some time I slept soundly, but finally the heated closeness of the place, which was among the least of its detractions, became unendurable, so, picking up my blanket, I quietly unfastened the door and slipped out. "Halt!" rang out the challenge of a guard from the nearest corner of the castle. Lying down on one of the stone seats at the side of the door, I pulled my blanket over me, vaguely heard some one slip the bolt of the door again, saw a dusky baracaned figure emerge around the corner of the lokanda and occupy the other seat, then fell asleep in the refreshing cool of the Desert night.

It must have been two o'clock in the morning that I was shaken awake by a Turkish soldier. The officer, by having placed my three men and

"His . . . hand shot out and seized me strongly by the wrist"

myself all night under the surveillance of a
guard, had seen fit to forestall any premature
departure, and now came in person, greeting me
with the remark, "It is time to start."

I was in none too gracious a mood, having
been so unceremoniously aroused. Further
sleep, however, was out of the question, and
other travellers were already bestirring themselves.

"I am travelling for my own pleasure and in
my own time," I said curtly.

The next half-hour was spent over our break-
fast while he stood insolently by. Then Mohammed and Ali secured the kit on the pack
donkey, Muraiche and I swung into our saddles,
and set out accompanied by the officer.

It was a glorious morning as we rode over
hillock after hillock of moonlit sand: one of
those Desert moods which leave their indelible
impress upon the traveller who seeks her arid
wastes. And I rode slowly that I might drink in
all that these great solitudes had to offer, too
slowly for my self-imposed escort. His restive
Arab mount was a superb animal, and the officer
tired, as I meant he should, of my slow pace.
Long before the pinks and greens of the sand

appeared in the early dawn he had given rein to his horse, ordering us to follow to the next army post, a half day's journey ahead. The order, however, was unnecessary, for only Bedawi and Desert thieves dare leave the main caravan trails.

The sun was scorching down on the Desert with a wilting heat when we slowly drew up at the outpost, typical of those which here and there are scattered along some of the main trade routes to protect caravans and prevent smuggling.

There was no need of dismounting, for our companion of the early morning came toward us, followed by two Turkish infantrymen, each of whom carried a loaded magazine rifle resembling closely the old Lee of our navy, while belts filled with ammunition sagged heavily about their waists.

"These two soldiers," said he, "will escort you to Tripoli. Adieu, Monsieur," and a malicious smile lurked about the corners of his pointed mustache.

He addressed a few words in Turkish to the soldiers, handed the younger one a heavily sealed document which he tucked in his belt, the two men saluted, and we set out.

"What did he say to the men, Muraiche?" I inquired shortly.

"He give orders they not lose you, keep their eyes on you always, and when we see Tripoli they go quick to the Bashaw with the paper."

The news was not welcome. I never had aspired to being personally conducted; besides, should the letter precede me it would be prejudicial to my future interests in Tripoli. My course was plain. I must anticipate its delivery by seeing the Pasha first.

My escort wore high red Turkish fezes and brown uniforms whose patched and dilapidated condition was characteristic of the Ottoman soldier of the Tripolitan frontier. The elder was a veteran upon whose sensibilities the untutored tactics of the younger seemed to rasp like the chafing of a bow across a Sudanese gimbreh. At first they marched with unslung guns and viewed my every movement with suspicion. Perhaps they were afraid that I would steal the Desert, as only mile upon mile of limitless sand lay about us. I mitigated this fear, however, by being content to carry away only a bottle full of it; but I am sure that the suspicions of these unsophisticated Ottomans were never fully allayed regarding my use of the camera, despite the fact that I eventually persuaded them to line up with my own men before it. On this occasion the veteran proved himself every inch a soldier.

As time wore on they slung their guns across their backs, unslinging them occasionally as I halted to use my camera. When I changed the films they watched, catlike, every movement. I could not resist the temptation to discard and surreptitiously bury in the sand with my foot the slip of paper containing the developing formula. Then the veteran would as surreptitiously slide up behind me, dig it out again with his foot, and stow it away in his pocket. In such a manner he secretly stored away in the recesses of his clothes some half-dozen of these slips, later to be produced as documentary evidence against me. I still wonder what sort of work was made of them when they came to translate those chemical formulæ into Turkish.

Hour by hour passed slowly. Again I made no stop, as is customary in the middle of the day, and the Turks with their heavy shoes and weighty accoutrements began to show signs of fatigue.

The veteran, however, was still game, despite

the lagging of the recruit, whom he naggingly admonished with all his surplus energy.

But at last the pace proved too much for even the veteran, who growled to Muraiche.

"He say to stop, go slow, Arfi," interpreted Muraiche. My plans were working well.

Mohammed and Ali on foot beside the pack donkey set the pace in front. I well knew that these half-naked, barefooted men of the Desert could walk the Turks to a standstill. So, turning to Muraiche, I said: "Tell him my men have marched many camels' journeys for days past. Ask him if an Arab can outwalk a Turk?" There is no love lost between the natives and their Turkish conquerors, and I knew that the question would be put with a relish.

We stopped a space at a Desert well. I now sent the men and donkey on ahead, and let the Turks take their fill of water and rest, while I studied the route carefully from a French officer's map which had been loaned me. Three kilometres away there was a double turn in the trail as it descended through a rocky sand-filled ravine.

If anything was to be done, it must be done soon and at that place. My men with the outfit had long since disappeared from view among the sand-hills. We at first rode slowly to give them a good start, at times gradually increasing or decreasing our lead. We were approaching the turn, and had almost imperceptibly opened up a hundred yards of daylight between us.

"Halt!" echoed over the sand as a hillock shut us from their view. "Ar-r-rah!" yelled Muraiche as he dug the corners of his steel Arabian stirrups into his horse's side. We gave the animals full rein, swerved around the second turn, and dashed down the ravine.

And it was here that the hardest riding must be done. A portion of the gully was exposed to the highest part of the trail. And I was not over sanguine that the Turks might not fire upon us, either by reason of their excitement or deliberately through a too rigid interpretation of their officer's orders.

This stretch was cleared none too soon, for as we disappeared behind the wall of the ravine, the red fezes of the Turks silhouetted over a distant sand-hill against the sky.

Not until we reached a point a mile away where the trail shelved on to a coast route did we slacken speed. Here, deep parallel and inter-

lacing camel paths were worn into the hard-packed surface by centuries of caravan traffic. The paths followed over clayey cliffs, literally the edge of the great Desert, which seemed here to pause before it emptied itself into the sea.

We soon caught up to the outfit. Not far ahead of us three mounted zabtie, a sort of rural constabulary who patrol the routes in the vicinity of the coast towns, were drawn up across the trail awaiting our approach. The sergeant, so Muraiche informed me, was a nephew of Sidi Hassan, the rightful successor to the throne of the deposed Arab house of Karamali. A satisfactory reply to their questions, and we were permitted to continue on our way.

The zabtie would soon meet the two hurrying soldiers, who might enroll them to apprehend us or to carry in the letter. So, as we passed the salt chotts of Malāha, I left word for the outfit to follow, and we set out at a steady canter along the Etreig-el-Kheiber [The Big Road] toward the five miles of palm groves and gardens of the oasis of Tripoli. An hour before sundown the horses and outfit were turned over to Mohtar, as per contract, before six o'clock that night, which hour is the beginning of the Mohammedan day.

Sunset found me over coffee in a cool chamber with his Excellency, Redjed Pasha.

As I passed out into the dusky street I encountered the escort! Handing them some baksheesh, I trudged over to my lokanda.

It was but an episode of Desert travelling in a land where the Occidental *voyageur* is not encouraged. But in spite of Mohammedan antipathy, it was the single annoyance shown me by a Turkish official. The officer, I afterward learned, was of Arab birth, but educated and trained in Constantinople for the Turkish service, and his temerity-may, perhaps, be ascribed to the enthusiasm of an overzealous proselyte.

The prismatic rays of passing wedding lanterns lit up my room and drifted like northern lights across the ceiling from the street below. But I was oblivious to the weird night sounds which break the quiet of a Desert town.

CHAPTER FOURTEEN

THE DESERT

IT would be well-nigh impossible for one who had heeded the call of those vast Desert solitudes to pass back through The Gateway to the Desert without a special tribute to the insidious charm of that great land of sand and silence which lies behind it. South, the interminable African main drifts on to the Sudan; west to east it sweeps the whole width of Africa. Even at the Red Sea it merely pauses for a moment at the brink, then dips beneath the limpid waters and continues across Arabia, Persia, and into northern India. For a thousand miles along the western half of North Africa this belt is screened from Europe by the Atlas Mountains, whose lofty peaks cut a ragged line against the sapphire welkin above them. At their base the Mediterranean, under the yellow light of the southern sun, breaks unceasingly against the dark coast rocks in a glistening band of gold, which at night, like a scimitar, flashes in phosphorescent streams of silver fire.

For a thousand miles along the eastern half of North Africa the Desert meets the coast, and its golden sands blend green with the sapphire of the middle sea. But here nature, as though timid of thus baring the Desert to the men and winds of the north, has shrunk back the coast-line three hundred miles from the main high-ways of water travel, and lined the barren shores with hidden reefs and dangerous quicksands.

The Desert eagle soaring far above the tawny surface of the Sahara looks down on great, won-derfully shaped sand reaches; here merging softly into broad expanses of Desert grass, or creased, where dry river beds have been etched into the plains; there vignetting among the foot-hills of heat-soaked mountain ranges, whose loftiest peaks are crowned with turbans of snow.

The fertile littoral and the mountainous region of Barbary, which extends as far back as the high plateau lands, are called by Arabs the *Tell*. It is a remarkably rich grain-producing country. Then comes the territory which they designate the *Sah'ra* [Sahara]—a country of vast table-lands, over which is sprinkled a veritable archipelago of oases. Here, under the shadow of their date-palms, the inhabitants grow gardens and graze flocks and herds on the open pasturages. Due to the imperfection of geographical knowledge, the name Sahara was erroneously applied by Europeans to the entire region of the Great Desert. Beyond these table-lands of the Sahara lies what, to the Arabs, is the real desert, called *Guebla*, or South, a vague term applying not only to the arid wastes which we call the Sahara, but also to its hinterland, the Sudan.

It is a mistake to consider the Desert one great waste of hot level sand. Sand there is in abundance and heat, too; but there are those rocky areas, high mountains, and table-lands, over which in the north, through the regions of Barbary, sweep the cold, penetrating winds of the African winter. Snow even has been known to fall in the highlands; but after the rains in the spring the whole country seems to burst forth in a wealth of flora.

As in Tripoli, the native races who make up the thirty to forty million people scattered over these three great natural divisions of northern Africa may be classed under the same three heads—Berbers, Arabs, and Blacks. The Berbers have settled throughout the mountains and plateau lands; the Arabs mostly in the towns and deserts, and the Blacks generally where fortune favors them most. Nearly all these people profess Mohammedanism, and intermarrying to some extent has gone on for centuries.

The Berber race is best represented in Barbary by the wild Kabyles of the Atlas, and in the heart of the Sahara by the fierce Tuaregs. Moor and Bedaween best typify the Arabs; the Moor is a town-dwelling Arab, the Bedaween a nomad. Of the Blacks there are two classes, the bond and the free.

On the rocky slopes of the mountains, among the parched, thorny shrubs, sparse tufts of rank, yellowed grass, and poisonous milk plants, can be traced the nocturnal wanderings of the hyena, by the huge doglike tracks he has left; there, too, the jackal howls as the moon lifts over a mountain crag; or the terrific roar of the lion suddenly breaks the stillness of the night, as though to shake the very mountains from their foundations and send their great boulders crushing down on some sleeping Arab *douar* [village] which, perchance, lies at their base, like a great glowworm in its stilly whiteness.

THE DESERT

In the sunshine, low down among the patches of halfa and grasses of the plains, the swallows eternally skim and the wild gazelle feeds. Here, too, the jerboa nibbles at the roots and grains, and the sand grouse and crested Desert lark hide away their nests from the watchful eyes of kites and falcons which here and there stain high against the clear vault on outstretched pinions. Now and again in barren stretches the lone sand lily nods its blossom in the soft wind, and little Desert snails hang like racemes of white flower bells to the under side of the tamarisk bushes and blades of rank Desert grass.

The daily aspect of the Sahara is the reverse of that of our country, for in the Desert the landscape is generally light against the sky, which in color so nearly complements the orange sand as to intensify greatly the contrast. When day breaks on the Sahara, the sun shoots long shafts of roseate light through the interstices of the palms; their dark red violet shadows wriggle and blend away over the gray-pinks and greens of the dew-wet sands. Soon the violet mists have turned to gold, and day has spread its brazen mantle on the sun-scorched Desert. One feels the strange weirdness, the uncanny solitude, the oppressive heat and monotony which make the day's work a constant fight against fatigue, ennui, and sometimes sun madness. Watch the sun sink and the color of its light sift through space as through gems: there, where the blue sky lowers to the hot sand, it might have filtered through some green peridot of the Levant. Such are some of the aspects of the Desert, whose charm places one under a spell which it is beyond the power of words to make real to the imagination of one who has never seen it.

It is little wonder that the ancients saw in the Sahara, dark dotted with oases, the graphic simile of the leopard's skin. The call of those limitless reaches is as subtle and insidious as must be the snow fields of the Arctic. Listening to it, one is beguiled onward against the gentle pressure of its capricious south-east breezes, under which date-palms nod their graceful crests over the murmuring oases; and to-night as I write I look out in imagination on that Leopard's Skin from under the broad lip of my sun helmet. No sound but the soft scuff of our horses and the creaking saddle leathers breaks the stillness; no shadows except our own paint splashes of azure upon the orange sand. Again white-walled, bastioned Tripoli lies many miles behind me on the edge of the coast like a great silver shell in a stretch of golden sand, and I feel that somehow I have again drawn back the veil of ages.

Oases practically determine the courses of the trade routes which for centuries have been the great arteries of the Desert, oft red-painted with the life-blood of caravans. The size of an oasis, like that of a caravan, is not a fixed quantity, but varies from a few date-palms around a Desert spring to areas over which thousands of these 'hermits," as the Arabs call the palms, raise their delicate shafts. One oasis south of Algeria contains over 280,000 trees, and the oases of Tuat, south of Morocco, cover many square miles of territory. Oases are practically all inhabited; most of them are the result of man's planting, and in many sandy regions a constant warfare must be waged by him against the encroaching sands—yes, and against men—for it is said that the most fatal disease in the Desert is the sword.

Outside the town walls and in many oases markets are held on certain days of the week. On market days, after breaking their lonely vigils on the far-off pasturages, multitudes of sombre-garbed Orientals troop in from every path, driving their flocks and herds. Here these human streams converge· toward the suks to mingle with their more brilliantly robed brethren of the towns. Inside the town gates they drift along the narrow streets, into which the sunlight sifts through a rainbow of sand dust. At these markets, town and country meet to trade—Berber, Arab, Turk, Jew, Ethiopian, and European barter their products, while Black women, their heads covered with woven plates, haggle and banter over their wares.

Water may be struck in almost any region of the Sahara and brought to the surface by artesian wells,[1] which are destined to be important factors in its development.

The presence of water there, is perhaps, not difficult to explain. One follows a river, which gradually lessens as the distance from its source increases until it is finally lost—drunk up by the

[1] Mr. Charles Robinson, the African traveller, writes of running across an artesian well in the Desert south of Tunisia. He says: "Pitched our tents at an oasis which had been formed by an artesian well constructed by M. de Lesseps, the water from which rises 25 feet in the air and is made to irrigate 400 to 500 acres of land, on which are growing date-palms, pomegranates, tomatoes, onions, and cucumbers. Previous to the construction of this well the whole of the oasis was nothing but barren sand."

sands. After disappearing, it follows underground courses and with other streams helps to
form vast subterranean lakes. Such is the case
with many rivers which flow from the southern
slopes of the Atlas. These, in all probability,
eventually find their way to that vast depression of which the salt wells of Taodeni are the
centre.

Water, of course, is an important feature of the
caravan trade. Where distances between oases
are great, Desert wells are sunk at intervals along
the trails, and in Tripolitania I have seen wells
faced with a stone curb. It is incumbent on the
last traveller who quenches his thirst in the Desert to cover the well, and failure to do so is the
greatest breach of honor and custom. However,
careless drivers do leave wells uncovered, and the
pursued will drink and then destroy the well, for
life as well as water is sweet. The next arriving
caravan finds the well filled with sand, or the
water fetid with the carcass of some dead animal;
and, in consequence, perchance another tragedy
of the Desert is written on the sands.

In some parts of the Desert, particularly in the
country of the Tuaregs, there are many hidden
wells known to them alone. These they conceal

with a cover of wood, brush, or skins, upon which they again spread the sand.

The concealment of wells in that land has become an art. The Tuaregs place secret landmarks about the Desert, and it is said they will find a hidden well within a day or two's journey from any point in the Sahara. Wells play an important part in Desert warfare, and the control of a well has more than once been the determining factor in a Desert fray, the besiegers being forced to retire for water. To wash with water in the Desert would be wilful waste to the Arab, who performs his ablutions there with sand, as his law prescribes. Since, in all lands, riches consist of the possession of that which is the greatest universal need and desire, it is not strange that, in some parts of those arid wastes, a man's wealth is reckoned by the number of wells that he controls.

Fatiguing travel and little sleep, with the relentless sun beating down from above and the everlasting, vibrating heat waves wriggling up from beneath, will, in the end, try the soul. The very watching of men and animals as, step after step, they sink ankle deep into the sand, is wearying. Sometimes it is over naked plains contain-

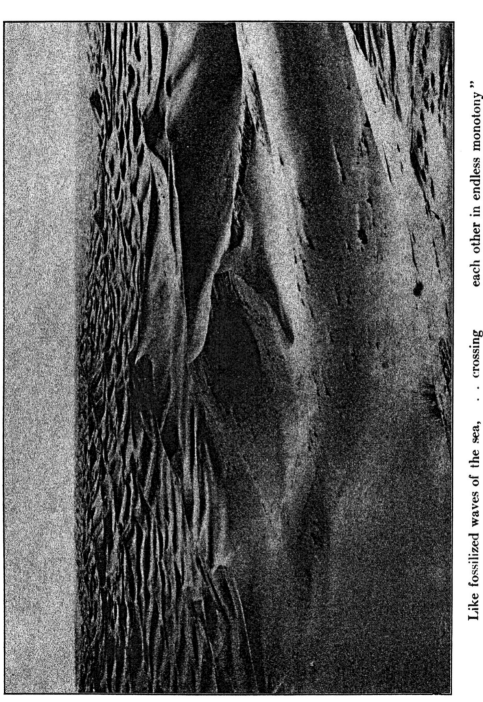

"Like fossilized waves of the sea, . . crossing each other in endless monotony"

ing nothing upon which the strained and roaming eye can rest; then, day after day, over rolling dunes of sand, unfolding, ever unfolding, phantomlike, away from one. Some take on shapes weird and picturesque: here, like fossilized waves of the sea; there, crossing and recrossing each other in endless monotony. Even its grandeur oppresses, and one feels as though a heavy curse had settled over this land, from which marvellous fables have arisen from the loneliness of its inhabitants.

Watch a light zephyr from the south-east as it playfully picks up and twirls the whiffs of sand dust swirling about legs of men and animals and stinging against their faces. Perhaps it dies down as quietly as it came; perhaps the wind increases and brings the terrific suffocating sand storm in its wake. Then after a week, perhaps, of the yellow, suffocating gloom, the surviving remnant of the caravan emerges, perchance to struggle on over a different country from that which surrounded it when the storm shut down on the landscape. From the level stretches of sand, which vary from a few feet to three hundred in depth, this wind will pile up dunes a thousand feet high; or, from those standing, it may twirl and twist out huge pillars or sand-devils—due, say the Arabs, to the caprice of passing demons.

Passing caravans always excite curiosity. A dark mass appears on the horizon; it seems to disintegrate as it comes nearer, and one soon discerns the great, lumbering camels. It may be a big trade caravan, taking the greater part of the forenoon to pass, during which the caravaneers and your men exchange news; then it passes, its tag ends flapping in the wind, for the fluttering rags of its caravaneers and the rents in the loads are the homeward-bound pennants of the north-bound trans-Saharan caravans. Perhaps the dark spot proves to be a caravan of Bedawi, who, like the will-o'-the-wisps that they are, sweep by with all their barbaric paraphernalia. Some of the women are hidden from view by wide-spreading, gaudily striped palanquins. At night they camp in a sunken spot where grow the spiny cacti and the withered camel thorn; by daybreak on the morrow they are a speck on the horizon.

The Desert as an obstacle to communication has, in many cases, been greatly exaggerated. However, the numerous bones which strew the trails bear ample evidence that the Desert, like the sea, claims its toll. Still, it is a practical and much-used highway to its several million inhabitants. The Black shepherds of the high steppes of the Adrar region, north-west of the Niger country, cross the Igidi Desert every year with their flocks, which they sell in the great markets in the oases of Tuat. In like manner, herds of cattle are driven from the south into the region of the Hoggar Tuaregs, and might easily continue north to Algeria if fodder were grown for them in the oases.

Before the advent of the draught camel into the western Sahara the ancients tell of a people called the Garamantes, who made the long trans-Saharan voyages with burden-bearing cattle; and many inscriptions, rough hewn on the Desert rocks, bear witness to the previous existence of these people.

Already the droning hum of the telegraph wire is heard in French Barbary and through certain sections of the southern and eastern Sahara; and, in Tripoli, even the unprogressive Turk has stretched a single wire six hundred miles south, connecting the sun-baked town of Murzuk with the outer world. France, with its Desert forts and systematic aggrandizement of the sands, will soon be the owner of the Sahara. Perhaps the day is not far distant when one may purchase a railroad ticket from Tangier to Timbuktu.

The central part of the Desert does not seem to have any great intrinsic value, although the high steppes between the Sahara and the Sudan could be converted into pasturages with a distinctly economic value. Such use is made of the plateau lands of northern Tripoli and southern Tunisia and Algeria. Tunisia has but a million and a half inhabitants; under the Cæsars it is said to have supported a population of twenty millions and still had enough cereals to stock Rome, acquiring, with Algeria and Tripoli, the proud distinction of being the granary of the Roman Empire.

Few now give credence to the theory that the sea once flowed over where now is the Desert, and there seems to be little doubt but that in prehistoric ages the Sahara was a veritable Garden of Eden. "Rivers which now traverse it in their underground beds originally flowed upon its surface and probably formed huge tropical streams, for unmistakable traces of the existence of still living crocodiles have been discovered within recent years in a small lake in the very heart of the Sahara."

There also seems good reason to believe that, while the Desert sands encroach northward, there is following in their wake the fertile, tropical vegetation of the Sudan—that the Sudan is encroaching on the Sahara. Thus empires depart, races dissolve, and religions change; but the great work of the Almighty on the eternal hills and trackless sands goes on.

Night everywhere transforms the commonplace into the realm of beautiful, but night on the Desert bewitches the imagination and allows all of the romance and vague fancy of one's nature to run riot. Go out after the dews have chilled the air and stand alone on the moonlit billows; hold communion with those mighty impulses which seem to issue from its sands; sound the fathomless depths of that dark blue African sky, resplendent with its million glittering stars; let your eye wander on and on over the undulating hillocks, ever rolling away to the horizon of the imagination, until the mysterious spirits of the Desert are rising dark and ghostlike out of the shades of the dunes. Then find your way back to your rug—spread, perchance, under the branches of some gnarled old olive tree—and fall asleep, to wander among the enchanted chambers of some Ali Baba, through the mysterious mazes of a thousand and one nights.

But of the morrow of the Tripolitans?

Through drought, inertia, and unbearable taxation, Tripoli's agricultural resources barely keep her inhabitants from starvation. Her caravan trade is leaking out to the south by way of the Niger, and what little intermittently trickles northward is unstable because of the insecurity of the routes. Thus the great decrease in her leading exports reflects unfavorably on the general commercial prosperity of Tripoli, but more saliently emphasizes the need of developing her agricultural resources. Turkey seems not only indifferent but averse to improvements of any kind, apparently not wishing to encourage either native or foreign interests, thereby attracting attention to the country. Yet with a jealous eye Turkey guards this province—perhaps that she may continue to squeeze from the flat, leathern money pouches of the Arabs more miserable verghi and tithes; perhaps that she may maintain a door between Constantinople and the hinter-

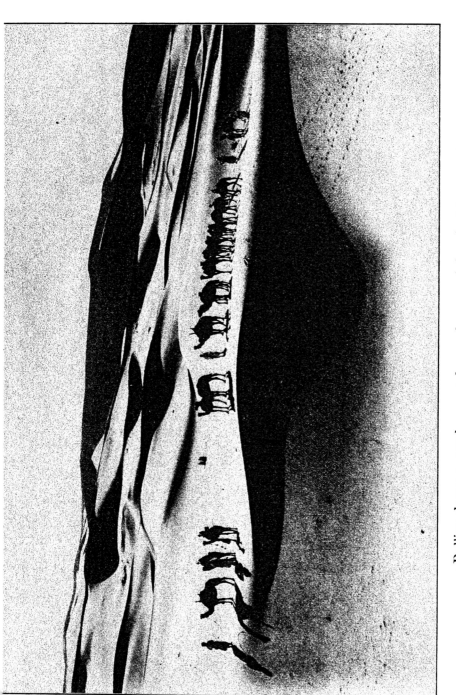

Rolling dunes o sand . . take on shapes weird and picturesque '

land of Tripoli, through which to secretly replenish her supply of slaves.

Along the rough trails back in the plateau
lands and the mountains of the Jebel Tarhuna
and the Gharian, I have occasionally run across
great broken-down coffer-dams. Along the
coast I have ridden for the greater part of a
day over the fine-crumbled remains of Roman
towns, now and again clattering over the tessellated pavement of all that was left of some Roman villa which had overlooked the blue expanse of the Mediterranean. The dams tell of
the previous conservation of vast water supplies
which once irrigated the fertile hills and plateaus upon which a great Roman and native
population depended. Other evidence is not
wanting which tells us that in those days much
of the land was thickly wooded, largely cultivated, and populated.

It is claimed that since those days great cli-
matic changes must have occurred to so alter the
face of the land and convert it to its present arid,
sun-dried condition. In those times it is said
that the rainfall was perennial—far in excess of
the present, and apparently sufficient for all
purposes of agriculture; so much so that some

modern travellers have sought to ascribe the construction of these dams to the necessity of providing against periodical inundations.

It is difficult, however, not to believe that the works in question which were thrown across wadis at different levels served as reservoirs for purposes of irrigation, as is shown to-day by the existence of remains of similar dams in eastern Palestine.

There is every reason to believe that it will be a Christian European power which will open for the Tripolitan that sesame which will arouse him from his inertia and usher him into fields where he will take new heart and courage; and Tripoli will be reclaimed from the Desert, not so much through the reconstruction of the coffer-dam of the Roman as by that modern agency, the artesian well.

Virtuous Europe no longer steals Africans from Africa. Her civilization, honesty, and hu manitarianism have frowned upon that; so now she reverses the order of things and steals Africa from the Africans.

A little over twenty years ago, just as Italy was spreading her wings over Tunisia, France alighted on the quarry. Chagrined and angered, Italy turned her attention to Tripolitania, a garden plot at her very back door, where to-day, next to Turkey, her interests and influence unquestionably predominate. To make future occupation secure, however, Italy must make some tacit arrangement with France for a free hand, and prevail upon the other Powers to admit her interests there; perhaps she has. It is to be hoped, however, that the accession of Mehemed V. to the Sultanate of Turkey is the beginning of a new and better order of things, for both Turkey and her colonies.

Whatever happens, Hadji Mohammed will but wrap his baracan more closely about him and mutter, "Fate is irrevocable; to oppose destiny is sacrilege. Allah, Allahu!"

CHAPTER FIFTEEN

LIBIA ITALIANA

ONE mid-afternoon Tripoli lay shimmering in white, peacefully basking under the glare of the North African sun, gleaming from skies of clearest blue. Through her streets and suks the quiet drone of voices and soft scuff of sandalled feet bespoke the peaceful industry of the townsman who sold and of the country-man who came in to buy. Outside the walls little was astir in the Tuesday Market and the near-by fondūks, while the tillers of soil and drawers of water in the oasis and the neighboring wadan worked to inveigle the sandy soil beneath the palms or in the open reaches into a more abundant yield. In fact, peace reigned in Tripoli, just as it had within the memory of the third and fourth generations.

The sun had begun to tinge to saffron and the shadow of the Old Castle to paint its way in blue across the little garden of the Turkish

Army and Navy Club. The long, level edge of the horizon was broken by a humping line of imposing Italian battle-ships under slow headway.

Boom! a column of white smoke belched from where a hostile shell struck the Spanish fort. Thus "the progressive aggression of" a "Christian power" began, and the cabled news of the daily paper hastily announced: "Tripoli Taken. The Last Ottoman Rule in Africa at an End."

This was October 3, 1911. A Christian European power had got in its deadly work. The city was demoralized, and within a month, in the little garden of the Turkish Army and Navy Club, where we Christians—European and American—as well as Jew and Greek, through the courtesy of the Turks, had sipped mastica and drunk coffee, Arabs now drank unflinchingly the cup of death and spilled their red blood against the blue walls of the Old Castle. The graceful palms of the oasis waved over devastated gardens and sands red-drenched with the blood of the Bedawi and Arab farmers; cholera, introduced from Italy, decimated the rest, those escaping being driven into the Desert.

In seeking the cause one is led into the seemingly inextricable yet fascinating maze of European politics. Almost day by day that mysterious European equilibrator, the balance of power, is insidiously shifting, in which the control of the Mediterranean and its littoral will ever be an important factor. Britain's control of Gibraltar, Malta, and Cyprus, the building of the Suez Canal, the crossing of the Frank into North Africa, the bottling of Russia at the Bosphorus, all have a direct effect on the *status quo* and were interwoven in the European-Mediterranean policies and in certain subsequent treaties, more particularly the Berlin Treaty of 1878, the Anglo-French Treaty of 1904, the Algeciras Conference, and the late Franco-German Treaty.

Those new motive powers of steam and electricity, the parents of machinery, applied science, and organization, have, through transportation and communication, bound the nations in a world-wide network of intercourse and exchange, and thus have made the cause of national developments and ambitions essentially industrial. In their understanding, development, and vigorous application, Germany has shown herself most scientific and efficient. Her neighbors, Italy and Austria-Hungary, awakening to a national consciousness, were essentially in the same situation regarding the necessity for colonies and their inability to acquire them, so, in 1882, occurred the creation of the Triple Alliance of Germany, Austria-Hungary, and Italy, primarily as a check to Russia and France, for they found little colonial territory left and most of that marked "reserved" by France, Great Britain, and Russia.

The Triple Alliance gave Germany allies having a sea frontage on the Mediterranean or its arms, an important feature in war or where naval prestige counted in the Mediterranean or policies affecting its command. No single member of the Triple Alliance could go the pace against the other great powers. Not only was Germany anxious to counterplay the French scheme of an African empire but also French aspirations of converting the Mediterranean into a French lake.

So it was not strange that the Berlin Treaty recognized certain Mediterranean aspirations of Austria and Italy. Austria's territorial possibilities lay to her south; Italy's toward that ancient granary of the Romans, Tunisia and Tripolitania—market gardens at her kitchen door. Tunisia had irretrievably gone to France just as Italy was reaching for it, so, disappointed, Italy naturally turned her attention to Tripolitania, where her interests, though small, predominated over any other European country except one—Turkey—the owner and sovereign power of Tripolitania. This fact complicated Italy's cause. Tripoli would have been more easily plucked had it been under an independent bey, as was Tunisia, or a heterodoxy of warring tribes under a nominal sultan, as was Morocco. But certain "powers" owning North African colonies containing millions of Mohammedans as subjects, with the Sultan of Turkey as their spiritual head, were not anxious to have "The Sick Man of Europe" stirred from his lethargy, arouse Islam and possibly leave a Holy War upon their hands.

Even Germany, at heart, by reason of her prestige and friendship with Turkey and her desired Turkish concessions and interests, had no desire to encourage her ally and was not averse to acquiring a slice of Tripoli for herself. War in Tripoli, too, might reopen the entire

Mediterranean problem and even the Turkish question itself.

At the extreme east of Tripoli, within eighty miles of the Egyptian frontier, lay a large, sheltered bay where the golden sands of the Desert mingled in emerald with the sapphire of the Mediterranean. On its shores clustered a few Arab houses on whose white walls the swaying date palms brushed their blue-violet shadows. Such was sequestered Tobruk, and Great Britain was pleased that it was so, for it did not take the practised eye of an engineer to see that Tobruk Bay could be converted into a second Biserta and become one of the greatest naval harbors of the Middle Sea.

Just prior to Italy's attack, the rumor gained strength that certain portions of the eastern section of Tripolitania, known as Barca (Cyrenaica), including Tobruk Bay, were about to be leased to Germany by Turkey. This may have had much to do with Great Britain's conceding Italy's position, for Tobruk in the possession of Italy, while strengthening the naval power of the Triple Alliance in the Mediterranean, would be the lesser of two evils. But Great Britain, through Kitchener, promptly counteracted this by shoving that movable quantity, a European-North African frontier, as many miles toward Tobruk as it could, saving the port of Sollom to Egypt and thus in a large measure neutralizing the menace of an Italian Biserta at Tobruk which might eventually have placed Alexandria at the mercy of the fleets of the Triple Alliance.

This rumor, too, may have precipitated Italy's action in her attack on Tripoli. But there were other impelling forces, possibly the faith in the old shibboleth that "trade follows the flag," for Italy, in 1870, saw the dawn of an Italian economic renaissance. It is, perhaps, the craze for conquest in Africa which has distinguished chiefly the successive administrations at Rome —stimulated and almost brought to a culmination by the greatest Italian statesman of his time, Crispi. The spirit he had stimulated and the effect of the propaganda he had so definitely launched continued to whet the Italian appetite for colonial extension.

It has been claimed that Italy was moved to launch her Tripoli adventure by certain advances and promises of the Triple Entente, possibly in thus awarding her this Desert which nobody

General Caneva proclaiming the sovereignty of Italy in the courtyard of the Castle

seemed to want, to offset the German move regarding Tobruk and so win Italy's favor and thus weaken her loyalty to the Triple Alliance, as the younger member of which she had fallen heir to nothing. Austria had acquired Herzegovina and Bosnia, which Italy desired for herself, and some considered Italy's coup a reprisal for this much coveted. territory.

Italy had seen Germany reach a number of times into the African grab-bag, and, following the sudden, unwarranted occupation of Fez by France, now, with the *Panther's* sudden spring at Agadir, making a fair bid for a slice of Morocco. If Italy was to have anything she must take it, and there could not be a better time than when Germany and France were in dead-lock over the Moroccan situation, for Germany, having less in compensation from Italy than Austria, might less readily sustain the Latins. Although France had undoubtedly given Italy a "hands-off" assurance regarding Tripolitania, Italy had reason to know how little French North African promises redounded to the benefit of the promisee. So Italy reached out across the Mediterranean, seized the psychological moment with one hand and Tripoli with the other.

Italy had, with patient impatience, kept vigil across the Adriatic on the derelict Ottoman Empire, watching its decay, but the moment of dissolution failed to come. Italy, like the rest of Europe, had confounded the Turkish people with its sovereign and the energy of Turkey with the acts of its government, and so, after a lethargy of half a century, the "Sick Man," through the ministrations of the Young Turk Party and the Committee of Union and Progress, turned over, sat up in bed, and, after being fed again on the spirit and traditions of Suleiman Pasha, the first conqueror of Roumelia, astonished Italy and the rest of the world with the proof that it was and probably would remain a European nation and power.

Turkey, convalescing rapidly, augmented her army and planned to enlarge her naval programme. This carried out would enable Turkey to transport troops and war supplies to her Tripolitan colony and to interfere with the transportation of those of Italy, and, above all things, would interfere with Italy's conquest of that territory.

By progressing, Turkey not only made the taking of Tripolitania more difficult for Italy but committed an unpardonable act against the foreign powers, and in valiant little Turkey's rapid convalescence lay the impelling motive of Italy's sudden move. She included both her note of complaint and ultimatum in the same official capsule which she handed Turkey. The complaint alleged certain indiscretions, claiming that all enterprise on the part of Italians in the regions mentioned (Tripoli and Cyrenaica) "has been systematically opposed and unjustifiably crushed," and the Italian Government, "having the intention henceforth to protect its interests and its dignity, has decided to proceed to the military occupation of Tripoli and Cyrene"—a case of heads I win, tails you lose. Such was the bitter pill which Italy handed to Turkey, giving her twenty-four hours in which to take it.

Turkey in vain sought a more homœopathic treatment through the powers and court of arbitration at The Hague, assuring Italy of her willingness to make any just reparation were the charges proved. But the court physicians of Europe were busy with other things and the soothsayers of The Hague were "not at home," so, on October 3, Italy proceeded to administer the dose, overlooking the most difficult part of the operation—holding Turkey's nose—and Italy, after years of careful planning, launched into a war for a Desert.

It was little to be wondered at that during my sojourn in that romantic land I was not only frankly accused of being a spy by certain members of the European chancellories, but as such was under constant surveillance by the Turks until my delightful associations with Rejed Pasha, the Military Governor. The fact that I was an American and had no political axe to grind did away to a great extent with that suspicion.

The Turks knew of Italy's methods and that she was constantly sending spies, commercial and political agents to Tripolitania, under the guise of merchants and scientists, to investigate the problems and possibilities and to map out the country; that the Banco di Roma had established branches in Tripoli and Benghazi to systematically buy Arab farm lands from the impoverished peasants for a few lire per hectare, which ultimately quadrupled in value at the landing of the first Italian soldier; and that inducements were offered Jews—in whose hands was the bulk of the country's trade—to become Italian subjects, thus furthering Italy's plans for the foundation of her claims of important interests in Tripoli.

Little wonder was it that certain scientific expeditions were not permitted and certain Italian business enterprises not encouraged. Furthermore, Turkey well knew that the least pretext of harm to an Italian citizen might be seized upon as a *casus belli*. So great care was exercised in the protection of the few hundreds of Italians resident in Tripoli, particularly when certain Italian correspondents were sent there, some months before hostilities broke out, and carried on an insidious newspaper campaign against Tripoli, magnifying unimportant incidents.

Regardless of the merits of the dispute, Italy's aggression upon Turkey in Tripoli, particularly the act and manner of opening the war, was in disregard of The Hague conventions, to which she was a party. Neither can the stigma of this disturbance of the peace of the world rest lightly on those governments which readily consented to recognize the annexation of the territory in Tripoli, without first insisting on reference of the dispute to arbitration. From a moral view-point, Italy had no justification for attacking Turkey in Tripoli.

Politically, Italy was justified even more than her European neighbors in thrusting her hand into the African grab-bag. Besides a common cause, the success of her newly developed army and the extension of a new Italy—an Italian empire—would do much toward welding together the disconnected elements of the Italian nation.

From a military stand-point, Italy's move was an admirable one. Turkey was resting on German assurance against attack, there was an interim between governors in Tripoli, and Europe was looking the other way, and so there was spread out before us a two years' wild and blood-letting campaign. Within forty-eight hours the coast of Tripoli was blockaded. The only Turkish vessel on the entire coast of Tripolitania was the old garrison ship *Seyadiderya*, which, covered with barnacles, had been swinging for years at her chains in Tripoli harbor.

Turkey's entire navy comprised on paper about five old battle-ships, a first-class cruiser, and some twenty smaller craft, as against Italy's seven modern battle-ships, five older ones, seven first-class cruisers, and one hundred and fifty-six smaller vessels. Such conditions did not permit the consideration of a naval programme on the part of Turkey, except to keep the few ships she had dodging about the shoals and islands of the Ægean Sea or to send them through the Dardanelles scooting for Scutari.

For three days an Italian torpedo-boat came and went under a flag of truce, each time demanding that the Turkish authorities surrender Tripoli and each time receiving the same courteous but firm reply from the Turkish commander that he had no authority to act as the cable had been cut. The Turks requested to be allowed to use the wireless of the admiral's warship, but when the Turkish officers arrived aboard they were in turn politely but forcibly told it was time for action and not for words. Meantime, however, before the bombardment began, the Turks had run the blockade with the *Derna*, under the very nose of the Italian fleet, succeeded in discharging her cargo of war munitions, and then scuttled and sank her; likewise the old Turkish gunboat *Seyadiderya*.

The city of Tripoli, the headquarters of the Turkish military and the capital of the provinces, was the natural centre of attack and subsequently formed the base of operations for the Italians. The defences were most inadequate, for, besides small, ineffective batteries at the Hamediah and Sultana forts on the coast, respectively to the east and west of the town, there were only the inadequate bastion walls of the Castle, when the blockade began at sundown the night of September 30.

The Turkish commander-in-chief, Nechet Bey, an able officer and a man of strong character, well knew the defence of Tripoli was impossible. A single Italian battle-ship could have wrecked the city without a shell of the meagre Turkish batteries ever reaching her. Consequently, a gun's battery or two of Turkish soldiers were left to draw the Italians' fire, while the entire Turkish force evacuated the city and took with them their supplies, including the *Derna's* cargo, and withdrew into the Desert. Before withdrawing it would have been good strategy and a justifiable military move to have razed Tripoli to the ground with fire and bomb, thereby leaving to the Italian soldiery a heap of smouldering ruins for barracks. In fact, this move was undoubtedly contemplated, and only through the secret meeting at night of certain members of the consular corps was Nechet Bey prevailed upon to relinquish this plan. Naturally, there was some looting by Desert Arabs who had worked into the town, but European residents of Tripoli were protected to the best of the Turks' ability, and later by the Arab police under the chief of police, Hassuna Pasha, of whom we shall hear more.

The Italian forces, under General Caneva, were soon ensconced in the town and among the palm groves, secure behind intrenchments, wire fences, batteries of machine guns, search-lights, and, to a great extent, under the guns of their battle-ships. Where the oasis edged the Desert, two miles eastward as far as Sciara-el-Sciut, they maintained a nerve-racking, defensive campaign. Beyond, somewhere in the Desert, were the Turks and Arabs, ever watchful for an opportunity to rise like phantoms from the sand-dunes and pounce upon the intruders; thus were the benefits of civilization bestowed upon Tripoli.

France, in her North African wars, had a country infinitely more fertile, mountainous, and with water supplies, inhabited by a people divided to some extent by internecine strife; from the start she was able to enlist many of these, and any one familiar with French North African history knows the important part Zouaves, Spahis, and Tirailleurs played, and still play, in the maintenance of the tricolor there. Both France and Great Britain in their North African conquests fought against natives unused to organized warfare, with practically no modern weapons or artillery and ignorant of the outside world.

The Turks had armed the majority of the Arabs with breech-loading rifles. With the Turkish troops as a nucleus, the Arabs, to some extent organized, carried out plans carefully arranged by the Turkish officers. Many of these officers were educated at the best military schools in Europe, knew internal Italian sentiment and financial resources, and, through that wonderful, mysterious "grape-vine telegraph" of Mohammedan countries, had their fingers on the pulse of Europe.

Great Britain in its Egyptian conquests had the Nile and the Nile Valley for its highway and subsistence, making possible a very definite and systematic control of the territory acquired by

the advancing troops. Italy, from a geograph-
ical-military point of view, had the most difficult of any European-North African campaign.
She had to land her troops on the edge of a
great desert without a navigable river, whose
sands, and clayey or rocky soil spread in hot,
shimmering, limitless reaches. Tripolitania, comprising the provinces of the Vilayet of Tripoli,
Fezzan, and Barca, and the recently annexed
region including Tibesti and the Bilma Oases,
totals an area nearly half that of the United
States.

Tripoli, the city, it must be remembered, is on
the edge of the Desert, in an oasis of palm-trees
running a mile back from the water's edge and
stretching five miles or so along the coast mostly
eastward of the city. The Italian navy co-
operated and covered the landing of the troops
at Tripoli, Benghazi, Derna, and a number of
the smaller coast towns such as Khoms, Tobruk, Zuara, Zan-Zur, Zleiten, Zafran. At
Benghazi and Derna there was desperate fighting before the actual occupation occurred. But
the Desert wilderness lay ahead, stretching for
fifteen hundred miles to the undefined boundary of the Fezzan.

Only certain sand-blown or clayey, rocky trails of a few trade caravans were available routes for penetration into the Tripolitan Sahara. Thus the opportunity for strategy by an invading army was limited. The character of the Tripolitan Sahara greatly interfered with flank movements, rear attacks, deploying, or work in any extended open order by the heavily accoutred invading army, yet all these military phases could be carried out to advantage by the Turks with the assistance of the lightly accoutred Desert Arabs versed in Desert life and warfare.

Furthermore, the invading army would have to follow the depressions and valley ways of the sand-dunes of almost dust-like fineness into which the weary troops, under a scorching sun, sank ankledeep at every step, practically prohibiting marching in column formation. The winding route would shut one section from view of the other, placing the invading forces in an exceptionally disadvantageous position to repel sudden onslaught.

The only available means of Italian transport would be the army mule; but the camel is the only animal in Tripolitania adaptable to Desert transport, and every camel worth taking was well behind the Turkish lines. Even water would have had to be carried over certain portions of the march, not to mention ammunition supplies and light artillery. Without adequate transport, the campaign into the interior was impracticable. Even under the most favorable conditions there was always that terror of the Desert, the sand-storm, brought by the gibli, which has taken its toll of many a caravan as the white-bleached bones of the death-strewn trails bear witness. Visions of Adowa, too, undoubtedly made Italy cautious, with the result that the army of over one hundred thousand men sat down on the edge of the Desert in the coast towns and oases.

Her plan of letting the enemy attack at her strongly intrenched bases of supplies, where she was under the protection of the guns of her battle-ships, was the most effective way to deplete the enemy's strength. However, the advisability may be questioned of keeping a force infinitely superior numerically, as well as in point of equipment and organization, on a defensive campaign for over a year on the outskirts of a vast territory. To the troops in trenches the cold winds and rains which swept down from the Mediterranean in the winter season, and the chill of nights with the sudden changes to the baking heat of mid-day and the sand-filled winds, were all nerve-racking and demoralizing to health. Those long vigils at the edge of the shadowy palms caused desert phantoms to rise out of the sands. But those in the field have pointed out that, outside of the occasional skirmish or pitched battle, the Italian troops did not have to endure the extreme hardship of an aggressive campaign.

The provisioning and sanitary arrangements were far better than during the annual military manœuvres at home. At night the cafés were run as gayly as in Naples; moving-picture shows filled the hearts of the soldiers with delight and the pockets of the proprietors with centesimi. One novel feature was an advertisement in Naples for all friends and relatives—sweethearts and wives in particular—to pass in review before a motion camera. The film shortly appearing in Tripoli proved a bonanza, as the place in which it was shown was daily and nightly packed with soldiers anxious to pick familiar faces from the passing throng on the screen. Even tanks of wine were shipped to Tripoli for the troops, which calls forcibly to mind the fact that the Turks and Arabs, through religious precepts, are total abstainers, which undoubtedly has much to do with their superb fighting ability and powers of endurance.

The men out in the oasis, off duty, made the short trip to town with its amusements, while the spirit of art, so strong in the Italian nature, was manifested in numerous ways—among the most interesting was the fashioning of miniature castles and ramparts ingeniously sculptured from the wet sand on the sunny days of the rainy season. But fifty thousand troops and the thousands of civilians who followed them could not be unloaded with impunity into a desert city of forty thousand, with its scant water supply and poor sanitary arrangements. Soon not only typhoid but that dreaded scourge of the Orient, cholera, brought from Italy, broke out. Both permanent hospitals and the camp hospitals formerly belonging to the Turks, with over one thousand beds, were soon filled, and then began a regular monthly migration of the very bad cases back to the hospitals of Sicily, Naples, and Tuscany, averaging two thousand a month.

Not only Tripoli, but Khoms, Benghazi, Derna, and Tobruk had been taken early in the war but no advances undertaken. Italy pursued a policy of waiting, and even nearly a year and a half after the war had begun was still only along the littoral, where she was forced to maintain five thousand men at Khoms, twenty-five thousand at Benghazi, seventeen thousand divided between Derna and Tobruk, and about fifty thousand at Tripoli and vicinity, an army of over one hundred thousand provided not only with inexhaustible munitions of war but greater luxuries than any army which we can call to mind ever had while engaged in a serious campaign.

Turn to the Turks and Arabs somewhere beyond the sand-dunes in the Desert wilderness. On paper, Turkey was supposed to have maintained an army of twenty thousand men in Tripoli, but to my knowledge the actual force did not exceed ten thousand men and, a few months prior to Italy's attack, half this contingent had been despatched to Yemen, Arabia, to put down an Arab uprising there, leaving in Tripolitania a meagre contingent of five thousand poorly clad, underpaid Turks to protect

the province and to face a great modern army
of over one hundred thousand

Italy firmly believed her show of military
force would not only impress the Arab and alien-
ate him from his Turkish conquerors, but ally
him to the Italian cause. Italy failed, however,
to understand the Arab mind or that spiritual
bond of Pan-Islamic union, and was bitterly
disappointed that the Arabs failed to welcome
her troops as liberators from the Turks. It
was but natural that a courageous and charac-
terful people like the Arabs should prefer to
side with their coreligionists and still recognize
Mehmed V, Caliph of all Islam, temporal and
spiritual head of two hundred and twenty million Moslems. So the Turkish forces were augmented by the Arab constabulary, formerly used
to patrol the coast routes, the Kol-oglu, a sort
of Arab militia organized under Arab chiefs,
and the larger contingent of Arab farmers of
the wadan, a contingent numbering, perhaps,
forty thousand, admittedly some of the finest
fighting material in the world, with wonderful
mobility, powers of endurance, and that valuable
asset, knowledge of the great Desert.

Then there was that ultra-Mohammedan secret sect, the Senūsi, whose influence the French found so hard to combat in North Africa. This sect had its origin in Tripoli, and its great central headquarters in the interior of the Libyan Desert in the wonderful Kufra Oases. Among many tales, fascinating and weird, it has been rumored by some authors that no non-Mohammedan could ever enter and return alive from their towns, within whose confines were vast arsenals for the manufacture of war munitions, to be used ultimately to repel and drive out the Christian from North Africa. While some writers will recount in a positive manner these facts, they inconsistently admit that the secrecy of this order has never been penetrated by an "infidel."

That valiant officer, Enver Bey—now commander-in-chief of the Turkish army—part Turk, part Arab, in whose veins flows blood of the famous Abd-el-Kadir, undoubtedly drew from that sect and the Kufra Oases much of the Arab contingent which fought the Italian troops so bitterly in Barca. At certain strategic points the Turks have Desert forts; at these and certain oases they encamped, established behind their lines field-hospitals and a daily caravan

service which brought food supplies from cultivated spots. A telegraph was strung east and
west, practically the length of Tripoli, and at the
western end, at Ouezzen, it was but six kilometres to the French Tunisian town of Dehibat,
on the boundary, and through this transfer by
runner undoubtedly many messages were transmitted.

The Draken balloon proved a valuable ad-
junct in directing the fire both of the navy and
army. In this war the aeroplane made its
début under fire, both monoplanes and biplanes
proving their worth in locating the enemy. In
fact, the Battle of the Oasis of October 23 to
26 would undoubtedly have resulted even more
direfully for the Italians but for the ascent
of a balloon on the 23d and the unexpected locating of the Turkish and Arab forces almost
within striking distance of the city. The automobile, too, has played its part well. At Zan-
Zur the dead and wounded were removed from
the field of battle by two auto ambulances, and
automobiles were constantly seen in and about
Tripoli as ambulances and couriers and convey-
ing supplies; while the first entrance to Ghadāmes, when that city opened its gates to

Italy, was made by Captain Pavoni by automobile, double rear tires being used over the sands.

Practically throughout the entire war the conquering army was besieged on the coast, affected by sickness, and fed from home. Italy was forced to seek reprisals along the Turkish coasts to induce Turkey to close the issue in Tripoli, indicating she had failed in her purpose to seize Tripolitania and oust Turkey by a sudden, powerful move. The Turkish commander in Tripoli conducted, under tremendously disadvantageous conditions, a remarkable military campaign. Severe engagements occurred with large losses on both sides. Yet Turkey consistently refused to sue for peace, and Italy, and later the Balkans, had it very definitely impressed upon them that they were fighting the great-great-grandchildren of those who had defeated the Allied Armies of Europe, the conquerors of the days of Necopolis, Varna, Kossovo, and St. Syndigi, those who vanquished the Knights, Hunyadi, and others, but who, as *Le Jeune Turc* expressed it, "are novices in the application of this new régime, because, after six years of absolutism and thirty-two years of

a terrible despotism, we have only three years
of parliamentary experience.

One late afternoon, over a year after hostilities had begun, at the hour when the tables
on the verandas of the Beau Rivage Palace Hotel
at Ouchy were filled with guests at afternoon tea
and the orchestra enlivened the scene by the
strains of a waltz, the Turkish and Italian peace
delegates passed through the gay crowd, after
one hundred days of arduous work conciliating
two extremes, and affixed their signatures to
the preliminaries of a peace treaty. But after
all, it had taken the foreboding shadow of the
Balkan War to force Turkey's hand and obtain
her signature to the Peace of Lausanne.

However, Italy's policy was to keep the Tripolitan question distinct from the complex Balkan problem. Italy had need of Turkey's good-
will and that of the Arabs in the new régime
in Tripoli, not to mention its relations to her
Levant trade, and, technically and politically,
Italy acquired the Hesperidian apple of her
dreams—Tripoli in Barbary.

Turkey could not, according to the Koran,
recognize the cession of Mussulman territory
to the infidels and did not recognize Italy's con-

quest. Consequently, according to the terms of the treaty, Turkey did not impose Italy's rule on her subjects, but, on the other hand, did not impugn it. She simply ignored it, granted autonomy to Tripolitania, and left it to its destiny; but with the proviso of free exercise of religious authority by the Caliph.

In place of the call of the Turkish sentry on the Castle ramparts, to which I had so often listened in the garden of the Turkish Army and Navy Club, when guard was changed, peace was proclaimed on October 20, 1912, also from the top of the fountain southeast of the Castle, and the decree of King Emmanuel solemnly confirmed Italian sovereignty over Tripolitania and Cyrenaica. Turkey agreed to withdraw her regular troops from Tripolitania, discountenance every and any assistance which Ottoman subjects might give to the Arabs, assume responsibility for every form of contraband of Ottoman subjects in Tripolitania, and make certain guarantees for the Christian peoples of the islands of the Ægean. It was the last ebb of the great tidal wave of the Jehad which had once flooded over half of Europe, reaching the very gates of Poitiers. On November 5, Royal

LIBIA ITALIANA

Decree annexed Tripolitania and Cyrenaica to Italy and christened it under its ancient name of Libia, and the Turk passed from Africa.

CHAPTER SIXTEEN

THE PRICE OF A COLONY

WE find Italy now possessed of a wild desert province with its burdens and responsibilities. But at what a price! Besides her original war cost, Italy must return the islands of the Ægean to Turkey; instead of an indemnity from Turkey, which was expected, the treaty terms entirely absolved Turkey from such payment, and Italy agreed to pay an amount equal to the value of all government properties which existed in Tripoli before the war as well as that part of the Ottoman debt guaranteed by Tripoli's revenues, deducting from this sum the cost of maintenance of the several thousand Turkish prisoners.

The Ottomans have effected by the terms of this treaty a most profitable real-estate transaction, for, aside from Italy's payments, Turkey is released from the maintenance of troops in a non-profitable province; these troops she can use to strengthen her army at home, which she is fast reorganizing under the new German régime. Turkey can now concentrate her whole attention on the maintenance of her connected empire, which, even eliminating the territory lost during the Balkan War, has a maximum width equal to the distance between Cape Hatteras and Los Angeles, with a coast line equal to that of the United States, without the peninsula of Florida, and a boundary line almost equal to the maximum combined length and width of the continent of Africa.

The cost of war is not to be reckoned alone in terms of money. The killing off of the large proportion of the flower of the nation for both victor and vanquished, the withdrawing of labor for military purposes, the disorganization of commerce, the suffering and hatreds engendered and the long aftermath needing recuperation, are only part of its toll. In consideration of the money cost of the Turco-Italian War, Turkey was under but a nominal expense. At the beginning, certain Italian newspapers estimated the war cost to Italy at $20,000,000, but within a year the special war fund of $150,000,-000 had been sunk in the sands of Tripoli; the people, already taxed four times as much as any other country in Europe, had additional tithes saddled upon them, and only on last New Year's Day (1914) advices from Tripoli told of nearly one hundred Italian casualties in one fight on those burning wastes.

It is reasonable to assume that the cost to Italy of the Tripoli campaign amounts to at least $220,000,000, and a year and a half after the war had begun and half a year after the peace treaty an additional $20,000,000 was appropriated to carry on the war with Tripoli. While we know little of the expenses of the past fifteen months, the total expenditure will probably eventually reach $300,000,000.

The monthly mortality rate rapidly rose from twenty-eight per one hundred thousand men from illness before the war to one hundred and thirty, and official statistics admit that during the first twelve months nearly twenty-four thousand were sent home, that nearly one thousand five hundred were killed in battle, and over four thousand two hundred wounded: during the first fifteen months nearly two thousand died by sickness and nearly one thousand in 1913, while in the ten months preceding August,

1913, twenty thousand sick were repatriated—totalling fifty-two thousand seven hundred casualties. However, so far as can be ascertained, no list of cases cured in Tripolitania has ever been published, and whereas the war in Tripolitania lasted over two years and is still (1914) going on in the hinterland, there are no statistics of those dead and wounded during the last ten months of the struggle. Subsequent to the peace proclamation some of the fiercest battles were fought, and conditions would point to the fact that Italy has paid the enormous toll of nearly eighty thousand casualties. The permanent loss to the commercial productive power of the country, through these, would directly and indirectly reach some stupendous total.

Considering $300,000,000 within the probable money expenditure for the last three years and a half, it would be necessary to add fully as much again in the near future, to construct dams, sink wells, improve harbors, construct roads and buildings, maintain an army, and develop the country generally before it is in working shape, which would give a total money expenditure of at least $600,000,000.

The interest accruing on the war expendi-

ture, as well as that on the development investment, would formidably raise the expenditure
and go far to swell the world's money cost of
war and armaments during the last fifteen years,
which has been estimated at $5,500,000,000.
One cannot but regret that Italy could not
have expended this cost in developing her unproductive regions, in lightening the burdens
of her overtaxed people and investing it in her
educational and commercial system.

For nearly thirty years prior to the war
Tripoli had a total average annual commerce
of about $4,000,000, a mere bagatelle, exports
and imports balancing with remarkable regularity, sponges, esparto grass (from which paper is
made), and the caravan trade forming seven-
tenths of the export trade, the other three-
tenths being made up of the products of the
oases and live stock brought to the coast-town
suks. The sponge industry can hardly be called
indigenous, the esparto grass is becoming scarcer
and its sale affected by wood pulp from Norway
and North America, while the caravan trade
with the Sudan is practically extinct and now
leaks out by way of the Niger, so that Italy
goes into a country which, at the time of her

Arab constabulary under Hassuna Pasha who have been enlisted in the Italian service

occupation, presented a meagre export trade of $600,000, and we may well ask what will she do with it.

That will depend primarily on labor, for which she has three natural sources upon which to draw—Italians, Maltese, and Tripolitans. The several thousand Maltese will naturally confine themselves mostly to the coast interests, so that they would be very useful as fishermen, lightermen, and stevedores. But the country depends fundamentally on agricultural and pastoral development, which in turn will be dependent upon the native Tripolitan and the Italian immigrant. It is estimated that over that great territory of Tripolitania there are scattered possibly a million inhabitants, the greater proportion being wild, independent nomadic Desert tribes. Many of the population, however, are agriculturalists, such as the Bedaween and the Arabs of the wadan, both of the more fertile coast strip, while the tribes of the Weled-bu-Zef and Orfella are great camel raisers.

It is upon this coast strip that Italy must depend, from forty to ninety miles in width and lying between the coast and the Tripoli Hills and comprising some four hundred thousand square miles of land, much of which can be used; but the unwise and indiscriminate slaughter of numbers of Arab farmers and Bedaween of this littoral not only greatly depleted the labor supply upon which Italy could have drawn but left a hatred and resentment rankling in the survivors which will undoubtedly affect the labor question. Only last year a large migration to Tunisia occurred, including thousands of Tripolitan agriculturalists. Inducements offered by a special commission of Italians sent to meet them at the border failed to stem the tide. Latest reports indicate that over forty thousand Tripolitans have migrated to Tunisia from the coast region of Tripoli alone and many other nomadic agriculturalists may prefer to withdraw to the innermost oases of the Libyan Desert or to the Nile Valley. Many, however, will remain and after a generation or two may be induced to "take up the shovel and the hoe" in the most approved Italian agricultural methods.

But it is upon the Italian emigrants that Tripolitan development must depend, and they should be picked for energy, sobriety, and farsightedness. But special inducements will probably be offered by Italy favoring cheap labor and, in many cases, perhaps the least desirable and least trained men, and difficulties will arise when these men labor side by side with the Arab, and the prestige of Rome will stand for naught. If there is but little Italian emigration, Libia will be a white elephant on Italy's hands, and foreign money will not be invested. Italy is overpopulated, not per capita to the square mile, but because so much of her country is not inhabited owing to the rough mountain lands. One of Italy's primary motives for her aggression was to obtain Tripolitania as an outlet for this surplus population; but it is all-important that the administration of this colony be eliminated from a cramping, hard-and-fast rack-and-ruin policy of centralization that swells and eddies about Rome.

Italy, politically and economically, was justified in seeking a new colony. The question of her wisdom lies in her choice and methods of obtaining it. But of the three hundred thousand Italians who emigrate from her shores annually, mainly to the United States and South America, how many will prefer to be diverted from those fertile lands—where comparatively high wages and ultimate success are assured—to the sunscorched Desert reaches of Tripoli to indulge in an agricultural undertaking which must, at least for some years to come, be an experiment. In fact, one direct result of the war has been the hard times in Italy, and that this condition has been foreseen by the laboring classes is evidenced from the fact that during the last six months of 1913 over one million immigrants left Italy; but, to the dismay of the Italian Government, their destinations were North and South America, save for a few thousands who straggled down to the new colony. The question of labor for many years will be one of the great problems confronting Italy and her new colonial venture.

Let Italy learn of her Roman forebears how they caused the Desert to blossom like the rose and made the region now known as Algeria, Tunisia, and Tripolitania famous as the granary of the Roman Empire. The crumbled remnants of Roman civilization with tessellated pavements of Roman villas laid down two thousand years ago, over which my horses clattered on my journey to Khoms, and the ruins of the ancient coffer-dams of the Cæsars in the low a vast population. To-day these scant remnants are revealed by the blowing away of the Desert sand, where the only inhabitant is the Bedaween, and in place of the call of the Roman guard at night, the weird howl of a Bedaween's dog, the jackal's yelp, or the idiotic laugh of the hyena greets the moon and echoes over the broad reaches or amongst the mountain crags.

The first requirement, then, in Tripoli's agricultural development is water, for the soil watered will cause an abundant yield from even the wind-blown sands of the Sahara, and the wells in many places have produced gardens out of the barren Desert. The wells depend primarily on the rains, but one can depend on but four good years of rainfall out of ten; and the year that hostilities opened drought was over the more fertile regions about Benghazi, making it necessary to import grain. However, during the years of plentiful rain there is more water than is needed, the market-places are flooded to the inconvenience of traders, the dry wadis become raging torrents, floods occasionally break down natural barriers, then rush across the Desert and in some cases have actually swept through the town of Tripoli, demolishing houses and taking lives.

The precious water spills into the Mediterranean and is lost; the tree-denuded land is soon a-bake with scorching heat, save where depressions form shallow lakes, lagoons, swamps, or marshes; these dry up, leaving a mud-cracked, mosaic bottom, upon which certain fruits or vegetables are sometimes grown. The water of the marshes, instead of being left to stagnate and evaporate, should be drained to feed the falling flood in the rivers, thus increasing the volume of water available for irrigation and leaving in place of the marshes greatly improved pastures.

It is my opinion that, while the artesian well will serve its purpose admirably during the seasons of good rain, it is for times of drought that Italy must prepare, involving the *conservation* of these innumerable millions of gallons which the absence of forests and, in many places, topsoil, assists in their hurried rush to the sea. Italy should appoint an engineering commission, whose specific purpose should be to make a care-

ful survey and to study conditions of the plateau lands of the Tripoli Hills and the coast
strip with its canyons and river beds. The ultimate result of this work should be to complete
the construction of a system of reservoirs from
which the entire littoral could be irrigated in
time of drought.

Careful consideration should be given to certain natural economic features in dam construction. There are some natural reservoirs in Tripoli Hills which need comparatively little in the
way of artificial construction to perfect. From
these vast reservoirs the slope of the land would
greatly assist in the distribution by canals and
sub-channels over the great productive plain
lying between the hills and the sea. It would
probably be feasible to construct reservoirs on
the southern side of the Tripoli Hills and to develop much of the Desert country to the south.

In heavy rainfalls the fertility of the country
is quickly evidenced, for much of it springs into
a paradise of verdure and flora. Italy will find
a leading product in the yield of the two million date palms of Tripolitania and will rapidly
increase the numbers of these regal beauties.
Under them the thrifty Italian market gardener

will grow the trees of the orange, pomegranate, and lemon, and raise from the semi-shaded soil leeks, red peppers, beans, tomatoes, and other vegetables and fruits, and on the hill-sides and valleys they will rehabilitate the olive, to the growing of which the country is particularly well adapted. Ten years ago the heavy Turkish tax on every olive-tree and the fruit thereof resulted in the Arabs cutting down the trees and selling them for fire-wood, thus depriving the country of one of its best products, since the olive will sustain itself in time of drought. Olive-oil will be extracted and oil-presses established in Tripoli, but on the plateau lands and open reaches wheat, oats, and barley will undulate under the hot breezes of the south and yield a great increase, and laws regulating the picking and preservation of the wild esparto grass will be instituted and this indigenous product preserved.

Pastoral development, too, will greatly increase, together with the agricultural products in both variety and quantity. This will call for direct and rapid transport to the markets of the Mediterranean, as a consequence of which railroads and steamships will be a necessity. Already one hundred kilometres of railway have been operated since last May by the Italian state railroad to Zuara east, Ain-Zara south, and to Zan-Zur west. The principal branch goes to Azizia, and it is planned to build two hundred kilometres each year for a period of three years, extending along the fertile coast section between the Mediterranean and the Jebel Gharian and the hills between Tripoli and Khoms. Railroads, too, will be a great assistance to Italy in collecting taxes and in establishing a strong and stable government over the independent Arab tribes who roam at will over the greater part of the country. They will give great impetus to the development of Tripoli, facilitating the construction of irrigation works, which, in turn, will furnish the railway with traffic.

Great regulating barrages across rivers and their branches and at the heads of important canals, as well as works connected with navigation, should be undertaken by the state, while the excavation and maintenance of the small canals should be intrusted to the cultivators themselves or to interested parties who, in turn, for title-deeds to the lands, would perform these services. Such canals in ancient times seared Mesopotamia but have ceased to exist. Their high-and-dry beds and lofty embankments, like ghosts recalling the past, form one of the striking features of the Desert. ' To a great extent the Arab of the Desert tribes has been a victim of circumstances and of environment, and Algeria and Tunisia prove that the Arab is not the hopeless person he is so generally supposed to be and that he may become a source of strength to the government.

To-day we find the whole country from the mountains to the sea scoured by Italian troops, and even beyond the mountains, nearly half-way to Ghadāmes, while over Ghadāmes itself the Italian flag has been hoisted with the approval and invitation of the chiefs. The entire country is occupied as far as Orfella toward the Fezzan, it being reported that many of the chiefs have submitted and *Residente* Italians been appointed and preparations almost completed for the journey to Murzuk and Ghāt. But in the province of Barca resistance has been quite marked, and the Italians met with severe defeat last May (1913) and were compelled to retreat to Derna, after which reverse the Italian Chamber of Deputies approved an appropriation of the additional $20,000,000, before mentioned, to continue the war in Tripoli.

The road between Benghazi and Derna is now in complete control of the Italians, and many of the chiefs are tendering submission. Italy, patterning after Great Britain and France, has already established the nucleus of a native colonial army of about eight thousand Arabs, well contented with the two lire a day and uniforms, and the New Year's Day despatch of the battle in the neighborhood of Murzuk, previously referred to, showed that these colonial troops stood by the Italian soldiers of the column and, after five hours of fierce fighting, routed the enemy. An engagement in Barca, March, 1914, also proved the loyalty of the native troops.

The proposed establishment of chairs of Mussulman law in Italian universities is one way Italy is seeking to foster friendly relations in Libia, while the Cadi of Tripoli represents there the Shiek-ul-Islam and will superintend all Mohammedan religious functions and appoint the local chiefs, the *naibs*, thus co-operating with the Italian Government in helping to bring about a better understanding. In Tripoli City many Arabs have been sworn into the police service and present a splendid appearance in their attractive uniforms; mounted Arab constabulary co-operate with the *carabanieri*. Hassuna Bashaw, a former officer in the Turkish constabulary, an Arab, heir to the Arab Bashawlic of Tripoli and direct descendant of Yusef Bashaw, the last of the Karamauli Bashaws, deposed by the Turks in 1835, was one of the few Arabs who had at the beginning of the war identified himself with the Italian cause. Now the city of Tripoli is run by a commission of three, with Hassuna Bashaw as President, and, I understand, with a comfortable salary from the Italians of three thousand lire ($579) per month.

Italy's plan is to expand the civil zone as rapidly as possible. With the powers' recognition of Italian sovereignty all extra-territorial rights of foreigners have ceased and resident consular officials no longer exercise any judicial prerogatives. For this zone there is a civil and penal tribunal and a court of appeals for the two provinces of Tripoli and Cyrenaica, into which Libia is divided. Outside the civil zone, cases are to be tried by the tribunal of war, or justice is to be administered by the local Arab officials appointed by the Italian Government under the supervision of the Italian *Residente*. Upon the tact and adaptability of these *Residentes* depends much of the success in procuring the submission of the chiefs in the southern districts.

Italy is also making medical researches in connection with the study of the pathology of those regions. The water supply has been doubled and new sources are being piped into town, one running around the southern wall, making it very convenient for the Jews of the Mellah. A number of new cables now connect Tripoli and Benghazi with the outside world; stringent land laws have driven away many speculators but prices on city property have risen very high; and rents increased to four hundred per cent more than during the Turkish régime. But this rise has not been confined to Tripoli, for Italy herself is at last facing this economic condition. The number of unemployed has increased, rents in Naples have gone up twenty-five per cent, and great suffering is already experienced there and in Sardinia through the high cost of food in general and milk in particular, which has risen to sixteen cents a quart. These elements are particularly fatal in southern Italy, where existence for the masses has always been a sort of hand-to-mouth routine, and when this equilibrium is destroyed starvation and lack of shelter ensue, and the present situation will involve the appropriation of several millions, at least, for relief work during the coming year. As a result of the war the cost of living has quadrupled, but that of garden truck has decreased since the Italian farmers have begun to grow vegetables.

The sanitary work in the city is a primary consideration. Within two hundred yards eastward from the old Turkish Club a local board-of-health building raises its white walls; the new quarantine station, costing $67,550, will be one of the largest and best equipped of the Mediterranean. The additions to the city hospital, costing nearly a third that amount, are already appreciated by the Arabs, who not only patronize it but even take their women, a thing never heard of before. After the peace proclamation thousands of starving Bedaweens came into the city and a sanitary camp was established. Here they were fed, given clothes, medical attendance, etc.; the majority were provided with seed for barley, but peace was declared too late for a successful crop that year.

One of the most interesting phases of the educational development is a school established for abandoned Arab boys by a captain of the Bersaglieri in the oasis of Tripoli. One hundred and twenty-five or more boys are provided with food twice a day, running water and baths, have military drill, athletic exercises, elementary instruction and instruction in agriculture. For this institution the government provides an appropriation.

Naturally, one of the first things to be done was to tear down the shacks about the old Arch of Marcus Aurelius, where I once purchased some supplies for my expedition from its occupant, a vender in dried fish and other commodities. The accumulations of years, Desert sands and rubbish, were cleared away from its base, so that this remnant of ancient Rome now stands impressively in the heart of Tripoli, and museums for archæology have been established in both Tripoli and Benghazi for the preservation of classic antiquities.

The maritime department has begun work on over fifty projects, most of which have been com-

pleted, so that now new piers thrust their pro-
boscides into the harbor; along the water-front
great electric cranes have sprung up and the
inner corner of the harbor will be filled in, giving more wharf and quay accommodation at
which vessels will be able to dock.

This large space, when filled, will entirely
cover in the spot where, in 1904, I located, sur-
veyed, and charted the skeleton remnants of the
old United States frigate *Philadelphia*. In connection with this there has recently been some
agitation in Congress to make an appropriation
to raise the hull. This would not be feasible
and the few remaining timbers would not seem
to justify the expense. But it is well within
the function and duty of Congress to perpetu-
ate, with approval and co-operation of the Italian Government, some adequate form of monu-
ment and tablet—a long-delayed tribute not
only to Decatur but to all those heroes who
played so gallant a part in defence of the flag
in Tripoli. What more appropriate spot could
be chosen than over the very grave where the
Philadelphia lies buried, consigned there by
Americans.

The most important harbor project is the

building of a great breakwater connecting the peninsula with two ledges lying parallel with the shore at a cost of $77,200, thus giving security to shipping from the northern gales of winter which sometimes cut the city off from mail service for twenty days.

Probably more passengers landed at Tripoli in the year of the war than during the whole of the last century. There naturally has been a sporadic and temporary increase in shipping and trade due to the abnormal conditions of the war, but many merchants, after the peace proclamation and withdrawal of many of the military, found themselves with large consignments on their hands. To the best of my knowledge, the only commercial American steamer that ever entered Tripoli with a cargo brought the year of the war a cargo of oats (worth $130,000) for the Italian cavalry. Over $500,000 worth of American products were imported in 1912, as against $20,000 worth, the greatest of any preceding year.

While the splendid developments which Italy is projecting in Tripoli are to Italy's credit, it must be borne in mind that they are also on Italy's credit. France needed more than forty years to pacify Algeria, and it is hardly to be expected that the Tibbus, Tuaregs, Darmaghu, and other wild, independent tribes in the unconquered fastnesses will peacefully capitulate, and Italy will undoubtedly be put to no little embarrassment and heavy expense before complete pacification is assured. But the conditions do not warrant their prolongation as in the Algeria conquest.

It has taken over three-fourths of a century for France to see some actual returns on her Algerian venture, and when the wild Desert tribes and Arabs eventually understand that their interests lie side by side with those of the Italians' a new era of peace, wealth, and prosperity will open up, at least for the Arabs, for Tripolitania—Libia—more expensive of occupation, less productive, less watered than Tunisia, cannot be expected to yield a commercial profit into Italy's pocket when we consider that, with all the frugality of the Frenchman, Tunisia, next door, has been an insatiable abyss into which France has poured millions in capital.

But nations play for a long game; their foreign policies must not be considered in the light of the events of a year or a decade. Italy has one wedge in Italian Somaliland and now has Libia. She has been thwarted in her scheme of an Italian-African empire, for the Gaul and the Briton have shut her off from contiguous communication with the Central Sudan, and diverted the Sudan trade from Tripoli to their own ports, to the Nile, Senegal, and Niger, which leaves Italy dependent on the pastoral and agricultural products of her colony.

Strategically, Libia gives Italy a certain control of the Sicilian-African Strait, through which all Mediterranean traffic must pass, and in the distant future its possession may be the first step toward Italy's recovery of Malta and the first growth of a colonial empire—who can tell? The new Italy is a young nation in the family of Europe and a novice at colonization; but her wonderful faculty for adaptation, scientific tendencies, willingness of her people to labor, her new enthusiasm, greater unity, common purpose and interest, well-organized army, increasing navy and economic growth, all will go toward making for her ultimate success, for Italy has found herself.

What a transformation within the old Arab town! Where one walked before, he now rides;

autos, with raucous warning, swing through the streets; the steam-roller adds its grinding on the Via Azizia; and boys shouting the *Nuovo Italia*, which arrives three times a week, mingle their cries with the cracking of whips and general hubbub.

The thousands of new-comers might divide their time between the moving-picture shows, a skating-rink, a new opera-house, or at the cafés which line the Via Azizia from the Turkish Club. The old Suk-el-Turc has been overhauled, painted, and spruced up, and as one wanders by the old Arab and Turkish booths one sees merchants of a strange caste and dye, for amidst the silks, cloths, and curios sit merchants from the East, and the Persian, Indian, and Japanese vend their wares to Italian officers and the inquisitive passenger who knows little or nothing of the Tripoli that has passed. In the Tripoli of yesterday the Turks' and Arabs' stores were few and were closed at sunset. As there was no business done in the evening there was little demand for lights, and the few there were sputtered or gleamed softly from oil lamps.

Now, as the last touch of saffron catches the

crescent of the minarets—yes, and the cross of the Cathedral—the electric lights garishly burst out in the new Tripoli of the Italian. Via Azizia is crowded with promenaders, all strangers to an old-timer, with only a barracaned and lonely Arab trying to find escape from the crowds, but—*mektub*—it is written.

GLOSSARY

a = *a* in father
ū = *u* in r*u*le

Adán, the call to prayer.
Addax, a North African antelope.
Akawali, [Hausa] a black horse.
Arbar-Arsāt, Street of the Four Columns.
Arfi, master—used in addressing Christians.
Ar-r-rah! used to start a horse.
Asben, a kingdom just south of Aïr, southern Sahara.
Asbenawa, people of Asben.
Asgars, Tuaregs of the Asgar tribe.
Awāsit, the second ten days of the Mohammedan month.
Baksheesh, a gratuity.
Baracan, woollen outer garment of Tripolitans.
Bashaw, or *Basha*, Arabic for governor, ruler.
Berbers, descendants of the white aborigines of Barbary [Berbery].
Bishna, millet.
B'is salamah!, On thy peace!
Būrro, go on, get out.
Chaca, Hausa gambling game played with cowries.
Chott, dried lake.
Cowries, beautiful white shells about an inch long used as currency in Sudan.
Damerghu, a place and a tribe in extreme southern Sahara on Ghāt-Kano route.
Dawa, [Hausa] bread.
Djema-el-Daruj, Mosque of the Steps.
Djibana, [Hausa] the place of the Cemetery of the Dog.
Douar, village.
Esparto, or halfa, a grass indigenous to Barbary.
Firman, [Turkish] a passport, requiring a special edict of the Turkish sovereign granting permission to travel, etc.
Fondūk, a caravansary.
Gangara, [Greek] sponge boats which use the trawl.

[355]

GLOSSARY

Gatrunys, people of Gatrun, a town in central Fezzan on Murzuk-Kanem caravan route.

Gedash ?, how much ?

Gibani ! an exclamation of surprise.

Gibli, or *gibleh,* south-east Desert wind which often terminates in the sand-storm.

Gulphor, a room in a seraglio for the exclusive use of the master.

Hadji Ahmed, a camel raiser and the master from whom Sālam escaped.

Haik, an outside garment of colored or striped cloth.

Halfa or *alfa,* Arab word for esparto grass.

Halfa Suk, Halfa Market where esparto or halfa grass is auctioned or sold.

Hashish, an intoxicating preparation made from tops of tender Indian hemp sprouts, smoked, drank, or taken in confections.

Hubba ! an exclamation used by Hausas.

Jamal, camels [draught camels].

Jebel, mountains or mountain region.

Jebel Nagahza, Nagahza Mountains, in northern Tripoli.

Jebel Gharian, Gharian Mountains in northern Tripoli.

Jehad, a Holy War.

Jemal, camel [draught camel].

Jinnee, a Mohammedan mythical order of beings, good and bad spirits.

Kafir, unbeliever.

Kanijar, dagger knife.

Kano, the great metropolis of the Sudan.

Kasrullah, knobbed stick carried by Tripolitans, principally at night.

Kelowis, Tuaregs of Kelowis tribe inhabiting vicinity of Aïr, southern Sahara.

Kibleh, sacred niche in a mosque placed to indicate the direction of Mecca.

Kief, dried hemp leaves, smoked in pipes.

Kouba, a saint's house, sometimes called a marabout.

Lah, no.

Lakby or *lagbi,* a palm wine.

Lasunvadi, Sālam's brother-in-law.

Lakoom, a Turkish candy.

Lazaretto, [Italian] quarantine.

Lingua franca, a mixture of Italian with Arabic, Turkish, etc.

[356]

GLOSSARY

Litham, Tuareg cloth mask.

Lokanda, hostelry.

Manometrom, the part of a scaphandra which indicates the atmospheric pressure.

Marabout, a holy man, a *M*ohammedan saint, also a kouba [saint's house].

Maria, [not Arabic] a bucket with a glass bottom, used in searching for sponges.

Mastica, a Turkish drink.

Mehari, a running or riding camel.

Mellah, Jewish quarter.

Meradi Katsena, a town in the state of Sokoto, Sudan.

Moor, a town dwelling Arab.

Orfella, a Tripolitan tribe.

Palanquin, a canopy on a camel or donkey under which women ride.

Para, small Turkish silver coin, one-tenth of a cent in value.

Pasha, [Turkish] governor, ruler.

Practique, quarantine clearance.

Ramadan, annual *M*ohammedan fast of thirty days during ninth *M*ohammedan month.

Redjed Pasha, military governor of Tripoli.

Roumi, a *M*ohammedan epithet.

Sala Heba, one of Sālam's masters, sold by him to Hadji Ahmed.

Sans firman, without passport.

Scandli, [Greek] a flat piece of marble used by naked divers to accelerate the descent.

Scaphander, [Greek] a diver's machine, consisting of air-pump, suit, helmet, and tube.

Scaphandra, [Greek] a Greek sponge diver who uses a scaphander.

Sciara-el-Sciut, a suburb of Tripoli, on the coast in the oasis.

Seraglio, a private *M*oorish palace.

Suk, market, generally held in open spots outside the towns or in the oases.

Suk-el-Halfa, Halfa market.

Suk-el-Thalat, Tuesday market.

Suk-el-Turc, Turk's market.

Tebus or *Tibbus,* a tribe inhabiting the Tibesti *M*ountain region east of the Fezzan-Chad caravan route.

Temenah, or *Teymeeneh,* greeting.

GLOSSARY

Tuaregs, a fierce confederation of tribes, who occupy and control great sections of the western half of the Sahara. The principal tribes are the Aweelimmiden, Hoggars, Asgars, and Kelowis.

Ugurra, an exclamation.

Verghi, poll and property tax imposed by Turks.

Wadan, country.

Wadi, a river or dry river bed.

Weled-bu-Sef, a Tripolitan tribe.

Yahudi, a *M*ohammedan epithet.

Yusef Bashaw, the last native ruler of Tripoli and of the line of Karamali.

Zabtie or *zaptiah*, a Turkish guardsman.

Zintan, a district back of Tripoli.

Zinder, a Desert town south of the Fezzan.

Zerebas, native huts.

INDEX

[359]

INDEX

Castle of the Bashaws, 2, 19, 20, 21, 68, 100, 125, 195, 259, 298, 299, 312, 326.
Ceremonies, 25–26, 71, 72.
Chad, Lake, 80.
Character, Tripolitan, 32–33, 36–37, 45–46, 234, 278, 297.
Cholera, 319.
Climate, 30, 196, 281.
Clothing, 8, 9, 16, 34–35, 45, 53, 62, 71, 72, 89, 98, 103, 149, 191–192, 216, 234–235, 265–266, 273, 274.
Commerce, 44, 45, 61, 62, 79, 81, 196, 206–207.
Committee of Union and Progress, 306.
Congo, 61.
Cortugna, Signor, 159.
Cowrie shells, 58–59.
Crête (war-ship), 117, 127, 129.
Crispi, 304.
Currency, 35, 45, 58–59.
Custom-House, 5.
Customs, Tripolitan, 49.
Cyprus, 300.
Cyrenaica or Cyrene, 307, 326, 327.

Damerghu, 81, 205–206, 350.
Dancing, 240.
Date-palms, 41–42, 285, 339.
Decatur, Lieut., 100–101, 112, 348.
Dehibat, 323.
Derna, 315, 320, 342, 343.
Derna, 311, 312.
Dewey, U. S. Dry Dock, 122.
Dickson, Vice-Consul, Alfred, 14, 102.
Dickson, Dr. Robert G., 14.
Divers, 131.
Diving, 131, 132.
Dragoman, 179.
Dwellings, 6, 27–30, 194.

Eaton, General William, xxv.
Education, 343, 347.

Egypt, 1, 2, 61, 157–158, 304, 314.
Enver Bey, 322.
Esparto grass, 48, 120, 124, 332.
Esparto industry, 124, 145–172.
Europe, 1, 9.
European occupation, xxiv, xxv, xxvi, 4, 296–297.
European politics, 300–305, 310.
Europeans, 16.
Evil eye, 18–19, 59.
Exports, 120, 123–124, 167, 171, 196, 294.

Fetiches, 19, 85, 99.
Fez, 305.
Fezzan, 4, 42, 315, 342.
Fighting, 31, 60, 64, 75, 81, 82, 110–112, 152, 205–207.
Firman. See Passport.
Flatters expedition, 86–87.
Floods, 23, 24, 337, 338.
Fondūks [caravansaries], 62, 184–188, 203–204, 259, 263–264.
Food, 39, 41–42, 48, 98, 185, 234–235, 292.
France, 1, 291–292, 296, 300, 305, 313, 343.

Gambling, 58–59.
Gardens, 188, 299, 340, 346.
Garflas. See Caravans.
Gatrunys, 80.
Ghadāmes, 65, 68, 77, 82, 83, 323, 342.
Ghāt, 77, 81, 342.
Germany, 301, 302, 305, 310, 329.
Gibraltar, 300.
Great Britain, 1, 300, 303, 343.
Greeks, 6.
Greeting, 9.

Hadj or hadji, 61.
Hadji-el-Ouchai, 105.
Hadji-Mohammeḍ Gabroom, 106, 112.

INDEX

Hague, The, 307, 309.
Halfa. *See* Esparto grass.
Hansaland, 54–55, 58–64, 174.
Hausas, 10, 52–64.
Herzegovina, 305.
Horses, 43, 180.
Hostelries, 6, 264, 269–270.

Immigration, 333–336.
Industries, 15–17, 193, 194.
Intrepid, U. S. ketch, 101, 112.
Irrigating, 40–41.
Italians, 6, 11, 318, 319, 333–336.
Italy in Tripoli, 297, 299, 351, 353.
  African Empire, 351.
  Arab police of, 343, 344.
  Casualties of, 329–331.
  Casus belli of, 328–332, 342.
  Civil government of, 343–345.
  Cost of war of, 328–332, 342.
  Defences of, 313.
  Development of, 331–353.
  Economic viewpoint of, 335,
    345, 346, 350.
  Hospitals of, 319.
  Labor supply of, 333–336.
  Military campaign of, 309–
    331.
  Military policy of, 317–320,
    324, 325, 342.
  Military viewpoint of, 310,
    315.
  Moral viewpoint of, 309, 310.
  Naval attacks of, 299, 304,
    310, 311, 316, 317, 320.
  Political viewpoint of, 310,
    335, 336.
  Sanitation of, 319, 346, 347.
  Sovereignty of, 326.
  Troops of, 313, 317, 319, 320,
    342–344.
  Ultimatum, 307.

Jefara, 263–264.
Jehad [Holy War], xxiv, 326.
Jews, 8, 10, 11, 45, 345.

Kabyles, 282.
Kairwan, 16, 62.
Kano, 16, 44, 61, 62, 81, 195, 196.
Khoms, 238–246, 315, 320, 336,
  341.
Kibleh, 27.
King Emmanuel, 326.
Kitchener, 303.
Knights of St. John, xxv, 96.
Kola nuts, 61, 63–64.
Kol-oglu, 321.
Kussabat, 258–259.

Lakby, or palm juice, 42, 59, 73.
Latins, 305.
Lebda, 241–242.
Libia, 327, 335, 343, 350, 351.
Libya, xxiii, xxiv, 334.
Lizards, 238.
Lokanda. *See* Hostelries.

Malta, 300, 351.
Maltese, 11, 333.
Marabouts, 16, 49–50, 83.
Marcus Aurelius, Arch of, 13–15,
  347.
Markets. *See* Suks.
Mecca, 27, 61.
Mediterranean, 1–2, 4, 100, 120–
  123, 124, 169, 279–280, 300, 302–
  303, 305, 318, 338, 340, 346, 351.
Mehara. *See* Camel, riding.
Mehari. *See* Camel, riding.
Mehemed V, 297, 321.
Military, 11.
Misurata, 16, 28.
Moors, 16, 282.
Morocco, 1, 123, 285, 302, 305.
Mosques, 26, 27.
Moving pictures, 318, 352.
Muezzins, 24, 240.
Murzuk, 21, 201–202, 207, 342.
Music, 183, 256.

Naples, 318, 345.
Nechet Bey, 312, 313, 324.

[361]

INDEX

INDEX

Lightning Source UK Ltd.
Milton Keynes UK
UKOW02f1134300117

293187UK00002B/732/P

9 781333 368579